Colorful LOUISIANA CUISINE
in Black and White

Colorful LOUISIANA CUISINE
in Black and White

**BY BIBBY TATE
AND ETHEL DIXON**

PELICAN PUBLISHING COMPANY
Gretna 1990

First printing, November 1988
Second printing, January 1989
Third printing, July 1990

Library of Congress Cataloging-in-Publication Data

Tate, Bibby.
    Colorful Louisiana cuisine in black and white / by Bibby Tate and
Ethel Dixon : illustrated by Ethel Dixon.
      p. cm.
    ISBN 0-88289-789-6
    1. Cookery, American-Louisiana style. I. Dixon, Ethel.
II. Title.
TX715.2.L68T38   1990   89-48163
641.59763-dc20   CIP

Manufactured in the United States of America
Published by Pelican Publishing Company, Inc.
1101 Monroe Street, Gretna, Louisiana 70053

We dedicate our cookbook to our better halves, El and George, without whose support, encouragement, and patience, it would never have come to fruition.

CONTENTS

SPECIAL THANKS GO TO ALL WHO SUBMIT-
TED RECIPES, WHO TOLD US STORIES OF
LOUISIANA CUISINE AND WHO HELPED US
PRODUCE OUR BOOK.

"COLORFUL LOUISIANA CUISINE"
A BLENDING OF BLACK AND WHITE CULTURES

INTRODUCTION

This cookbook was written by two Louisianians, one black and one white, one a descendent of slaves and the other a descendent of a plantation family who owned slaves. Both of us have roots deep in the South and both come from families that "set a good table". So much of Louisiana cooking came from French, English, Spanish, Indian and African cultures. These culinary recipes have blended together through the years to give Louisiana cooking a distinct taste that is known worldwide. Many call it Creole and many call it Cajun (although Cajun properly refers to South Louisiana culture only). However, it is distinctly Louisiana, no matter what it is called and with whom it originated. One of the secrets of Louisiana cooking is how to season. We will try to be as accurate as we can in seasoning when we give a recipe; however, when we have in a recipe "season to taste", we mean just that. Each person has an individual preference for how much seasoning to use, such as pepper, curry, basil, oregano, cumin, dill, chili powder, just to mention a few. We will list the ingredients, the amount we use and if there is some doubt, we'll have "season to taste" by the recipe.

I am an ardent cook and party giver. I met Ethel Dixon when she rented space in the shopping center I was managing. Ethel is an artist and she has done all of the illustrations for our book. She has also added many recipes that came directly from her black history. As recipes have been handed down through the years, they have changed and been added to. If the recipes appear modern it is because we have written them as they appear today. You will find others that are the same as they were in the 1800's.

9

Ethel's paintings at the front of each chapter have put us in the role of a little black girl and a little white girl enjoying and experiencing events of old Louisiana days. I have written a short explanation with each painting.

With this cookbook we are attempting to bring all Louisiana cultures together and show that through the years, black and white recipes have been intermingled to make for Bon Appetit Louisiana.

We hope you enjoy it!

Bibby Tate

TO DIFFERENTIATE BETWEEN ETHEL'S RECIPES AND MINE, YOU WILL FIND A B (BLACK) BY HERS AND A W (WHITE) BY MINE, TO SHOW THE ORIGIN.

Colorful LOUISIANA CUISINE
in Black and White

Morning Bells Are Ringing

Chapter I

"Morning Bells are Ringing"

Breakfast & Brunch Foods

When there were plantations and plantation owners, slaves, and independent farmers; and cotton, corn, rice, sweet potatoes and sugar cane were the mainstay of Louisiana, folks went to the fields at daybreak and worked till mid morning when the sun got too hot. Each plantation had a big bell and when the temperature had risen and breakfast was ready, the bell was rung to signify "quittin time". The workers then went home and had a big breakfast. From this came the brunch which is a combination of breakfast and lunch. It has become a popular social event for Sundays after church. A real treat for Louisiana visitors is brunch in one of the hotels or restaurants.

The following recipes work well for breakfast and brunch.

Picture Explanation

Usually the "house man" rang the plantation bell to call the workers in from the fields. Ethel depicts our little girls taking over the "bell" duty.

GRILLADES - W

Use either veal steak or thinly sliced round steak. Cut in pieces 3 or 4 inches long and wide. Put flour, salt, pepper and cajun seasoning in paper bag and add meat pieces. Lightly flour pieces by shaking in bag. Fry to golden brown in small amount of oil (cover bottom of skillet). After frying meat, fry diced onion, celery, and green pepper in same oil. Keep drippings in skillet. Add tomato sauce (1/2 cup) and meat pieces. Add water to cover. Simmer till meat is tender and gravy is brown. Add a little thyme and bay leaf while simmering. Serve over grits or rice.

BAKED GRITS - W

For this recipe, you will need 6 cups water, lightly salted, 2 cups grits, 2 cups milk, 2 eggs beaten, 2 sticks oleo. Cook grits to a slow boil in the salted water, stirring constantly. Turn heat to low and cook till done. While still hot, add eggs and oleo. After cooking a short while, add milk and put in preheated 375° oven and bake for 1 hour. Serve with Grillades or ham.

CHEESE GRITS - W

This recipe takes 8 cups water, lightly salted, 2 cups grits, 1 roll garlic cheese, 2 sticks butter, 1 tbsp Worcestershire sauce, 2 eggs beaten, a dash of tabasco and pepper to taste. Cook grits in water till done. While still hot, add cheese, eggs and seasoning. Cook in 375° oven about an hour till firm.

FRESH HAM - W

This recipes takes a 10 to 12 lb ham. Put oven temperature at 350° and cook 30 to 35 minutes a pound. Temperature according to meat thermometer should be 185°. Before ham stops cooking, remove some rind with sharp knife, then score fat on top. Season with brown sugar, dry mustard and pineapple juice and chunks.

PORK CHOP CASSEROLE - W

Lightly flour and season chops with cajun seasoning. Brown in oil in skillet and drain on paper towel. Pour off most of oil to leave crusts and 1 tbsp oil. Add 2 tbsps flour and brown on high heat, adding water and stirring until smooth. Cook till thickened. Pour over chops in casserole dish. Put sliced thin onions and half fresh mushrooms over top. Cover with foil and bake in 325° to 350° oven approximately 45 minutes till tender. Serve with grits or rice. Sweet potatoes or fruit can be added instead of onions and mushrooms.

COMPANY OMELET WITH HAM OR SAUSAGE - W

Plan on 2 eggs per person. Break eggs, whip, and set aside. Grate sharp cheddar cheese. Dice green onions, bell pepper, pimento, fresh mushrooms, celery, tomatoes, cooked potatoes, ham or cooked sausage. Melt butter in pan; add beaten eggs and cook, loosening the bottom with a spatula. Put the grated cheese on top of eggs on one side of skillet and the chopped mixture on top of the cheese. Fold over other side of cooked eggs to cover ingredients. Let cook a short while then carefully turn whole mixture to put top on bottom. Slip on warm platter and garnish with sour cream and parsley.

CREAMED CHICKEN ON TOAST - W

Cook chicken the day before and debone. Cut up chicken in good size pieces. Saute green onions, bell pepper, mushrooms, and celery in butter. Make white sauce and add sauted vegetables and chicken to sauce. Add cayenne pepper, Worcestershire sauce and creole seasoning. Serve on layer of toast points garnished with pimento, parsley, and grated egg yellows. Add sliced eggs to mixture.

CORNED BEEF HASH AND EGGS - W

Use left over corned beef or canned corned beef. Saute in oleo, chopped onions, bell pepper, and diced potatoes. When potatoes are cooked, add diced corned beef and add a little milk to keep from drying out. Have toast points ready. Put a mound of mixture on toast and a poached egg on top of each. Sprinkle tabasco on top of each egg.

BRUNCH CHICKEN WINGS - W

5 lbs. chicken wings
3 sticks of oleo
Orange marmalade or apricot
  preserves
Hot barbecue sauce
Worcestershire sauce

Steak sauce
Tabasco
Juice from 2 lemons
Sliced oranges, lemons, pine-
  apple and whole cherries

Pan broil chicken wings in oleo after seasoning with cajun seasoning and pepper. Sprinkle lemon juice, Worcestershire, tabasco and steak sauce over wings. Cook till tender and transfer wings and juice to a casserole dish. Make a sauce of marmalade or preserves and barbecue sauce and pour over wings. Garnish with oranges, lemons, pineapple and cherries and run in oven at 350° for 45 minutes. Check to see if juices are cooking off and add water, if so.

TOAST, BACON AND CHEESE - B

Fry bacon, drain on brown paper. Toast bread in a hot skillet with butter. Place on top of toast, the cheese and the bacon. Run it in the oven until the cheese has melted. Serve hot. If you like, you can pour Cane or Maple Syrup over it, or for lunch, add a seasoned tomato.

EGGS BENEDICT - W

Make Hollandaise sauce (see sauce chapter). One egg for a person, one slice of ham or canadian bacon per person. 1/2 English muffin a person, splitting, buttering and toasting muffins. Poach eggs in boiling water to which a teaspoon of white vinegar has been added. Saute ham or canadian bacon in butter. Place slice on muffin, then poached egg, then Hollandaise sauce. Dash tabasco on top of each and serve immediately.

QUICHE LORRAINE - W

Line muffin tins with pie dough. Crumble 6 or more slices of bacon in bottoms. Grate swiss cheese over bacon. Over this pour custard made of 4 eggs, 1 tbsp flour, 1/2 tsp salt, 2 cups half & half. Bake in preheated oven (350°) for about 30 minutes. If making big pie, cook approximately 10 minutes longer. Sprinkle top with nutmeg.

SAUSAGE QUICHE - W

Brown 1 lb hot sausage. Bake frozen pastry shell according to directions on package. Combine 1 cup grated swiss cheese, 1 cup grated sharp cheddar, 1 cup fresh parmesan cheese. Combine cheeses and sausage. Beat 3 eggs with 1 cup sour cream and 1/2 cup evaporated milk. Add cheese mixture to egg mixture and put in pie shell. Bake at 375° for 45 to 50 minutes till firm in center.

SWEET AND SOUR SAUSAGE - W

Use package of small sausage links. For party of 25 with other foods being served, use 4 packages. Boil links to remove extra grease and drain water from links. Add a bottle of hot barbecue sauce and a jar of pineapple or apricot preserves. Add a small can of diced pineapple. Bring all to boil, cut down heat and keep warm in crock pot or chafing dish. Serve with tooth picks.

BREAD FOR BRUNCH

LOST BREAD OR PAIN PERDU - W

Take stale bread slices and soak in sugared milk to which a tbsp of brandy has been added. Drain and turn each slice in beaten eggs. Fry in hot oil and brown on both sides. Sprinkle with powdered sugar. If you cook ahead, keep warm in low oven.

SHORTNIN' BREAD - B

2 cups flour
2 1/2 tsps baking soda
1 pinch salt
1 stick butter

2 eggs
1 tsp vanilla
1 cup sweet milk

Cream eggs and butter. Add remaining ingredients. Oil and flour a 9 x 12 loaf pan. Pour batter in pan. Bake in 350° oven for about 1 hour. Let cook. Cut and serve with jam or jelly.

COUNTRY CRACKLING SHORTNIN' BREAD - B

Cracklings are the crisp, brown bits off the pork skins and a little fat off fresh pork. A modern version of cracklings can be crisp fried, not burned, bacon. Chop up fine and use in recipe.

1 1/2 cup corn meal
3/4 cup sifted flour
1/2 tsp baking soda

1/4 tsp salt
1 cup sour milk
1 cup cracklings

Sift the dry ingredients together. Add milk and stir in cracklings. Pour into a greased baking pan. Bake in hot oven (425°) for 30 minutes or until brown. Makes one loaf.

HOE CAKES - B

2 cups flour
2 tsps baking powder
1 tsp salt

3 to 4 tbsps shortening
1 cup sweet milk
1 tbsp oil (for frying)

Mix all dry ingredients together. Make a well in center and pour in sweet milk, mix well. Form the dough into small patties. Fry on both sides in 1 tbsp of hot oil.

BISCUITS PERFECT - B

5 cups flour (before sifting)
1 cup shortening
1 1/2 cups Pet milk

3 heaping tsps baking powder
1 tsp salt

Mix shortening in sifted flour with fingers. Add salt, baking powder and milk (more or less depending on type of flour used). Mix well, roll about 1/2 inch thick and cut with biscuit cutter. Bake in fairly hot oven (375°) in greased pan.

NOTE: Making biscuits is a trial and error process. If dough is allowed to rise for about 30 minutes before baking they tend to bake better. Always use cold milk or water to prepare biscuit dough. Do not use too much flour on board when rolling.

SYRUP BREAD - B

3 cups flour
2 tsps baking powder
1/2 to 1 tsp soda
1/4 tsp salt
2 sticks of butter
1 cup cane syrup

3 to 4 eggs
1/2 tsp nutmeg
1 tsp cinnamon
1 cup buttermilk
2 cups sugar

Cream butter until soft, add sugar and blend well. Add eggs and mix. Add milk, syrup, flour, baking soda and spices and mix well until blended. Pour into 9 x 12 loaf pan, greased and lined with wax paper. Bake at 350 for 55 minutes to one hour (or until cake springs back when touched with finger tip). Cool in pan, then turn out.

NOTE: Batter rises a full 2 inches when baking, so do not fill pan too full.

DROP BISCUITS - B

2 3/4 cups flour
4 tbsps baking powder
1 tsp salt

6 tbsps shortening
1 1/4 cups milk

Sift flour, measure and sift with baking powder. Cut in shortening. Add milk, stirring sufficiently to blend well. Place mixture in teaspoon size droppings onto a well oiled baking sheet. Bake in hot oven about 12 minutes. These biscuits may be split, buttered and used with various fruits as the basis for an emergency shortcake. Makes about 14 biscuits.

PLAIN OLD COUNTRY DOUGHNUTS - B

3 tsps butter
1 cup sugar
2 eggs, beaten
3 3/4 cups sifted flour

4 tbsps baking powder
1/2 tsp salt
1 tsp vanilla
3/4 cup milk

Cream butter and sugar together, lightly. Stir in beaten eggs. Mix and sift flour, baking powder and salt. Add to creamed mixture, alternating with the milk. Stir in vanilla. Chill thoroughly. Roll out 1/3 inch in thickness on a lightly floured surface. Cut with floured cutter. Fry in deep hot cooking oil, letting float to the top. Flip and brown on other side. Drain. Sprinkle with powdered sugar and cinnamon.

FRENCH TOAST - B

3 eggs
2 cups milk
1/2 tsp salt
12 slices of bread, toasted (1/2 inch thick)

1/2 tsp vanilla extract
1/2 cup sugar

In a large bowl pour in milk. Add eggs, salt, vanilla extract, and sugar. Pour in a large flat pyrex dish. Dip slices of bread into mixture, and saute in a little fat until golden brown on both sides. Serve hot. Sprinkle with confectioners' sugar or serve with Maple or Cane Syrup.

CEREAL AND PANCAKES FOR BRUNCH
OR BREAKFAST

BUCKWHEAT PANCAKES - B

2 cups milk
2 cups boiling water
1 cake yeast
4 cups buckwheat flour

1/2 tsp baking soda
1 cup hot water
1 tbsp molasses
1 tsp salt

Scald milk, add boiling water. Cool to luke warm and soften yeast in mixture. Sift in enough flour to make a batter thin enough to pour. Let it rise over night. In the morning dissolve soda in hot water and add to batter with molasses and salt. Mix together thoroughly. Drop from a large spoon into a hot greased skillet and cook until you see tiny bubbles and the underside is golden brown. Turn and brown on other side. This makes about 3 1/2 dozen cakes. If you want to have cakes again soon, this will keep for about 3 to 4 days in the refrigerator. Keep 1/2 cup batter out and proceed with above instructions.

OLD FASHIONED RICE CAKES -B

Nothing went to waste in our refrigerator that a little flour, milk, and eggs would not fix. The rice was leftover from the night's supper and Mom got up and made breakfast from it.

2 cups sifted flour
3 tbsps baking powder
1 tsp salt

2 cups rice, cooked
2 eggs, separated

Heat rice to take the chill off. Mix all dry ingredients into a large bowl including rice. Add milk and beaten egg yolks. Combine the two mixtures together, then fold in beaten egg whites. Spoon into a hot black iron greased skillet. Makes about 12 cakes.

OATMEAL WITH RAISINS - B

1 cup oats
2 cups cold water

1 tsp salt
2 tsp raisins

Place in a 2 quart saucepan with a tight fitting lid. Set over high heat until oats boil vigorously. Stir with a fork. Cover and reduce heat to very low. Add raisins and stir. Cook about 15 minutes longer. Serve hot. Add milk and brown sugar.

OLD FASHION COUNTRY SYRUP PANCAKES - B

1 cup sifted flour
1 1/2 tsp baking powder
1/2 tsp salt
1 tbsp syrup

1 egg, beaten
1 cup milk
3 tbsps melted shortening
    or cooking oil

Sift flour, baking powder, and salt together. Combine syrup, egg and milk. Add gradually to flour, mixing only until smooth. Add shortening or cooking oil. Cook on hot griddle or iron skillet. Makes about 10 to 12 pancakes.

POTATO PANCAKES

This can be used with left over mashed potatoes or you can cook potatoes.

2 cups sifted flour
3 tsps baking powder
2 cups mashed potatoes
1 tsp salt

2 eggs, beaten
1 cup milk
4 tbsps nutmeg

Combine potatoes, sifted flour, salt, and baking powder. Mix together the eggs and milk and stir lightly into the potato flour mixture. Add corn syrup and nutmeg, then beat vigorously. Other syrups can be used. Cook in a hot greased skillet and brown on both sides. Serve hot with butter and syrup. Makes about 12 cakes.

FRUIT FOR BRUNCH

BAKED PEARS, PEACHES OR APPLES - W

Halve and core fruit. Put on cookie sheet. Heat oven at 325°. Sprinkle fruit with cinnamon, clove, and lemon juice. Bake slowly till done, approximately 10 to 15 minutes. Garnish with cherry and mint.

BAKED BANANAS - W

Choose not too ripe bananas. Peel and half. Sprinkle cinnamon over top, squeeze a little fresh lemon juice on top and dot with butter or oleo. Cook in 350° oven till butter is melted.

BROILED GRAPEFRUIT - W

Halve and carefully seed grapefruit. Cover with brown sugar. Put under broiler until sugar melts. Garnish with cherry and mint leaves.

CURRIED FRUIT

1 can fruit for salad
1 can dark bing cherries
1 can pear halves

1 can peach halves
1 can pineapple chunks

Drain and dry fruit and mix with 1/2 c light brown sugar, 1/2 tsp, curry powder. Place mixture in shallow casserole. Drizzle with some fruit juice mixture and dot with butter on the top. Bake in 350° oven for 30 to 40 minutes.

HOT LEMONADE SPICED FRUIT - B

2 6 oz cans concentrate lemonade
Water (2 lemonade cans full)
1/2 cup raisins (set in hot
   boiling water)

4 pear halves
2 tbsp cinnamon
2 tbsp cloves
2 bananas, cut in 2 chunks

Mix concentrate for lemonade with water and spice. Arrange well-drained fruit in deep baking dish and pour the lemonade mixture over fruit. Bake in moderate oven (350 degrees) for about 20 minutes. Serves 4 to 6.

SUMMER WATERMELON DELIGHT - B

24 marshmallows
2 stiffly beaten egg whites
1/4 cup lemon juice

2 cups diced watermelon
   (approximately)

Squeeze and drain juice from watermelon saving 1 cup juice. Melt marshmallows in watermelon juice over hot water, stirring until marshmallows are melted and smooth. Cool and add lemon juice. Combine marshmallow mixture with stiffly beaten egg whites, stirring gently until smooth and blended well. Do not beat. Pour into pyrex bowl and freeze. When partially frozen, turn into chilled bowl. Beat quickly with hand mixer. Return to freezer in serving dishes or custard cups. Makes about 5 servings.

BAKED TOMATOES - W

Use small, firm tomatoes and slice top off. Put a slice of onion on top of each tomato and sprinkle Italian bread crumbs and parmesan cheese on top. Bake at 300° for 15 to 20 minutes. Do not let them get too mushy.

DRINKS FOR BRUNCH

BLOODY MARY OR VIRGIN MARY - W

1 lg can V8 juice
Juice from 1 whole lemon
3 or 4 good size dashes of
    Worcestershire sauce

4 or 5 dashes of tabasco sauce
Salt and pepper to taste

Put all above ingredients in pitcher and mix well. Fill individual glasses with
ice and mixture. For Bloody Mary, add 1 1/2 jiggers of Vodka. For Virgin Mary,
serve as is. Garnish with celery stalk. Salt and pepper to taste.

ICE MILK PUNCH - W

2 qts vanilla ice milk
3 tbsps sugar
2 cups cold milk

1 1/2 cup bourbon
1 tsp vanilla

Add bourbon to ice milk, sugar and vanilla, then add milk. Fill tall glasses with
mixture and sprinkle with nutmeg on top. This can be mixed in blender.

JIMMY'S SUNDAY MORNING MILK PUNCH

1 jigger bourbon
1 jigger vodka
2/3 cup milk

1/4 tsp vanilla
2 drops almond extract

Put in blender on low and mix with small amount of ice. Pour over ice and
sprinkle nutmeg on top.

ORANGE BLOSSOMS* - W

1 fifth gin
1 fifth orange juice
1/2 fifth apricot brandy

Juice of 1/2 lemon
Shakes of orange bitters

Chill mixture till cold in refrigerator. Serve in champagne or wine glasses with a slice of orange and a cherry. Makes approximately 16 to 18 4-oz servings. Delicious but deadly!

*This recipe is from Senator John Overton's wife, Ruth, who obtained it from Pearl Mesta while Senator Overton was in Washington. This is also excellent for a bride's cocktail party.

LOUISIANA STRAWBERRY AND WINE PUNCH - B

1 qt hulled strawberries
2 cups sugar
1/2 cup water

3 bottles chilled wine
(your favorite)

Place berries in a fruit jar with sugar and water. Cover the jar and chill for 6 to 8 hours. Stir gently occasionally to blend fruit and juices. Combine strawberries with wine in a punch bowl. Use no ice. Makes about 30 servings. This is very good.

DRUNKEN HOT BUTTER RUM - B

1/4 lb light salted butter
6 tbsps brown sugar
1 tbsp mace
1 tbsp allspice

2 tbsps crushed cloves
Dark Jamacian rum
Boiling water
Ground nutmeg

Cream butter, brown sugar, mace, allspice and cloves until smooth. Place 1 tbsp of butter into each 8-oz glass mug. Add 1 1/2-ozs rum and 4-ozs boiling water to each mug. Stir until smooth. Add more butter, if desired. Garnish with nutmeg.

Note: To avoid possible breaking of the glass mug, pour the hot liquid over a metal spoon in the mug. Makes 6 to 8 servings.

CREOLE DRIPPED COFFEE - W

Use a drip coffee pot with dark roast coffee ground fine. For every cup of coffee, allow 2 heaping tbsps of grounds. Pour boiling water slowly over grounds until desired amount is made.

CAFE AU LAIT - W

2 cups black coffee, 3 cups sweet milk are needed for this recipe. Heat each of above separately. Pour half cup of coffee and top with half cup of hot milk. Serve in big cups and pass the sugar.

CAFE BRULOT - W

(For after Brunch or holiday entertaining)

Plan on 2 after dinner coffee cups for each guest. Combine 2 cloves, 2 all spices, 2 lumps sugar, a thin slice lemon and orange rinds, a whole cinnamon stick, 1/2 after dinner coffee cup of cognac into a brulot bowl or large silver one. Put 2 sugar lumps in a tbsp of cognac. Light a match, holding it near the spoon till cognac is lighted. Ladle slowly with contents in bowl. Let flames melt sugar and blend spices and peelings. Then add hot coffee to bowl. Ladle into after dinner coffee cups.

COFFEE LOUISIANIAN - B

3 cups strong coffee, freshly brewed 1/2 tsp ground cinnamon
Grated rind of one orange   1 tbsp curacao
6 tsp sugar   3 tbsp brandy
1/2 tsp ground cloves

Heat orange rind, sugar, spices, and liquors in a small container or sauce pan over low heat, until sugar melts. Pour into coffee and serve at once, in after dinner coffee cups. Makes servings for 6.

A Louisiana delight. One of the old ways of serving this good coffee is to place the half of an orange shell fitted snugly into a cup. The brandy is floated on top and is ignited before the drink is sipped.

Put on the Pot

CHAPTER II

"Put on the Pot"

Soups, Gumbos, Stews

and Sauces

Long a favorite of Louisiana have been the delicious soups, gumbos and stews. Most of these originated with the black culture, for these people had to stretch food, usually for a large family, and created these gourmet delights more to fill stomachs than to create exotic recipes. Nevertheless, they did, and because of the abundance of seafood, wild game, fowl and vegetables, these are among the most famous of Louisiana dishes. An interesting sidelight to the Louisiana gumbo comes from the Choctaw Indian squaws. They lived on the north shore of Lake Pontchartrain and would journey to the French markets on weekends where they would sell herbs and fruits, including plantain and ground leaves of the sassafras plant that came to be known as filé and was used for thickening and seasoning gumbo. It is still a must with Louisiana gumbos.

Picture Explanation

As was done so often, Grandma and Aunt "B" have gone out in the yard to prepare a big meal. You could smell the meal cooking throughout the area. Fieldhands, houseworkers, and land owners all know that today they will have a very special meal. As seen on the drawing the girls are anxiously awaiting the completion of the cooking.

POT-AU-FEU - W
(Bouillon)

The Pot-au-Feu is made by boiling a good soup bone in water a certain length of time until all nutrients are extracted. It takes four or five hours to boil the soup bone, skimming the scum as it rises, and adding the vegetables when the soup is boiling well.

Most Louisiana grocery stores sell a "soup bunch" that consists of cabbage, a turnip or two, carrots, parsley, celery & onion. Many famous Creole cooks add bay leaf, thyme, cloves & allspice. Strain after cooking.

This serves as a base for many soups.

MAKING A ROUX - W

To make a roux, add 1 tbsp of flour to each tbsp fat, usually drippings from meat. To make a brown roux, brown the flour to a deep brown. When dark brown, pour in liquid, water, milk, stock or other sauce. To make a white roux, smooth flour into under browned fat for a white paste, season to taste and add liquid. This is the basic white sauce. From the brown roux, most Southern gravies are made. There are now roux mixtures already made up that are good and will save worry of burning.

SEAFOOD GUMBO - W

Start with a roux, either store bought or made from lard and flour. When browned, add 1 chopped cup celery, 1 cup chopped bell pepper, 1 can tomatoes, 1 cup chopped onions, yellow and green. Add approximately 3 or 4 qts of water, slowly, stirring as you do. Season to taste with salt, pepper, bay leaf, garlic, and cayenne. Add 1 lb crab meat, 1 lb peeled shrimp and the frozen package of gumbo mix with cracked, whole crabs and shrimp. Simmer for another 30 minutes and then add oysters and their liquid, chopped parsley, and more green onions and chopped okra. Serve over hot rice. Pass the filé!

SALLY'S OKRA GUMBO - B

Put on ham bone to boil for stock. Slice 2 lbs of okra. Have ready one large can of tomatoes, 1 large can of tomato sauce, 1 can diced Rotel tomatoes, 1/2 bunch celery, 1 large onion, 4 green onions, 3 garlic pods, 2 lbs shrimp (uncooked). Make roux from 1 cup flour and 1 cup shortening. Saute okra and garlic, adding to ham stock, roux, tomatoes, sauce, celery, and onions. Season to taste. Simmer for 1 1/2 hours and add shrimp last 20 minutes. Serve over hot rice and have filé at table.

CHICKEN GUMBO - W

Cut up a 3 lb chicken for frying. Salt and pepper and dust with flour. Fry chicken in cooking oil till brown. Remove chicken and add 1 cup chopped onions, celery, and bell pepper, along with a can of tomato sauce. Add 2 lbs sliced okra to this and simmer. Add 2 qts of water slowly and cooked chicken. Cover and simmer for 2 hours. If you wish to add sausage, slice it and add after 1 hour of simmering. If you also wish to add oysters or shrimp, add in last 20 minutes.

DUCK GUMBO - W

In a large pot, make the roux and saute onions, peppers and celery. Cut up ducks and brown in another pot. Add water to roux mixture, a little at a time, and then add ducks, salt, pepper, Worcestershire sauce, cayenne, garlic powder, bay leaf, and a small amount of filé. When duck is cooked, approximately 2 hours, take out and take meat off bones. Return meat to gumbo and if you wish, add sausage at this time, also okra.

TURKEY GUMBO - W

Turkey carcass from holiday dinner. Put whole carcass in big stewing pot and boil in water with chopped onion until meat falls off bones. Remove the bones and make a roux by taking some of your seasoned water and mixing with flour, or use one of the prepared rouxs like "Iron Pot". Return mixture to pot and add chopped bell pepper, a can of Rotel, chopped basil, thyme, okra, rosemary, salt, and pepper. Cover and let simmer at least an hour. Add crab meat, fresh or frozen, and shrimp that has not been cooked before. You may also add gumbo, crabs, and oysters. Cool till shrimp are done and serve over rice.

CREOLE GUMBO - W

1 onion
1 bell pepper
2 pieces celery
2 tbsps bacon drippings
1 tbsp flour
1/4 tsp black pepper

1 tsp salt
1 large can tomatoes
1 box frozen okra
Chicken parts
Shrimp
1 tbsp gumbo filé

Cook and season okra and drain. Cook chicken parts, remove from bone. Cook shrimp. Put diced onions, pepper and celery into large pan with bacon drippings. Add flour and stir constantly for about 5 minutes. Add tomatoes and about 1/2 can of water, salt and pepper. Next add okra and meat. Let simmer for about 20 to 25 minutes. Add more salt and pepper if needed. Add gumbo filé and simmer for about 5 minutes.

FILÉ - W & B

Beware of filé that is made from ground leaves of the sassafras tree. It is delicious, if used sparingly, and gives gumbos that delicious smell. It is best to use only a little and have it on the table for individuals to use as they see fit.

COURT BOUILLON - W

Start with a roux, adding onions, celery, bell peppers and garlic. Add a large can of tomatoes and a small can of tomato puree. Cook all of this slowly for 20 minutes, then add a qt of water. Let this simmer down. Then add 4 lbs red fish, snapper, cat or trout. Add Worcestershire sauce, salt and pepper, cayenne, and creole seasoning. Simmer about 30 minutes adding a little white wine, lemon and parsley at last 10 minutes. You can add crab meat and shrimp to the court bouillon, if you wish. Serve over hot rice.

TURTLE SOUP - W

In oleo, saute diced onions, celery and bell pepper till softened. Add chopped turtle meat. Cook longer if meat is fresh, not canned. Add a little flour to thicken and then add chicken stock and a small can of tomato sauce, tabasco, Worcestershire, chopped peeled lemons, chopped parsley, salt and pepper and 2 sieved hard boiled eggs. Simmer 1 to 2 hours. Just before serving put a tsp of sherry in each bowl and add the soup garnished with the hard boiled egg whites and fresh parsley.

SIDONIE'S MOCK TURTLE SOUP - W

Cook a 1 lb package of red beans (see recipe under vegetables). Save water from beans. Brown flour in butter and add to beans and 3 cups bean water. Mash cooked beans. Add minced garlic, tabasco, chopped onions, lemon juice and simmer for 1 hour. Add more water, if this gets too thick. Add a cup of sherry. Serve with chopped hard boiled eggs, lemon slices, and mint on top.

CRAYFISH BISQUE - W

See fish chapter for boiling crayfish. After eating all the boiled crayfish you want, break tails off heads, save fat and clean largest heads. Make a dressing of chopped tails, chopped onions and green onions, parsley, bell pepper, bread crumbs, and fat. Saute all of this in oleo, seasoning with garlic powder, cajun seasoning, cayenne pepper, and black pepper. Stuff the heads with dressing.

For stew:

Make a roux with flour and oil. Add chopped onions, bell pepper and celery. Let simmer. Add water and simmer more. Add 1 tsp tomato puree, crayfish tails, and some fat, letting cook longer till mixture becomes rather thick. Put stuffed heads in stew and simmer for half hour. Serve over cooked rice.

Some people roll the stuffed heads in flour and fry before adding to stew.

CRAB SOUP

1 can cream of mushroom soup	1 can cream of split pea soup
1 can cream of chicken soup	3 cans milk
1 can cream of potato soup	3 or 4 green onions
1 can cream of celery soup	1 medium bell pepper
1 can cream of onion soup	2 lb lump crab meat
1 can cream of tomato soup	(can use claw)

Saute green onions and chopped pepper in oleo in large pot. Add soups and milk, blending well till no lumps remain. Add crab meat until blended. Season with tabasco or cayenne pepper. Serves from 16 to 20 people. Add more ingredients for a larger crowd. Excellent for a supper party with salad and fresh bread.

OYSTER STEW - W

2 sticks oleo
1/4 cup flour
1/2 cup chopped green onions
1/2 cup celery
2 pts oysters with liquid

1 qt milk
1 pt half & half
Tabasco, Worcestershire sauce,
    salt and pepper, and cayenne

Saute onions and celery in oleo. Add drained oysters and simmer till they curl. Set oysters aside. Add milk and half & half to celery onion mixture, slowly and then add oyster liquid, stirring all the time. Season at this time and cook slowly about 10 minutes. Add oysters. Just before serving, sprinkle with chopped green onions.

SPLIT PEA SOUP - W

Soak 2 packages of split peas in water overnight. The next morning start the soup with a ham bone, from left over ham or from the grocer. Boil for 15 minutes with chopped onions and celery. Clean bone and chop ham in water. Add peas that have been washed and drained. Cut up some carrots and add. Also add a little thyme, cayenne, bay leaf, and marjoram. Season with salt, tabasco, and pepper to taste. Cook slowly for at least an hour, using a potato masher to mash the peas when they get tender. Left over soup freezes well and when reheating, add water to thin.

VEGETABLE SOUP - W

Start with beef short ribs and a soup bone. Cook a long time with diced onions and celery. When beef falls off the bone start adding vegetables, fresh and canned. Vegetables include peas, beans, corn, cabbage, carrots, turnips, rutabaga, tomatoes, green onions, potatoes, parsley, and tomato paste. Add basil, oregano, chili powder, cajun seasoning, black and red pepper, and salt to taste. Simmer a long time. For supper, remove some of the meat and serve with horseradish sauce, soup, cornbread, and sweet potatoes.

BROCCOLI SOUP - W

Saute green onions in oleo. Add chicken broth (1 pt) and chopped broccoli. Cook till broccoli is done. Either make a cream sauce with cheese and add, or use a can of cream of celery, cream of mushroom and cheddar cheese soup. Add 2 cans of low fat evaporated milk, salt, pepper and cayenne. Simmer for 30 to 45 minutes.

EGGPLANT SOUP - W

Saute 1 1/2 cup chopped onions, 1 1/2 cup chopped celery, 1 1/2 cup diced cooked potatoes and 2 small eggplants, peeled and diced. Add a quart of chicken stock, thyme, basil, curry and simmer. Mash or puree ingredients, adding salt and pepper, cayenne and 2 cups heavy cream. Simmer for an hour and serve with fresh parsley and a dash of sour cream on top.

HOT POTATO SOUP
OR
VICHYSSOISE (COLD POTATO SOUP) - W

2 cups chicken broth   **1 cup green onions**
5 or 6 good sized potatoes   **1 cup white onions**

Boil peeled potatoes till falling apart. In skillet, saute onions in stick of oleo till tender. Add to pot of potatoes from which water has been drained. Add seasoning and cover pot and simmer 30 minutes. Strain soup and then add 2 cups hot milk and 1 can condensed milk. Bring to boil and then strain again. Chill well and serve with chopped chives on top for vichyssoise.

OYSTER ARTICHOKE SOUP - W

1 package frozen artichoke hearts
2 sticks oleo
3/4 cup chopped green onion
1 stalk celery, chopped
1 small chopped carrot
2 tbsps chopped parsley

1 clove chopped garlic
1 qt oysters
1/4 cup dry vermouth
1/2 cup evaporated milk
1/4 cup white wine
1 qt chicken stock

Seasonings: salt, pepper, flour, bay leaf, thyme, cayenne pepper, anise, dash of Worcestershire sauce, dash of lemon juice.

Cook artichokes and chop. In saucepan, melt oleo and saute onions, celery, carrots, parsley, and garlic. Add chopped artichokes and stir well. Add 2 tablespoons flour and slowly stir it in mixture, but do not brown. Stir in chicken stock and add seasonings. Simmer slowly over low heat. Chop oysters in food processor and add to artichoke mixture. Add wine, Vermouth, and 1/2 cup evaporated milk. Remove bay leaf and put mixture in processor or blender till smooth. Add a little water, if too thick. Serve warm.

TURNIP SOUP - B

2 tbsps oleo
1 small chopped onion
2 cups chicken broth
3 cups water
3 lbs turnips, peeled and cubed

3/4 cup half & half or evaporated milk
3 tbsps chopped parsley
Salt, pepper, tabasco, sugar, basil, bay leaf, lemon juice

Saute onions in oleo till soft. Add broth, water, bay leaf, and turnips. Cook till turnips are tender. Remove bay leaf and add seasoning. Cook a little longer. Puree in processor or blender. Return to pot and add cream and heat. Before serving, garnish with parsley and a lemon slice.

GAZPACHO - W

2 lg can tomatos or fresh,
   chopped
1 cucumber, peeled and finely
   chopped

1 green pepper, finely chopped
1 med onion, chopped
4 stalks celery, chopped

Place above ingredients in blender or food processor. Blend in the following:

6 ozs white wine
3 ozs oil
3 ozs white wine vinegar
1 clove garlic
Juice of half lemon

4 sweet pickles, chopped
Pimento, chopped
Salt, pepper, and cayenne
   to taste

Chill till very cold

HAM HOCK SOUP - B

4 to 5 lbs ham hocks, fresh
   or smoked
2 tsps salt
1/2 tsp pepper

1/2 cup bell pepper
1/2 cup celery
1 bay leaf
1 1/2 cups cooked rice

Cook rice and set aside. Cover ham hocks with water and add salt, pepper, bell pepper, celery, and bay leaf. Cook on high fire until it comes to a rolling boil. Lower heat and cook for 1 hour or until ham hocks are tender. Add rice and cook 2 more minutes. Serves 8.

OYSTER STEW

3 doz. shucked oysters with liquid
1/4 cup butter
1 qt milk
1 tbsp. flour
Salt and pepper to taste (do not add salt until you have tasted the oyster liquid, sometimes the oysters are very salty and more salt may not be needed.)

Carefully pick over oysters to remove bits of shell. Heat butter in deep sauce pan. Add flour and stir until well blended, but not browned. Add seasonings and oyster liquid . Simmer for a few minutes. Add oysters and heat until edges of oysters curl slightly. Add milk and heat quickly, but do not boil. Serve in bowls with a dash of paprika and a lump of butter. Serve with crackers. You may add a sprinkling of finely minced parsley to the top.

EGG DROP SOUP

Homemade chicken broth or 2 cans
As much water as broth
2 tbs chopped parsley
1 tsp soy sauce
2 eggs
2 or 3 shakes tabasco or
   black pepper

Heat broth, water, soy sauce, seasonings and parsley. Beat eggs slightly and stir into boiling liquid, continuing to stir till eggs separate in shreds.

CREAM OF GREEN BEAN SOUP

2 cans green beans
1 can cream of onion soup
1 can cheddar cheese soup
1 can milk
Tabasco & cumin

In a blender, blend green beans and their liquid till smooth, and combine in saucepan with soups, milk and seasonings. Heat to boiling, then turn to a simmer. Serve 4 to 6

FRENCH ONION SOUP - W

1 lb onions	Gruyere cheese, grated
Butter or oleo	Seasoning to taste
Flour	2 cans consomme
French bread	

Peel and slice onions and cook slowly in oleo until soft, but not brown. Stir in flour and then add consomme and stir till bubbling. Simmer for 20 to 25 minutes. Slice French bread, spread oleo on one side and top with cheese after you have toasted the other side. Run bread back in oven to toast cheese side. Put a piece of French bread on top of each serving and sprinkle a little parmesan cheese on top. Serve hot!

BEEF STEW - W

Coat 2 pounds beef stew meat with salt, pepper, and flour. Brown in 3 tablespoons oil. When meat is brown on both sides, pour off excess oil and add a little water to crust and cook till thick. Add chopped onion, a bay leaf, a teaspoon Worcestershire sauce, salt, pepper, and cayenne pepper. Cover and bring liquid to a boil. Reduce heat and simmer about 1 hour. Add small onions, potatoes, and cut carrots to stew and 1/2 cp burgundy wine. Cover pot again and cook till vegetables are tender. Add 2 cans mushroom steak sauce or 1 can beef gravy. Serve over toast or rice.

NAVY BEAN STEW - B

2 qts water
1 1/2 cups dried navy beans
Salt and pepper to taste
1/2 cup chopped onion

2 cloves chopped garlic
1 lg bell pepper, chopped
2 lg ham hocks or
   1 lg ham bone

Cover beans with water; cover and bring beans to a rolling boil. Lower heat and add salt, pepper, onion, garlic, bell pepper, and ham hock. Cover and cook 1/2 hour. Take large spoon and press beans against side of pot. Cook another 1/2 hour. Add additional 1/2 cup water if bean liquid becomes too thick. Cook 1/2 hour longer or until beans become souplike in liquid. You can remove ham bone or bone from hock. Serves 6.

SIMPLE MEAT BALL STEW - B

2 lbs ground beef
2 cloves garlic, minced
1/2 cup chopped onion
1/4 cup chopped bell pepper
1 egg, beaten
2 cups corn
1 cup carrots, thinly sliced
2 med cubed potatoes

1 can tomato sauce
1 can water
1 can tomato paste
1 can water
2 bay leaves, crumbled
Salt and pepper to taste
1/2 tsp red pepper
2 tbsps cooking oil

Mix ground beef with garlic, onions, bell pepper, beaten egg, salt, and pepper. Shape into 1 1/2 inch meat balls and brown in cooking oil. Drain. Add tomato sauce, tomato paste, water, carrots, corn, potatoes, bay leaf, and red pepper. More water may be needed. Make sure meat balls are almost covered to the top. Cover and cook for 1 hour on low heat, stirring occasionally. It may be necessary to thicken with flour. Use your own judgement. To thicken with flour, blend with some sauce and mix and stir until smooth. Mix into sauce and cook 10 minutes longer. Serve over rice.

COQ AU VIN - W

1 stick oleo
2 tbsps oil
2 chickens, cut in pieces
4 bacon slices, cut in strips
8 ozs fresh mushrooms
6 to 8 small white onions

1 cup red wine
1 cup chicken stock
1 bay leaf
2 chopped garlic cloves
Flour, salt, pepper, tabasco

Brown chicken pieces in oleo in heavy skillet. Remove chicken and add bacon, mushrooms, and onions. Brown. Add a little flour to skillet and add some of the stock, garlic, bay leaf, salt, pepper, tabasco, and the skillet ingredients in a big heavy pot. Simmer till chicken is done and the liquid has thickened.

CORN CHOWDER - W

1/2 stick oleo
1 small chopped onion
1/3 cup flour
3 cups chicken stock
3 potatoes, diced, peeled,
    and cooked

2 can whole kernel corn or
    fresh corn
1 cup milk
Salt, pepper, cayenne

Fry onion in oleo till soft. Stir in flour and cook, stirring constantly for about a minute. Slowly add chicken stock and bring to a boil. Turn heat down and simmer till thickened. Add corn, potatoes, and seasoning for 5 minutes. If using fresh corn, put it in before potatoes and cook a little longer. Add milk at the last and heat thoroughly being careful not to burn. Sprinkle chopped parsley on top of chowder.

STEWED RABBIT - W

Prepare and season 2 rabbits and cut into pieces at the joints.

3 onions, chopped
1 small hunk of ham
Clove of garlic, finely chopped
Flour
1 med bell pepper, chopped

3 tbsps chopped celery
1 (6 oz) can sliced mushrooms
1/2 cup red wine
1/2 cup oil
Salt, pepper, cayenne

Use a heavy dutch oven, if possible. Heat oil and brown rabbit pieces in hot oil. Remove rabbit and saute onions, garlic, bell pepper, celery, and mushrooms till soft. Cut up ham and add to pot after pouring off any excess oil. Add a little flour and brown slowly. Add the rabbit again and a bay leaf, thyme, and parsley. Add the red wine and some boiling water. Stir well, season, and cover pot. Simmer for 1 to 1 1/2 hours or until rabbit is tender. Serve over rice.

SMOTHERED SQUIRREL - W

1/2 squirrel (Per person)
1 chopped onion for each
  squirrel cooked
1/2 chopped bell pepper for
  each prepared squirrel
1 tbsp chopped celery for each
  person

Flour
Oil to cover bottom of pot
1/3 cup red wine for each
  prepared squirrel

In heavy dutch oven, brown squirrel in oil till rich brown color. Remove squirrel and saute vegetables till soft. Add a little flour to pot and brown for roux. Add salt, pepper, cayenne, or tabasco. Return squirrel to pot and add red wine. Turn heat to low, cover, and simmer till squirrel is tender, approximately for 1 hour. A little water may be added while cooking if gravy gets too thick. Serve with rice.

MAKING A WHITE SAUCE - W

2 tbsps butter   Dash of pepper
2 tbsps flour   1/4 tsp salt
1 cup milk or half & half

Melt butter over low heat. Stir in flour and cook till bubbly, stirring constantly. Add salt and pepper. Remove from heat and slowly stir in milk till mixture is smooth. Cook again over low heat till thickened, stirring constantly. A little more cooking and stirring improves taste.

BECHAMEL SAUCE - W

Make a basic white sauce, sauteing 3 tbsps onions in butter before adding flour. Stir in 2 tsps minced parsley. To make sauce thicker, add 1 beaten egg yolk. Use with fish, eggs and poultry.

DIJON SAUCE - W

Make basic white sauce and add 1 tbsp dijon mustard and a dash of lemon juice when you add flour.

CURRY SAUCE - W

1 carton sour cream
1/2 cup mayonnaise
2 or 3 tsp curry powder
1 tsp Worcestershire sauce

1 tsp lemon juice
Dash of tabasco sauce
Black pepper

Cook over slow fire to keep from burning. Use with poultry, meat or shellfish.

BEARNAISE SAUCE - W

Add 1/2 tsp tarragon leaves and 1/2 tsp chervil or parsley leaves and dash of cayenne to Hollandaise sauce. Great with beef, fish and eggs.

MORNAY SAUCE - W

Make basic white sauce and then add 1/2 cup of heavy cream or low fat evaporated milk. Stir in grated fresh parmesan cheese and swiss or cheddar cheese till cheese is melted. Use with poultry, seafood or vegetables.

HOLLANDAISE SAUCE - W

Needed for this recipe is 1/2 cup butter, 4 egg yolks, 3 tbsps lemon juice and a dash of salt and cayenne. Melt butter on top of double boiler over hot water. Remove from heat, add egg yolks, then heat approximately 2 minutes till mixture doubles. Return boiler to hot water, cook, stirring constantly till sauce thickens.

MOCK HOLLANDAISE SAUCE - W

3/4 cup mayonnaise
3 or 4 shakes of
   Worcestershire sauce

1 tsp lemon juice
3 shakes of onion juice
1/2 tsp dry mustard

Mix all thoroughly and sit on side of stove to warm.

HORSERADISH SAUCE - W

Add 2 to 3 tbsp prepared fresh horseradish to Hollandaise sauce. Use with beef, ham, or corned beef.

MOCK HORSERADISH - W

For use with beef, add horseradish to mayonnaise. For corned beef or ham, add prepared mustard to horseradish.

BORDELAISE SAUCE - W

This quick recipe calls for 1 can mushroom or beef gravy, 1 tbsp minced shallots or green onions, 2 tbsps butter, 1/8 cup red wine, 1 tsp wine vinegar, 1/8 tsp thyme, 1 bay leaf, and chopped parsley. Combine all ingredients and simmer about 12 to 15 minutes. Remove bay leaf and stir in parsley. Use with steak or egg dishes.

Party Time

CHAPTER III

"Party Time"

(hors d'oeuvres, canapes, appetizers,
drinks, sandwiches)

Sweets for party time can be found
under Chapters XI and XII

Hors d'oeuvres and appetizers as we know them today were not the same in by gone days. There were tea parties for the ladies and "drinking parties" for the men. Much of the entertainment for the blacks and the poor whites was centered around the church and from these weekly church meetings came the fanciest party food they would dream up. Weddings, among whites and blacks, were special and tables were laden with goodies. Cajuns and creoles were most imaginative with their special occasion cooking and thus were born some of the finest party foods. In a later chapter we will deal with sweets. In this one we wish to deal only with the party foods that came of age with cocktail parties and receptions as late as the early 1900's.

PICTURE EXPLANATION

Playing house was one of the girls' favorite pastimes and having a tea party was the best. If the cook in the big house had time, she would fix cookies or a sweet bread or give the girls something left over from dinner. With imagination, water became tea and the party was complete. Ethel shows our girls enjoying their tea party with a tea set handed down, that would, in later years, become a priceless memory.

CANAPÉ SPREADS

Canapé Spreads

Cut bread into different shapes or use melba rounds. Spread bread with any of the following:

Liver paté mixed with mayonnaise and green onion.

Sardines, mashed, mixed with diced onion, mayonnaise, tabasco, and lemon juice.

Minced turkey or chicken with diced sweet pickle, mayonnaise, and dijon mustard

Tuna fish or salmon with sour cream, relish, mayonnaise, and grated lemon rind on top.

Canned crab meat with mayonnaise, chopped, hard boiled egg, and relish. This can be topped with fresh parmesan cheese and put in oven till cheese melts.

Minced cucumber mixed with sour cream, cream cheese, and dill.

Chopped shrimp (little canned ones) mixed with mayonnaise, celery salt, sweet relish, and chopped capers.

Cream cheese, hard cooked, chopped eggs, and sour cream, topped with caviar.

Party Sandwiches

Fillings:

Grated cheese, chopped, hard boiled egg, minced onion, minced sweet pickle and chopped pimento, softened with mayonnaise.

Softened cream cheese combined with chipped beef, chopped onion, chopped corned beef, minced chives, chopped green pepper or chopped dill pickle. Add tabasco to any of the above mixtures.

Softened cream cheese with minced nuts and crushed pineapple and a dash of curry; or softened cream cheese with apricot preserves, chopped, and a dash of horseradish.

Cottage cheese with chopped ham and sweet pickle relish. Cottage cheese with your favorite preserve or jam. Cottage cheese with pepper jelly.

Thinly sliced red onions with mayonnaise spread. Thinly sliced bell pepper with mayonnaise spread. Thinly sliced tomatoes with mayonnaise spread.

Diced,cooked chicken or diced, cooked ham mixed with chopped celery, a dab of dijon mustard and mayonnaise. Chopped, hard boiled eggs with minced pickle, meat or chicken or fish and mayonnaise.

Chopped,hard boiled eggs with mashed sardines or anchovies with a dash of lemon juice and some mayonnaise. Chopped,hard boiled eggs with caviar, cream cheese and sour cream.

Flaked, cooked salmon with mayonnaise and cucumber, diced. Flaked tuna with minced capers, lemon juice and mayonnaise.

Crab meat with minced pimento, green pepper, diced, sweet relish and mayonnaise.

Chopped almonds with chicken, tuna or crab meat and mayonnaise to moisten.

Cream cheese, chopped nuts,and chopped olives. Cream cheese, chopped nuts,and crushed pineapple. Cream cheese, chopped nuts, and any jelly.

Crisp, chopped bacon with dill pickle and mayonnaise. Crisp, chopped bacon with shredded, sharp cheese, and mayonnaise.

Ground ham and ground American cheese with sweet or dill pickle and mayonnaise to moisten. Ground ham, chopped, hard cooked egg, chopped green pepper, dash of yellow mustard, sweet relish, and mayonnaise.

Deviled ham with grated onion, sweet relish, and mayonnaise.

Thinly sliced corned beef with thinly sliced onion, and mayonnaise. Thinly sliced roast pork with thinly sliced onion, sliced dill pickle, and mayonnaise. Thinly sliced turkey or chicken with dijon or creole mustard and mayonnaise.

Quickie Hors D'Oeuvres

Mushrooms: Stem mushrooms and pat dry. Make mixture of cream cheese, bleu cheese, and bacon bits. Stuff mushrooms and chill.

Cucumbers: Peel, cut ends and take out middle seeds. Stuff with cream cheese mixed with chopped, green onion and mayonnaise. Chill in refrigerator for one hour before slicing.

Cucumber sandwiches: Cut bread rounds. Mix cream cheese, chopped chives, mayonnaise, and 2 to 3 dashes of tabasco. Peel cucumbers and put a thin slice on each bread round, after icing bread with cheese mixture. Sprinkle paprika on top.

Cherry tomatoes: Cut top off tomatoes and hollow out. Make cream cheese mixture as with cucumbers. Fill tomatoes, chill, and sprinkle with bacon bits on top just before serving.

Celery: Mix diced ham, pickled relish (dill or sweet), and mayonnaise. Stuff celery pieces with mixture.

Deviled eggs: Make stuffing mixture of hard boiled egg yellows, mashed, mayonnaise, relish, and dijon mustard. Can be used for egg or celery stuffing.

BLUE CHEESE CHICKEN SPREAD - W

1 3oz package cream cheese,
  softened
2 ozs blue cheese, crumbled

1/2 cup chopped, cooked chicken
1/3 cup drained, crushed pineapple
1/3 cup chopped pecans

Mix softened cheese and add other ingredients. Makes approximately 1 cup.

CAP'N BILL'S CRAB CLAW FINGERS - W

1 container crab claws
2 cups fish fry breading
1/2 cup milk

Salt, pepper and cayenne
  to taste
2 eggs

Drain crab claws and put on paper towel to absorb moisture. Mix egg and milk in bowl, adding salt, pepper and cayenne. Dip crab fingers in egg batter and then roll in breading. Deep fry until golden brown. For spicy flavor, add 1/4 tsp of liquid crab boil to egg batter.

COCKTAIL MEAT BALLS AND MUSHROOMS - W

Make small meat balls of ground chuck, chopped onion, garlic powder, Italian bread crumbs, whole beaten egg, cajun seasoning and black pepper. Fry in hot oil till brown. Drain meat balls. Make gravy of mushroom steak sauce, A-1 sauce, Worcestershire sauce and tabasco. Wash large mushrooms and add to gravy. Let them cook in gravy a short while and then add meat balls. Simmer all and serve in chafing dish. Freezes well.

CHEESE STRAWS - W

1 lb Kraft Old English cheese,
   grated
1/2 lb oleo

1 tsp salt
4 cups cake flour
Large tsp red pepper

Soften cheese and oleo in bowl. Mix cake flour and red pepper with cheese and oleo. Put mixture in cookie press and squeeze out strips on an ungreased cookie sheet. Cook in 400° oven for approximately 10 minutes.
* Sharp cheese may be used if Old English is not available.

SHRIMP MOUSSE - W

2 small cans medium shrimp
1 can tomato bisque soup
6 ozs cream cheese, softened
1/2 cup minced onion or
   green onions (2 bunches)

1/2 cup celery, thinly sliced
1 cup mayonnaise
1 1/2 tbsp Knox unflavored gelatin
1 cup water
Parsley flakes to taste

Spray mold with Pam. Mix water and gelatin; let set to dissolve. Stir cream cheese and soup over low heat until well blended. Don't over cook. Add onions, shrimp, celery, gelatin and mayonnaise. Stir and pour into mold. Mold overnight. Unmold and serve with Wheat Thins or other crackers.

CAP'N BILL'S SPICY CRAB DIP - W

1/2 cup margarine
1/2 cup diced onion
1 8 oz package cream cheese
1 can cream of mushroom soup

1 lb crab meat
1 can Rotel tomatoes
Garlic powder
Salt and pepper to taste

Saute onions in oleo and add cream cheese, breaking the cheese into pieces. Let melt in skillet. When this has melted, stir in mushroom soup, crab meat, tomatoes and seasoning. Heat thoroughly. Serve in chafing dish.

SHRIMP DIP - W I

1 can tomato soup
1 (8 oz) package cream cheese, melted
1 package unflavored gelatin dissolved in 1/4 cup water

1 cup mayonnaise
1/2 cup chopped celery
1/2 cup chopped bell pepper
1/2 cup chopped onion

Mix all together and add 2 cans shredded shrimp. Put in mold and let set overnight. Serve with Saltine crackers.

HAM OLIVE LOG - W

1 (4 1/2 oz) can deviled ham
1 package cream cheese
1/4 cup chopped, stuffed olives

1/2 cup chopped onion
Tabasco

Combine ham, cream cheese, and olives. Chill. Roll into log and sprinkle with parsley.

OYSTERS IN SHERRY WINE - W

2 dozen oysters
Flour for dredging
Salt and pepper to taste
1 tbsp vegetable oil
1/3 cup fresh lemon juice

1 cup A-1 sauce
2 tbsps Worcestershire sauce
3 ozs pale dry sherry
1 tsp tabasco

Salt and pepper oysters. Dredge in flour. Grill on lightly oiled griddle on top of stove until crisp and brown on both sides. Sprinkle oysters with remaining oil while grilling on each side. Combine lemon juice, A-1 sauce, Worcestershire, and wine in a saucepan. Heat thoroughly over low heat. Remove from heat. Correct seasoning (sauce will be thin). Place oysters on a hot serving plate or in a shallow chafing dish. Pour sauce over oysters to completely cover. Insert toothpicks and serve. Serves 8.

GEEGEE'S SALMON BALL - W

1 can salmon
2 8oz packages cream cheese

1/2 tbsp lemon juice
4 shakes Wright's liquid smoke

Soften cream cheese. Drain salmon and mix all ingredients in a bowl. Make into one large ball and harden in refrigerator till serving time.

CHEESE PUFFS - W

1 lb sharp cheese
1/2 lb butter
1 tsp salt

2 cups flour
Red pepper to taste

Cream cheese and butter. Add salt and flour and mix in red pepper. Roll to marble size balls and put on cookie sheet 1 1/2 inches apart. Press down with fork. It will make waffle pattern on top. Bake 8 to 10 minutes in 450° oven.

SHRIMP DIP - W II

3 cans small shrimp
1/4 cup lemon juice
1 1/2 8 oz packages cream cheese
1 cup mayonnaise

1 med grated onion
1 tbsp Worcestershire sauce
Dash of red pepper

Combine all ingredients and serve as a party dip with crackers. Serves 10 to 12.

PICKLED SHRIMP - W

1 1/4 cup salad oil
3/4 cup white vinegar (warmed)
1 tsp salt
2 1/2 tsp celery seed
2 tbsp capers with juice
1/3 cup Worcestershire sauce

1 tbsp yellow mustard
Dash of hot sauce
Bay leaves
Fresh onion rings
3 - 5 lbs shrimp, peeled and cooked
   (best to boil and then peel)

Mix marinade and pour over boiled shrimp. Lightly toss to moisten all shrimp. Let shrimp sit in marinade in refrigerator overnight.

AUDREY'S FROSTED PATE - W

1 lb liverwurst
4 green onions, chopped
4 good sized sprigs of parsley, chopped
1 can beef consommé
2 envelopes gelatin

1 8oz package Philadelphi cream cheese
Worcestershire sauce
Hot Sauce
Mayonnaise

Mix onions and parsley with liverwurst, adding 3 dashes of hot sauce. Warm beef consommé and add the 2 envelopes of gelatin to it. Pour some consommé mixture in bottom of mold. Mix some consommé mixture with liverwurst mixture and put on top of first layer. Mix remaining consommé mixture to softened cream cheese that has been mixed with mayonnaise, 2 dashes Worcestershire sauce and 3 dashes hot sauce. Top other layers with this. Refrigerate until it congeals or freeze for future.

SHRIMP DIP - W III

Whip ingredients in order given until mixture is light and creamy.

1 cup peeled, canned shrimp, chopped fine (use cans of small shrimp)
2 8oz or 1 16 oz. package of cream cheese
1/2 cup mayonnaise
1 tbsp grated onion

1/2 cup bottled steak sauce
2 tsp horseradish
1 tbsp Worcestershire sauce
1 or 2 dashes hot sauce
Pinch of salt
Lemon juice
Paprika

63

BLACK BEAN DIP - W

1 lb black beans
3 bell peppers, chopped
2 lg onions, chopped
1 tbsp vinegar

1/4 tsp cumin
1/4 tsp oregano
1 cup oil
Salt and tabasco to taste

Soak beans overnight. Cook till they get real soft when mashed with fork. In skillet, saute onions and peppers in 1/2 cup oil. Add vinegar, cumin, oregano and rest of oil to cooked beans and let thicken. Add seasoning and mash beans. Serve hot or cold with chips.

PIMENTO CHEESE DIP - W

1 lg jar of chopped pimentos
1 lb sharp cheese, grated

1 med onion or 4 or 5
    green onions, grated

Add enough mayonnaise for "dip" consistency. Also add 4 or 5 shakes of tabasco. Let sit a while before serving so onions can blend with cheese. Serve as dip with chips or tortilla chips. Also great for sandwiches. Simply cut down on amount of mayonnaise.
For hotter dip, chop jalapeno peppers in mixture.

LIZ'S ARTICHOKE BALLS - W

1 14 oz can of artichoke hearts
1 cup bread crumbs
2 eggs
2 tbsps oil

2 tbsps lemon juice
3 cloves chopped garlic
3 tbsps parmesan cheese

Drain and mash artichokes. Add other ingredients except cheese and put in refrigerator for 4 hours. Roll in cheese and heat in oven at 400°. Makes 4 dozen.

HAM AND CHEESE BITES - W

Combine an 8 ounce package of cream cheese with a small can of drained, crushed pineapple, dash of powdered mustard, tabasco, and chopped pecans. Refrigerate mixture till hard. Make into small balls and roll in minced ham, corned beef or dried beef. Keep in refrigerator till serving time.

LIPTAUER CHEESE - W

1 (8 oz) package cottage cheese, lowfat if desired
1 stick unsalted butter
1 to 1 1/2 tsps caraway seeds

2 tbsps chopped onion
1 tsp chopped capers
Carton of sour cream

Put cheese in food processor or blender and blend till smooth. Add softened butter and mix till smooth. Put above mixture in bowl and add onion, capers, caraway seed, salt, pepper, powdered mustard, and sour cream. Mix all with mixer and shape into ball. Decorate with chives and paprika and refrigerate for 2 to 3 hours. Serve on a party tray with small slices of rye bread and small slices of baked ham. Makes a pretty tray with cheese in middle, ham slices around, and bread in outside ring. Garnish with parsley, radishes, and cherry tomatoes.

CAMEMBERT OR BRIE MOUSSE - W

1 tbsp unflavored gelatin
1/2 cup water
1/2 lb camembert cheese, shredded
Chopped pimento, parsley, and chives

1 egg white, beaten stiff
1/2 cup heavy cream, whipped
Dash of red pepper

Soften gelatin in water over low heat till it dissolves. Add cheese and stir till melted. Mix in pimento, onion, and parsley. Refrigerate till cool. Fold in egg white and whipped cream and put all in fancy party mold. Chill till firm. Serve with fresh vegetables: celery, zucchini, radishes, pepper strips, cucumber slices, green onions or crackers.

HOT SHRIMP CANAPES - W

1 cup small shrimp or other size,
   finely chopped
1 cup of sharp cheese, grated
1 dill pickle, finely chopped

Tabasco to taste
Mayonnaise to make mixture
   stick together

Toast bread on one side, trim crusts and cut in fourths. Spread mixture on toasted side. Bake in moderate oven for 10 minutes. Can substitute shrimp with crayfish, crabmeat, salmon or sardines.

EGGPLANT CAVIAR - W

1 lg eggplant
1 lg onion, chopped
1 green bell pepper, chopped
1 bud garlic, crushed

1/2 cup olive oil
2 fresh tomatoes, chopped
3 tbsps dry white wine
Salt, pepper and cayenne to taste

—Much faster in microwave.— Put whole eggplant in 400° oven and bake until soft (approximately 1 hour). Saute onion, garlic and pepper till tender but not brown. Peel and chop eggplant; mix with tomatoes and add to sauteed vegetables. Add wine and seasonings and mix thoroughly. Cook till thick. Cool and refrigerate. Great on party rye or melba rounds.

FRESH VEGETABLE DIP - W

1 cup mayonnaise
1/2 cup chili sauce
1/4 cup ketchup
1/2 cup salad oil
1 clove garlic, chopped fine

1 small onion, chopped fine
1 tbsp Worcestershire sauce
1 tbsp dijon mustard
Couple dashes tabasco sauce
Black pepper to taste

Great as a dip or as salad dressing.

66

JALAPENO COCKTAIL PIE - W

3 or 4 seeded, chopped jalapeno   6 beaten eggs
  peppers
4 cups shredded sharp cheddar cheese

Grease a 9 inch square baking pan and cover bottom with cheese. Sprinkle peppers over cheese and pour eggs over mixture. Bake at 350° for 30 minutes or until firm. Cool and cut in 1 inch squares. Mild chili peppers may be used instead of jalapeno peppers.

MATTIE'S LAYERED SHRIMP PARTY PLATE - W

Use either a spring form pan, a 10 to 12 inch serving platter or fix on regular platter.

Bottom Layer:

Blend together 2 (8 oz) packages softened cream cheese, 2 tablespoons Worcestershire sauce, 2 tablespoons tabasco, and 2 to 4 minced garlic.

Second Layer:

1 medium size bottle (9 oz) Kraft Cocktail Sauce

Third Layer:

1 lb boiled shrimp, chopped in thirds

Fourth Layer:

1/2 to 1 lb grated mozzarella cheese

Fifth Layer:

Mix together 6 to 8 chopped green onion, 1 green pepper, and 2 to 3 chopped, peeled tomatoes

On a 12 inch serving platter, begin with cheese mixture and spread flat, adding layers in order. Cover layers evenly and well. Decorate rim of plate with fresh parsley and boiled shrimp. Serve with melba rounds and party crackers.

CRAB & SHRIMP BISCUITS - W

Original recipe created for Our Lady of the Gulf Crab Festival, 1987

6 Tbsp margarine
1 large garlic clove, chopped
1/2 C. shallots, chopped
1/4 C. fresh parsley, chopped
1/4 tsp Tony Chachere seasoning
1/8 tsp salt
1/8 tsp black pepper

8 oz (2 C.) crab meat
1/2 C. raw shrimp, chopped
2 Tbsp seasoned breadcrumbs
1 C. grated Swiss cheese
1 10 oz can butter biscuits

In a heavy skillet, saute the first seven ingredients on a medium heat until seasonings are limp. Add crab meat and chopped shrimp and continue cooking until shrimp are pink (about 2-3 minutes).

Remove pan from heat and allow to cool. Add breadcrumbs to mixture in order to absorb any excess margarine from the seafood mixture. Excess margarine on the biscuit will make it difficult to form & seal the biscuit into a ball. When mixture is completely cooled, add grated Swiss cheese and mix well.

Next, roll each canned biscuit individually between two pieces of wax paper until about 5 inches in diameter. Biscuit will handle easily if waxed paper and biscuit are lightly dusted with a little flour. Remove the flattened biscuit from the paper and hold in the cupped palm of your hand. Add approximately 1 to 2 tablespoons of the seafood mixture into the center of the biscuit. By pinching the outer edges of the biscuit together, you can seal the biscuit into a ball about 2 inches in diameter. It is important to completely and uniformly seal the biscuit or it will come apart when frying. Place the stuffed biscuits seam-side down on a cookie sheet and refrigerate 2 hours before frying. Can also be frozen individually for later use.

TO COOK: Heat about 2 inches of corn oil to 400 degrees in a heavy duty Dutch oven and deep fat fry the biscuits. Drop biscuits into the oil one at a time, making sure the biscuit does not stick to the bottom on initial contact. The biscuits will float while cooking; turn them occasionally to insure even cooking. Remove biscuits when golden (about 2-3 minutes) and drain them on paper towels. Serve. If cooking frozen biscuits, let them partially thaw before dropping into hot oil.

CAJUN PATE DE FOIE GRAS

1 lb goose (or chicken) livers, cooked
3 onion chopped fine
8 ripe olives, pitted
1 teaspoon chili powder

Salad oil or dressing
1 clove garlic chopped fine
Dash of cayenne
1/8 c chopped parsley

Grind all ingredients together and mix with enough salad oil or dressing to form spreading consistency. Spread paté on potato chips or toasted bread or small party biscuits.

LITTLE HAMBURGERS

1 lb. ground meat
1 egg
1 tsp salt

1 tbsp prepared mustard
Juice of 1 small onion
Dash of Lowry's seasoning salt

Spread small rounds (4 out of 1 slice of bread) of bread with Horseradish sauce. Place small patty of meat on top (covering completely). Put under broiler for 5 or 6 minutes until brown. Makes 48.

CURRY CHEESE BALL

8 oz. Philadelphia cream cheese
1/2 cup chutney (Major Gray)

1/2 - 1 tsp curry powder
1/2 cup chopped nuts

Mix together and put in refrigerator till easy to handle. Shape in ball and roll in 1 cup chopped nuts and 1 cup coconut. Serve with crackers.

WELSH RABBIT - W

1/3 cup butter
2 lbs sharp cheddar cheese, grated
1 tsp dry mustard
1 tsp Worcestershire sauce

4 eggs, lightly beaten
1 cup half & half cream
Cayenne

Melt butter slowly in double boiler. Add cheese and stir occasionally till cheese melts. Add mustard and Worcestershire and some cayenne pepper. Blend eggs, cream, and strain into cheese mixture. Cook until thick, stirring constantly. Garnish with parsley. Serve in a chafing dish with toasted French bread cubes or melba rounds.

DEVILED DELIGHTS

1 lg can Underwood deviled ham
1/2 stick butter (stored at
  room temperature)

1/2 tsp mustard

Mix altogether until it becomes a paste. You may have to add a little mayonnaise. Spread on bread rounds top with thinly sliced cucumbers or onions. Add small shrimp for decoration.

HOT CHEESE CANAPES - W

Cut bread rounds from white or rye bread. Toast one side of bread and turn over for filling. Filling includes 1 cup Hellmans mayonnaise and 1 cup grated provolone or mozzarella cheese. Put a slice of ham, corned beef, or roast on each round. Mix mayonnaise and cheese and top meat with mixture. Broil till bubbly. Can top with onion, olive or tomato.

DEVILED GOODIES - W

1 (8 oz) package cream cheese　　**Cut bread rounds**
1 lg deviled ham

Mix cream cheese with 1 egg yolk, one half teaspoon baking powder, onion juice, lemon juice, Worcestershire sauce, and red pepper. Toast bread rounds on one side. Turn them over and spread deviled ham on rounds and ice with cream cheese mixture. Run in a 350° oven for 15 minutes. Can be topped with a slice of onion or olive.

CHEESE DIP - W

Mix 1/2 stick melted oleo with 4 tbsps flour. Cook over low heat for 1 minute. Add:

1 tsp paprika　　　　　　　　**3/4 tsp cummin seed**
1 tsp ground mustard　　　　**1 tsp pepper juice from can**
1 tsp chili powder　　　　　　**　of Jalapeno peppers**
6 ozs sharp cheddar cheese

Mix well. Then add 2 cups milk, 1/2 pod Jalapeno pepper (finely chopped), 6 ozs grated sharp cheese and 1 bud of chopped garlic. Cook over low heat till thick, stirring constantly to avoid lumping. More chili powder and pepper sauce can be added if you want it hotter.

MINT JULEP - W

There are many different versions of the Mint Julep, but this one I learned from "Mama".

Bibby

Make a simple syrup of equal parts sugar and water and bring to a boil. Add some crushed mint leaves to mixture. Boil syrup till thick. Pack julep glasses, silver goblets or tall glasses with ice. Put 1 1/2 tea of syrup over ice. Add whiskey to glass and garnish with fresh mint. Straws are good for sipping.

SAZERAC - W

1 tsp simple syrup	1 jigger whiskey
3 drops Peychaud bitters	Dash of Pernod
2 drops Angostura bitters	Twist of lemon

Combine first four ingredients and stir. Chill a glass and then coat inside with Pernod. Put ingredients in cocktail shaker and then pour into chilled glass. Add lemon twist.

FROZEN DAIQUIRIS - W

1 fifth white rum	1 can fresh lemon juice
2 cans frozen limeade	8 small cans water
2 cans frozen lemonade	2 scant cups powdered sugar

Blend well. Put in freezer jars in deep freeze. Take out right before serving.

A STREET DANCE PUNCH - B

In French (Fay-doh-doh)

1 12-oz package frozen strawberries
2 tbsps grated lime rind
Juice from one lime
1 bottle (4/5) sparkling burgundy

1 bottle (4/5) dry champagne
1 bottle (4/5) sauterne
Block of ice for punch bowl

Combine strawberries, lime rind and lime juice in saucepan. Simmer together 10 minutes, put through blender. Cool.

Pour fruit mixture over ice in punch bowl. Add wines just before serving.

Garnish with whole strawberries and lime slices. Makes about 25 servings.

LOUISIANA MINT JULEP - B

6 mint leaves
1/2-oz simple syrup mix

2 ozs bourbon
1 mint sprig

Place 6 mint leaves in tall 12 oz glass. Add simple syrup mix. Muddle mint leaves. Add remaining bourbon. Stir thoroughly. Garnish with mint sprig.

Simple Syrup Mix

Place 4 tbsps granulated sugar and 1/2-oz water in sauce pan. Cook until sugar is dissolved, stirring occasionally.

Makes one serving.

SOUTHERN WINE LEMONADE - B

Prepare lemonade in the usual manner with ice.

For each glass, add 2 to 4 ozs of any red or white table wine. Sweeten to taste.

73

OLD HOME STYLE ICE CREAM SODAS - B

In a tall soda glass put about 1/3 cup crushed sweetened fruit such as strawberries, raspberries, peaches, pineapple or chocolate and 3 tbsps of your favorite syrup.

Stir in a spoonful of ice cream; whipped cream or light cream.

Fill the glass three fourths full with chilled carbonated beverage. Float in the carbonated mixture two dippers or two full tbsps of ice cream and then add more carbonated beverage to fill to the top. Suck with a straw or use a long handled teaspoon.

PLANTATION LEMONADE PUNCH - B

4 6-oz cans frozen concentrate
    for lemonade
4 cansful water (from juice cans)
4 6-oz cans frozen pineapple juice
4 cansful water (from juice cans)

2 qts ginger ale
1 qt sparkling water
1 qt dry champagne
Ice cubes (crushed) or
    block of ice

Make sure you fill cans to the top with water. Combine the juices and water to keep chilled. When ready to serve, add ginger ale and sparkling water and pour over ice cubes or other ice in a large punch bowl. Then pour the well chilled champagne as evenly as possible over the punch and stir it gently through the punch. Makes approximately 50 4-oz servings.

CREOLE SUMMER PUNCH - B

2 qts orange ice or sherbet
3 (3/4 quart) bottles sauterne or
    other white wine, chilled
2 6-oz cans frozen orange juice

Sugar to taste
1 lg bottle sparkling champagne,
    well chilled

Place sherbet in punch bowl. Pour in sauterne and frozen juice diluted with water according to directions on can. Stir until no lumps of sherbet remain.

Add sugar, if desired, and stir until dissolved. Add champagne. Makes about 75 (1/3 cups) servings.

SOUTHERN JULEP CHAMPAGNE - B

4 mint sprigs
1 tbsp sugar

2 ozs brandy
Champagne to fill

Crush mint sugar and 2 tbsp of water in a large glass. Half fill with crushed ice. Add brandy and pour in champagne to fill glass, stirring slowly.

Decorate with pineapple or orange, several sprigs of mint and serve with straws. Juleps should be sipped.

BRANDY EGGNOG - B

1 egg
1 tbsp sugar

2 ozs brandy
3/4 glass of milk

Shake well with cracked ice. Strain with nutmeg on top. Other ways to serve this eggnog is to substitute port, rum, sherry or whiskey.

HOLIDAY EGGNOG - B

6 eggs, separated
3/4 cup sugar
2 cups milk, chilled
1 to 1 1/2 cups cognac or brandy

1/4 cup rum
2 cups heavy cream, chilled
Nutmeg

Beat egg whites until almost stiff enough to hold a peak. Add sugar gradually, beating until stiff but not dry.

Beat egg yolks until thick. Stir in milk, cognac, and rum blending well with whipped cream until stiff and fold into egg-milk mixture. Fold in beaten egg whites.

Keep cold until ready to serve. Pour into punch bowl. Sprinkle each serving with nutmeg. Makes 3 quarts.

ROOSEVELT HOTEL'S RAMOS GIN FIZZ - W

This came from Ramos, one of New Orleans' most famous and colorful bartenders. Although it is not exactly the same because it has been passed down through the years, this is our version.

1 jigger gin
1 tbsp powdered sugar
2 dashes lime juice
2 dashes lemon juice

1/2 egg white
Dashes of orange flower water
1/3 cup cream
Seltzer water and crushed ice

Combine all ingredients and shake in shaker with crushed ice till foamy. Pour into cocktail glasses and add a dash of seltzer water to each drink.

CRANBERRY PUNCH - B

2 (12 oz) cans frozen lemonade
1 lg can pineapple juice
4 cans cranberry sauce, whipped
4 fifths ginger ale

2 (16 oz) cans frozen orange juice
3 1/2 bottles cranberry cocktail

Serves 150.

Company Comes to Dinner

Chapter IV

Company Comes to Dinner

Casserole Dishes

In plantation times visiting was a problem for people who lived miles apart and horses and wagons were the only mode of transportation.

When people did visit it was usually for a very special occasion like weddings and balls and most of the folks stayed overnight.

When these occasions took place it was always a big event and cooking was done in advance to take care of the extra guests. Although casseroles as we know them today were not called that, the kitchen was filled with big pots of delectable combinations that would feed a crowd. Thus were born the casseroles because it was a way to cook for many. In this chapter we will present some old recipes that have been updated and some casseroles of our modern times.

Nowadays, the casserole has become a way of life for feeding a big family or informal entertaining.

Picture explanation

Our girls were always excited when it was announced that "company comes to dinner" because this meant they would have new playmates for a day or two. They would wait at the gate and run behind the carriage, anticipating the excitement of a two day party.

CANNELLONI A LA NERONE - W

3 dozen thin pancakes (should
  be like crepes)
3 chicken breasts
1/2 lb chicken livers
1/2 lb prosciutto (any ham will do)
1/2 cup flour

1 qt milk and cream
1/4 cup sherry
2 cups parmesan cheese,
  freshly grated
Salt and pepper to taste

Cook chicken breasts and livers till tender. Grind chicken, livers and ham together. Make white sauce of flour, milk, salt, and sherry. Mix enough sauce with ground meats to spread on thin pancakes. Roll up pancakes. Place in shallow casserole dish. Pour remaining white sauce over mixture. Add parmesan cheese on top. Bake in 375° oven for about 25 minutes. Can be made a day ahead of time.

CHICKEN CATCH ANYTHING - B

1 whole frying chicken
  (liver, neck and gizzard)
1 stick of margarine
1/2 cup onions
1/4 cup parsley flakes
Salt and pepper to taste
1 can corn (16 oz)

3 carrots chopped in small pieces
1 can peas (16 oz)
1/2 cup chopped bell peppers
1 med package spaghetti
1 can tomato sauce (16 oz)
1 can water
1 can tomato paste (12 oz)

Wash and cut chicken in serving sizes. Peel and cut carrots into small pieces. Chop onion and bell peppers. In a large skillet, melt margarine and saute onions, bell peppers, parsley flakes and chicken (using all parts). Skin if you prefer. Stir constantly until light brown; do not burn. Add carrots. Saute, stirring constantly for 10 minutes on low flame. Remove from heat. Boil spaghetti and drain. Place in large roasting pot the spaghetti and chicken mixture, mixing well and seasoning to taste with the salt and pepper. Pour tomato sauce and paste over chicken and spaghetti mixture. Add water and mix well. Place in a large well greased casserole baking dish with a cover and bake for 1 hour on 200° to 225° until chicken is tender. Add water if necessary. Check often. Serves 6 to 8. Serve with green salad or just with cornbread.

CHICKEN AND SPAGHETTI - W

2 hens or 3 small fryers
Boil with 2 stalks celery chopped,
  1 onion quartered, salt and pepper.
  Cook till done and put in refrigerator
  overnight in chicken stock.

The next day saute in oleo:

3 lbs ground chuck
4 stalks chopped celery
1 bunch of chopped green onions
1/2 bunch of chopped parsley
4 cloves garlic, minced
1 lg bell pepper, chopped

When above mixture is done, put in big pot that contains the cut up chicken. Add 2 cans tomatoes, 3 cans mushrooms (stems and pieces) and 1 lb sharp cheese, grated. Cook slowly till cheese melts. Add a little margarine and basil, salt, pepper and cayenne pepper to taste. Cook 2 lbs spaghetti in another pot and add to above mixture. Sprinkle parmesan cheese in mixture. Put in large casserole dish and top with more parmesan cheese. Keep warm in oven. Great for large crowds.

CHICKEN AND SHRIMP CANTONESE - B

6 cups cooked rice
3 chicken breasts, cooked and
    cut into cubes
1 5 lb bag fresh shrimp, cut
    into bite size pieces
1/4 tsp celery salt
1/4 cup butter or margarine
2 cloves garlic, minced
1 small can mushrooms, drained
    and cut up

1 cup shredded red cabbage
1/2 cup sliced bamboo shoots
2 cups sliced water chestnuts
2 1/2 cups chicken stock
2 tsps soy sauce
2 tsps Worcestershire sauce
3 tbsps flour mixed with water
    till smooth

In a large skillet, melt butter or light cooking oil. Add garlic and celery salt. Then add your chicken, shrimp and mushrooms. Saute for 3 to 4 minutes on a low fire, stirring constantly. Add bamboo shoots and water chestnuts, also stirring constantly. Saute for 2 to 3 minutes longer. Add remaining ingredients: chicken stock, soy sauce, Worcestershire sauce, flour and water mixture. Simmer 4 to 5 minutes longer and serve over rice or add rice a little at a time until rice is mixed well. Serve then with a green salad.

MARGUERITE'S CRAB DISH - W

1 stick butter or oleo
1 small bunch green onions,
    chopped
1/2 cup chopped parsley
2 tbsps flour

1 pint breakfast cream
1/2 lb grated swiss cheese
1 tbsp dry sherry wine
Salt, black and red pepper
1 lb white crab meat

Saute onions and parsley in melted butter. Blend in flour, cream and cheese till cheese melts. Add other ingredients and gently fold in crab meat. Serve in chafing dish or on toast or patty shells.

EGGPLANT CASSEROLE - W

1 can tomatoes
1 can cheddar cheese soup
Chili powder to taste
1 cup crushed Fritos

1/2 bell pepper, chopped
1 onion, chopped
1 med eggplant, cut up
  and peeled

Saute onions, peppers and eggplant in oleo. Add vegetables to other ingredients in a casserole dish. Sprinkle romano cheese and Italian bread crumbs on top. Bake at 350° till heated through.

GOOGSIE'S SHRIMP STEW - W

Saute 1 cup chopped onions, 1 cup chopped pepper, 1 cup chopped celery and 1 cup chopped parsley. Boil 3 lbs shrimp; peel shrimp and save heads. Wash heads well. Boil heads in a little water and add seasoning. Remove heads and add flour to water to thicken. Add 2 cans tomatoes and 1 can tomato paste. Add cooked vegetables and simmer mixture for 30 to 45 minutes. Add shrimp at end and cook a little longer. Serve over rice. Remember, if you do not want to make white sauce, use one of the cream soups.

CRAB CASSEROLE - W

6 tbsps oleo
4 tbsps flour
2 cups milk
2 tbsps grated onions
1 egg, beaten

1 cup grated sharp
  cheddar cheese
1 lb crab meat
1 lb fresh mushrooms
1 can cream of mushroom soup

Make white sauce of flour, butter and milk. Add onions and cook till thickened. Add small amount of sauce to beaten egg and then stir in hot sauce. Add cheese and stir till melted. Add crab meat, mushrooms, soup, and season to taste. Pour into casserole dish; sprinkle bread crumbs and parmesan cheese on top. Bake 15 to 20 minutes in 350° oven. Serves 4.

CHICKEN NOODLE CASSEROLE - B

4 chicken breasts, cooked and
　chopped (skins removed)
4 chicken upper thighs, cooked
　and chopped (skins removed)
1/2 cup chopped onions
1/2 cup chopped green peppers
1/4 cup hot red peppers
1/4 cup chopped celery

4 tbsps butter
4 tbsps flour
1 1/2 cup milk
Salt and pepper to taste
1 8 oz cooked noodles
1/2 cup sour cream
1/2 cup crushed potato chips
　(sour cream flavored)

Saute onions, green peppers, hot red peppers and celery on a low heat in a large skillet in butter. Cook for 5 minutes. Add flour to mixture, stirring often. Slowly stir in milk over the mixture. Mix well. Then add the chicken breasts and thighs. Mix well. Season to taste with the salt and pepper. Add cooked and drained noodles. Mix well and stir in sour cream. Put in greased baking dish. Place in oven at 250 to 300° and cook for 20 minutes. Sprinkle with potato chips and bake for 5 to 10 minutes longer. Serve hot with toasted bread.

ELLA'S SHRIMP CREOLE - W

2 to 3 lbs cleaned and deveined
　shrimp
4 tbsps fat
1/3 cup flour
1 4 oz can tomato sauce
1/2 cup chopped onions
1/2 cup chopped bell peppers
1/2 cup chopped celery

1 garlic clove, minced
1/2 tsp thyme
1 bay leaf
2 tbsps chopped parsley
2 tsps sugar
1 3/4 cups hot water
Salt and pepper to taste

Saute shrimp in fat in large skillet until pink. Remove from pan and add flour and brown slightly. Add chopped seasoning and saute. Add tomato sauce, water, thyme, bay leaf, sugar, garlic, salt and pepper. Stir well and simmer in covered pan for 20 minutes, stirring occasionally. Add shrimp and cook till tender. Add parsley just before serving. This may be made several hours earlier and reheated till piping hot. Serve over hot rice. Makes 6 servings.

MILDRED'S CRAB CASSEROLE - W

1 pint half and half
1 lb oleo or butter
1 lb cheddar cheese (grated or
  melt block)
2 green onions, chopped

1 small jar pimento
1 medium bell pepper, chopped
1 small bunch parsley,
  finely chopped

Mix oleo, half and half and cheese in double boiler until cheese melts. Add 2 lbs of crab meat, onions, parsley, pepper and pimento and large can of mushrooms. Cook 1 package of vermicelli and drain. Combine all ingredients and vermicelli. Top with paprika and parmesan cheese. Bake at 325° for 30 to 45 minutes.

DEVILED OYSTERS - W

1 cup chopped onions
1 cup chopped celery

1 cup chopped bell pepper
2 tbsps butter

Boil above ingredients in 1 cup water. Combine 1 pint chopped oysters, 2 cups crushed crackers that have been soaked in milk. Also add 2 tbsps oil, 2 tbsps ketchup, 2 tbsps Worcestershire sauce, salt, pepper, cayenne (to taste), 2 whole eggs, boiled vegetables and a cup of chopped parsley. Put in casserole dish with bread crumbs on top and bake for 20 minutes at 300°.

CLARA'S SALMON LOAF OR CASSEROLE - W

1 cup scalded milk
2 cups soft bread
1/4 tsp dry mustard
1/4 lb sharp cheese

3 eggs
2 cups salmon
Salt and pepper to taste

Soak 2 cups soft bread in 1 cup scalded milk. Add dry or prepared mustard, sharp cheese (cut in small pieces) and mix over low heat till cheese melts. Cool. Add 3 beaten egg yolks. Fold in 2 cups flaked salmon and add stiffly beaten egg whites. Pour in greased casserole dish and bake in 325° oven for 45 minutes. Serves 6.

SEAFOOD FONTENOT - W

3/4 cup green onions, chopped
3/4 cup celery, chopped
3/4 cup bell pepper, chopped
2 small cans stems and
   pieces mushrooms
2 cans mushroom soup
2 packages frozen broccoli,
   chopped

1/2 tsp Worcestershire sauce
1/2 tsp Tabasco
1 can low fat evaporated milk
1 lb grated sharp cheddar cheese
2 lbs crayfish or shrimp (cooked)
1 lb white crab meat

Saute vegetables in butter or oleo until soft. Boil broccoli and drain well. Add mushrooms, mushroom soup and evaporated milk to the vegetables and cook over low fire till it becomes medium sauce. Add grated cheese and melt in the mixture. Then, add broccoli and stir through mixture. Add crayfish or shrimp and crab meat. Season to taste with Worcestershire, tabasco, salt, pepper and garlic. Serve 25 as a hot dip with crackers or 12 for lunch or dinner in patty shells or on toast. Freezes well.

CAJUN FETTUCINI - W

2 lg onions, chopped
3 med bell peppers, chopped
1 clove garlic, minced
1/3 cup flour
1/2 bunch parsley
1 pint half and half
1 8 oz jalapeno cheese

1 lb velveeta cheese
1 lb crab meat
1 1/2 lbs shrimp, cooked
   and peeled
1 1/2 lbs crayfish tails,
   cooked and peeled
1 lb fettucini noodles, boiled

Saute vegetables in oleo till wilted. Add flour and parsley. Add half and half and cheeses, stirring till cheeses have melted and blended with vegetables. Add seafood and blend. Then add seafood, vegetable mixture to pot that contains noodles. Mix well and put in large casserole dish. Garnish with fresh parsley and sprinkle with parmesan cheese. Heat in slow oven (325 to 350°) till heated through.

OLD-TIME JAMBALAYA - B

1/2 lb fresh pork
1 onion
1 clove garlic
1/2 lb cured ham
6 fine (pork sausage)
2 tbsps lard or butter

1 bay leaf
1 whole clove
1 1/2 qts beef or chicken broth
1/2 tsp tabasco
3/4 tsp salt
1 cup uncooked rice

Cut the pork (lean and fat) into cubes about 1/2 inch thick.   Chop the onions and garlic very fine. Dice the ham and sausage into pieces. Melt the lard in a heavy iron pot or dutch oven. Add the onions, garlic, pork and ham, and brown slowly, stirring frequently. Add sausage, bay leaf, clove, and cook about 5 minutes. Add both tabasco and salt and bring mixture to a boil. Add the rice, which has been washed. Cover and simmer gently a half hour or longer until rice is tender. Stir often to mix well. Season to taste.

JAMBALAYA TODAY - B

1/4 cup butter
1/2 cup chopped onion
1/2 cup chopped green pepper
1 clove garlic, finely chopped
1/2 lb cooked ham
  (1 1/2 cup diced)

1 lb shelled raw shrimp, cleaned
1 can (1 lb, 12 ozs) tomatoes
1 tsp salt
1/2 tsp tabasco
1 3/4 cups packaged
  precooked rice

Heat butter in skillet. Add onions, green pepper and garlic and sauté until lightly browned. Add ham and shrimp and cook over low heat until ham is lightly browned and shrimp are pink. Add tomatoes, salt and tabasco. Cover and simmer about 5 minutes. Stir well; add rice and continue to simmer for 5 minutes longer. Yields about 4 to 6 servings.

SOPADASODIL - B

2 tbsps shortening
1/2 lb spaghetti
1 lb ground beef
1 tsp salt
1 tsp black pepper
1 tsp garlic salt
2 cups onions, thinly sliced

2 cups celery, thinly sliced
1/2 cup green peppers,
    thinly sliced
1 can tomatoes
1 can whole kernel corn
2 tbsps chili powder
8 oz package American cheese

Preheat skillet to 300°. Sauté spaghetti until lightly browned. Stir in meat, cook until meat loses red color. Drain off fat. Add other ingredients, except cheese, saving the tomatoes and water for last. Simmer for 30 minutes with cover on. Put cheese on top.

LOUISIANA DIRTY RICE - B

1/2 lb chicken livers
1/2 lb chicken gizzards
1/2 lb chicken necks
1/2 lb ground meat
1 lg onion chopped
3 green onions chopped
1 bell pepper chopped

4 ribs of celery chopped
3 cloves garlic chopped
1/4 tsp white pepper
1/4 tsp red pepper
Salt to taste
2 cups water
2 cups uncooked rice

Chop up all onions, green onions, bell peppers, celery, garlic, red pepper, white pepper, and salt in a large bowl. Boil chicken livers, gizzards and necks until done. Using 1/4 of the above chopped ingredients, put the ingredients into a skillet with ground meat and season to taste. Drain. Pour oil off ground meat and set aside. Put chopped chicken livers, gizzards and deboned necks through the blender. Add the blended meats and meat mixture with the rest of the chopped seasonings, and 2 cups of water, into a large pot. Simmer for 30 minutes. Set aside and cook rice alone until done. Mix with the heated dressing. Remove from heat for 10 minutes before serving. Be sure not to leave dirty rice on heated stove after being done. It will spoil quickly. Use serving portions to reheat.

CHICKEN CASSEROLE - B

In a large, lightly greased casserole pan, arrange the following in layers:

1 package Doritos (med bag)
1 boiled chicken, deboned
  (save broth)
1 can cream of mushroom soup
1/3 can water
1 can mushrooms
1 chopped onion

1 chopped bell pepper, sauted
1/2 lb Velveeta cheese, sliced
1 tbsp chili powder
1 can cream of chicken soup,
  mixed with 1/3 can chicken broth
1 can Rotel tomatoes

Bake 35 minutes at 375°. Do not stir.

CASSEROLE WITH TOMATO SAUCE - B

2 lbs ground beef
2/3 cup tomato sauce
1/3 cup onion, chopped

1 can cut green beans (drained)
Salt and pepper to taste

Mix ground beef with tomato sauce. Add chopped onions. Sauté until meat is tender. Drain fat. Add salt and pepper to taste. In a separate bowl, toss green beans and season to taste with salt and pepper. Toss again. Add green beans to ground meat and tomato sauce mixture. Place in casserole dish and bake at 250° slowly, for two to two and a half hours, sprinkling with water or Worcestershire sauce. A few strips of bacon can be added for a richer flavor. Serve with corn bread sticks or green salad.

PORK CHOP CASSEROLE - B

6 pork chops
6 sweet potatoes (cut in slices)
Salt and pepper to taste

1/2 cup brown sugar
1 to 2 cups milk

Season pork chops with salt and pepper; place in a well greased casserole dish. For quick results, place cut sweet potatoes, brown sugar and milk in a sauce pan on top of stove. Cover and cook until almost tender, but firm. Remove from heat. Pour sweet potato mixture over pork chops. Cover pork chops well. Bake in oven at 350° with pork chops covered with aluminum foil for one hour. Remove cover and cook chops again until they are tender and the sweet potato mixture is a little crusty on top.

SEAFOOD CASSEROLE - W

Drain and sauté 2 jars of oysters in oleo till they curl. Be sure and save the liquid. Put oysters aside and saute green onions and bell peppers in oleo. Add 1/3 cup white wine, oyster liquid, a can of cream of celery soup, cream of onion soup and shrimp soup. Add 1 lb white crab meat, 2 lbs cooked and peeled shrimp and oysters. Add 1/2 cup evaporated milk and pour all in casserole dish. Top with seasoned bread crumbs and grated Mozzarella cheese, bake at 350˚ for 30 to 40 minutes. Serve on toast points, rice or noodles.

RUTH'S MARINATED GREEN BEANS - W

2 cans green beans
1 sliced onion
3 strips bacon, cooked and
  the drippings

3 tbsps vinegar
3 tbsps sugar
Salt and pepper to taste

Cook bacon; save drippings. Put green beans and onions in casserole dish. Crumble bacon in mixture. Make dressing with 3 tbsps bacon drippings, 3 tbsps vinegar, 3 tbsps sugar and seasonings. Pour dressing over beans and marinate overnight. Cook in 350° oven for 30 to 45 minutes. Double, triple, quadruple, etc., for bigger groups. Makes 4 servings. Loved by all.

FRITO-RED BEAN CASSEROLE - W

1 lb ground beef
1 onion, chopped
1 green pepper, chopped
1 tbsp chili powder, dissolved
  in 1/2 cup water
1 can tomato sauce

1 can kidney beans, undrained
  or fresh cooked ones
1 small can chopped ripe olives
3/4 lb grated sharp cheddar
  cheese
1 med bag regular Fritos

Brown onions, peppers and meat. Add all the other ingredients in casserole dish with meat and vegetables. Let stand an hour or so. Heat in 350° oven.

CHICKEN BREASTS WITH MUSHROOMS - B

4 chicken breasts, skinned
Salt and pepper
1/4 tsp parsley flakes

1/2 cup mushrooms, sliced
1/2 cup chopped onions
White sauce

Skin chicken and season with salt and pepper. Arrange in baking dish. Sprinkle with onions, mushrooms, and parsley flakes. Cover and bake for an hour to an hour and a half or until chicken is done. Make white sauce and pour over chicken. Serve over rice.

FIVE SPICES CASSEROLE - W

1 lb ground beef
3/4 cup chopped onions
1 1/2 tsp salt
Dash of pepper
1/8 tsp each of oregano, garlic
  powder, thyme
1/2 small bay leaf

1 can (1 lb) tomatoes
1 can cream of mushroom soup
1 cup minute rice
Slice of American cheese
Sliced stuffed olives
1 tbsp oil

Brown meat. Add onions and cook. Stir in seasoning, tomatoes and soup. Add minute rice. Bring to a boil. Reduce heat and simmer 5 minutes. Spoon into 1 1/2 quart baking dish and top with cheese. Place under broiler till cheese is melted. Garnish with olives. Makes 4 to 6 servings.

SHRIMP AND RICE CASSEROLE - B

2 lbs boiled fresh shrimp, cleaned and peeled and seasoned with salt and pepper. Dot with melted butter. Mix with 1 cup cooked rice and 1/2 cup green onions and tops. Place in large baking dish. Bake for 15 minutes covered. Serve with favorite gravy or seafood sauce.

HAM AND POTATO CASSEROLE - B

6 potatoes
1 lb raw smoked ham
3 cups milk (more, if necessary)
1 green pepper

1 small chopped onion
Flour
Salt and pepper to taste

Cover the bottom of a well greased casserole dish with raw potatoes, sliced about 1/4 inch thick. Sprinkle with flour and add sliced square pieces of ham. Season with salt and pepper. Repeat until dish is full. Pour in as much milk as the dish can hold without spilling over the top. Cover and bake at 350° or until potatoes are tender. If desired, sprinkle with grated cheese on top and cover. Then bake until cheese has melted.

POTATO CASSEROLE - B

1 1/2 bags of frozen hash brown
    potatoes
1/4 cup onion, chopped
1 can cream of mushroom soup

1 pt sour cream
6 to 8 slices of cheese
Salt and pepper to taste
1/2 cup crushed potato chips

Grease bottom and sides of baking dish. In a separate bowl, mix sour cream and cream of mushroom soup. Using layering techniques, place a layer of hash brown potatoes, spread the soup mixture over the top of potatoes, then cover with the onion, then the cheese. Repeat layers again. Bake for one hour or until potatoes are done. Remove and sprinkle potato chips over the top. Bake again till chips brown on top. Serve hot. Can be put in freezer bags and heated as needed.

BEEF AND VEGETABLE PIE - W

4 green onions, chopped
1 green pepper chopped
2 cups cooked beef
1 can beef gravy or left over gravy

1 can carrots
1 can peas
1 can green beans

Sauté vegetables in oleo and add cooked meat. Add beef gravy, carrots, peas, and beans. Season with Worcestershire sauce, salt, pepper and cajun seasoning. Put mixture in greased baking dish and top with biscuits or pastry. Cook in hot oven 400° till crust is brown, approx 20 to 30 minutes.

CHILES RELLENOS CASSEROLE - W

1/2 lb ground beef
1/2 cup onion, chopped
1/2 cup celery, chopped
1/4 cup green pepper, chopped
1 tsp salt
1/2 tsp pepper
2 (4 ounce) chopped green
  chiles, drained
1 1/2 cup (6 ounces) sharp
  cheddar cheese, shredded

1 cup (4 ounces) Monterey Jack
  cheese with jalapeno pepper,
  shredded
2 or 3 corn tortillas, sliced in strips
6 eggs
2 1/4 cup milk
1/2 tsp salt
1/4 tsp pepper
1/4 cup & 4 tsp flour
2 drops Tabasco sauce

Combine first 6 ingredients in a medium skillet; cook until meat is browned, stirring to crumble. Drain off pan drippings.

Mix cheeses together.

Layer meat in a lightly greased 10x6x2 inch baking dish. Layer strips of tortillas on top. Layer peppers, then cheese on top. Combine remaining ingredients, stirring well. Pour over casserole. Bake uncovered at 350° for 45 to 50 minutes or until set. Let stand 5 minutes before serving. Yields 8 servings.

PECAN MEATBALLS WITH VEGETABLES - B

2 cups soft bread crumbs
2 cups green beans
1/2 cup milk
1 tbsp soy sauce
1 1/2 cloves garlic, chopped

1/4 cup onions
1/2 lb ground beef chuck
1/2 lb pork sausage meat
1 cup chopped pecans
1 tbsp melted butter

In a baking dish, season beef and pork sausage. Bake for 25 minutes. Remove from oven. Combine milk, soy sauce, garlic, onion, and green beans. Toss well. Pour over meat and bake for 15 minutes longer. Remove again and sprinkle with pecans and bread crumbs. Return to oven and bake for 20 minutes longer. Serve with tossed green salad.

PORK WITH SAUERKRAUT - B

4 tsps Worcestershire sauce
1 tsp salt
4 cups chopped pork (fresh)
2 tbsps brown sugar
1/4 tsp pepper

1 can (1 lb., 11 oz) sauerkraut, drained
1 small can pineapple chunks, drained

Season pork with salt and pepper and Worcestershire sauce by using a barbecue sauce brush. Place in a greased baking dish. Sprinkle brown sugar and pineapple over meat. Add sauerkraut and pepper on top of brown sugar and pineapple. Bake in oven at 350° for an hour to an hour and a half.

CHICKEN CONTINENTAL - B

6 pounds (about) frying chicken pieces
2/3 cups seasoned flour
1/2 cup butter
2 cans (10 1/4 ounce each) condensed cream of chicken soup
5 tablespoons grated onion
2 teaspoons salt

Dash of pepper
2 tablespoons chopped parsley
1 teaspoon celery flakes
1/4 teaspoon thyme (optional)
2 2/3 cups water
2 2/3 cups Minute Rice
1 teaspoon paprika
Additional parsley (optional)

Roll chicken in seasoned flour and saute in butter in a dutch oven until golden brown. Remove chicken.

Combine soup, onion, and seasonings in Dutch oven, mixing well. Blend in water. Bring to a boil over medium heat, stirring constantly. Place rice in a 3 quart casserole. Reserve 2/3 cup of soup mixture. Pour remaining soup mixture over rice in casserole. Stir just to moisten all rice. Top with chicken and pour reserved soup mixture over chicken. Cover and bake at 375° about 30 minutes, or until chicken is tender. Sprinkle with paprika and garnish with parsley. Makes 8 servings.

MOUSSAKA - W

1 eggplant
1 lb. ground beef
4 medium onions, chopped
1 clove garlic, minced

1 can tomatoes
Italian bread crumbs
Grated parmesan cheese
Seasonings

Cut eggplant crosswise into 1/2" thick slices. Dip in beaten egg and then in Italian bread crumbs and fry on both sides in hot oil. Remove slices and drain. Add onions and garlic to skillet and add ground beef, cook till brown. Chop tomatoes and add to beef mixture. Cover and simmer for 20 minutes. Lightly oil a 2 quart baking dish and put alternating layers of egg plant and meat mixture in dish.

Make a white sauce and stir in 2 beaten eggs and nutmeg. Stir mixture over casserole and top with parmesan cheese.

Bake at 350° for about 1 hour until top is bubbling.

CRUNCHY CHICKEN CASSEROLE - B

6 chicken breasts
Water to cover
1/2 sliced lemon
4 ribs sliced celery
3 bay leaves
1 tablespoon pepper corns
Black pepper to taste
1 teaspoon salt
2 large carrots (peeled sliced and
    cooked 15 min. in salted water)

1/4 cup butter
1/4 cup all purpose flour
8 oz. shredded cheddar cheese
1 2 oz. jar chopped pimento
1 1 oz. chicken broth (from
    cooked chicken + 2-3 tsp.
    chicken broth granules)
1 cup chopped mushrooms
8 oz herbed seasoned stuffing
1/2 cup butter

Slowly cook chicken in ingredients listed above carrots until meat falls off bones. Strain liquid into container and store meat and liquid overnight in refrigerator. When ready to use, skim fat off broth and dice chicken. In 3 quart saucepan melt 1/4 cup butter over medium heat. Stir in flour, add broth stirring constantly until mixture thickens. Lower heat, add cheese and stir until cheese melts. Remove from heat. Stir in chicken, carrots, pimento and mushrooms. In 10 inch skillet, melt 1/4 cup butter. Add stuffing and mix. Spread chicken mixture in 2 quart shallow baking dish. Cover with stuffing mix, top with 5-6 teaspoons butter and bake at 375° (uncovered) for 30 minutes. Makes 8 (1-cup) servings.

PORK CHOP CASSEROLE - B

16 loin pork chops 1 to 3/4 inch
    thick (about 5 lbs)
Salt and pepper
2 tablespoons shortening
1 cup chopped onions
1/4 cup butter

2 2/3 cups Minute Rice
2 2/3 cups water
2 cups diced peeled tart apples
1 tablespoon salt
1/4 teaspoon pepper
1/4 tsp poultry seasoning

Trim excess fat from pork chops: season to taste with salt and pepper. Brown chops quickly in shortening in a large skillet. Drain on absorbent paper. Pour drippings from skillet.

Sauté onion in butter in the skillet; place in a lightly greased shallow 4 quart casserole. Add remaining ingredients: mix well. Arrange pork chops on top of rice mixture. Cover and bake at 350° about 45 minutes, or until chops are tender. Makes about 8 servings.

CRAB AND SHRIMP BAKE - B

2 1/2 cups shrimp
1 lb crab meat
1 1/2 cup finely chopped celery
1/2 cup finely chopped parsley

1 cup mayonnaise
Salt and pepper to taste
Bread crumbs

Mix shrimp and crab meat, celery and parsley with mayonnaise. Salt and pepper to taste. Put into buttered 2 1/2 quart casserole. Sprinkle bread crumbs on top and pour melted butter over crumbs. Bake in oven at 325 degrees for 45 minutes. This can be frozen until ready to bake. Double recipe, if necessary. This serves four.

OYSTER SPAGHETTI - B

1 lb spaghetti
1 c of pear shaped tomatoes
  (1 lb) 12 oz size,
  chopped fine or sieved
2 tbsps. oregano

2 tbsps. finely chopped garlic
1/2 med size can tomato
  sauce (16 oz)
2 pts. oysters chopped or whole

Place oil and garlic in large skillet and heat till garlic turns light brown. Add drained oysters (save juice) and brown, slightly. Add tomatoes, tomato sauce and oyster juice and cook for about 10 to 15 minutes. Add sweet basil and oregano, salt and pepper and cook for 5 minutes longer. Boil spaghetti in salted water for about 7 minutes. Drain, place in dish and cover with sauce.

BROCCOLI CORN BAKE - B

1 can cream style corn
Fresh or frozen broccoli
1 beaten egg

Onion powder or diced onion
1 cup Pepperidge Farm crumbs
2 tbs oleo

Combine ingredients and put in 1 quart casserole. Combine crumbs and some of oleo for top. Sprinkle over vegetables mixture. Bake uncovered in 350 degree oven 35 to 40 minutes.

GROUND MEAT AND VEGETABLE CASSEROLE - B

1 lb ground beef
1 can corn, drained
1 can cut green beans

1/2 cups onions, chopped
1/2 cup grated cheese
Salt and pepper to taste

Crumble meat in baking dish and bake at 350° for 30 minutes. Remove and drain fat. Place meat in a large bowl and mix the meat, onion, corn and green beans together. Place the mixture once more in the baking dish. Sprinkle with cheese and cover. Bake for 15 to 20 minutes longer or until the meat and vegetables are tender. Serve with hot french buttered bread.

SPAGHETTI CASSEROLE - B

1 onion
1 large green pepper
1 cup pimento stuffed olives
8 ozs spaghetti, cooked
   and drained
1 can (16 ozs) tomatoes

1 lb fresh mushrooms, sliced
2 cups grated American or
   cheddar cheese
Toasted bread crumbs
1/4 cup butter
1/2 cup heavy cream or milk

In a blender, place the onion, olives, green pepper together. Blend well. Then mix these ingredients with the spaghetti, tomatoes, and mushrooms. Season to taste with salt and pepper. Place into a greased large baking dish. Sprinkle with cheese and bread crumbs. Dot with butter. Pour cream over top and bake at 350° for one and a half hours. If you want to, omit milk and pour white sauce over top and serve.

VEGETABLE CASSEROLE - W

1 box frozen broccoli
1 box frozen cauliflower
1 box frozen brussels sprouts

1 can cream of onion soup
1 can cream of mushroom soup
1 can chedder cheese soup

Sauté green onions, celery and bell pepper in oleo. Add cans of soup and a little milk to this. Boil vegetables and drain. Add vegetables to mixture and a little mayonnaise. Put in casserole and top with parmesan cheese and french fried onion rings. Run in oven at 350° for 30 minutes.

BEEF NOODLE CASSEROLE - W

1 lb. ground beef
1/2 cup chopped onions
2 cup cooked noodles
1/2 cup chopped green pepper

1 can mushroom stems
  & pieces
1 carton sour cream
1 can mushroom soup

Sauté beef, onions and peppers. Pour off grease and add mushrooms, soup, sour cream and noodles and season with salt, pepper, cayenne pepper. Top with grated sharp cheddar and cook in 350° oven for 30 minutes.

TURKEY, RICE AND CHEESE - B

1 small onion
1 tablespoon fat or oil
3 cups water and broth
1 cup uncooked rice

1 1/2 cups cut up canned
  boned turkey
1 cup cut up cheese
Salt and pepper to taste

Chop onion and cook in fat or oil until tender. Drain broth from the turkey and add enough water to make 3 cups liquid. Add to onion. Heat to boiling and add rice. Lower heat. Cover and cook 20 minutes. Add turkey, cheese, salt and pepper and cook over very low heat until cheese melts. Makes 6 servings, about 2/3 cups each.

MOUSSAKA - W

4 med eggplants
2 lbs lean ground beef
3 med onions, chopped
1/2 cup oleo
1/2 cup dry red wine
2 tsps salt
1/4 tsp black pepper
1 tsp oregano

2 lightly beaten eggs
1 cup grated sharp cheese
1/2 cup soft bread crumbs
2 cans tomatoes, drained
6 tbsps flour
3 cups milk
4 egg yolks, lightly beaten

Peel eggplant and cut crosswise in 1/4 inch or smaller slices. Sprinkle with salt and place heavy plate on top. Let stand to drain. Cook beef and onions in 2 tbsps butter until well browned. Add wine, salt, pepper and oregano. Simmer until liquid is absorbed. Stir in 2 beaten eggs, 3/4 cup cheese and 1/4 cup bread crumbs. Brown slices of eggplants, dipped in crumbs, lightly on both sides. Grease large casserole dish. Sprinkle crumbs over bottom. Put layer of eggplant, meat mixture and tomatoes. Sprinkle with cheese and continue to fill casserole dish as described above with layer of eggplant on top. Melt remaining butter and blend in flour and add milk. Slowly pour a little, not much, into 4 beaten egg yolks. Return to remaining sauce. Pour sauce over casserole. Sprinkle with cheese. Bake at 350° for 45 to 60 minutes. Makes 10 to 12 servings.

TOP OF STOVE CASSEROLE - B

1 small onion
1 pound ground beef
2 cups canned tomatoes
  (1 pound can)
1/2 cup rice

1/2 cup water
1 tablespoon sugar
2 1/2 cups cooked split peas
Salt and pepper to taste

Chop onion; put ground beef and onion in a pan and cook until meat is browned. Drain off any extra fat. Add tomatoes, rice, water and sugar. Cover and cook slowly 20 minutes, until rice is tender. Add split peas, salt and pepper. Cook slowly until mixture is hot. Serves 6 - 1 cup each.

HOT TAMALE PIE - W

1 tbsp fat	1 tbsp sugar
1 cup chopped bell pepper	1/2 tsp salt
1 lb ground beef	1 tsp chili powder
1 package onion soup mix	Dash of pepper
2 cups canned tomatoes	1 cup grated American cheese
1 1/2 cups corn	1 recipe corn meal topping
1/2 cup chopped ripe olives	1 clove garlic, minced

Saute peppers, adding meat and brown. Stir in onion soup mix, tomatoes, corn, olives, garlic, sugar, and seasoning. Simmer 30 minutes till slightly thick. Mix in cheese. Pour into a well buttered casserole dish.

Corn Meal Topping:

Stir 3/4 cups corn meal and 1/2 tsp salt into 2 cups cold water. Cook and stir till thick. Add a tablespoon of butter. Pour over meat mixture.

SPAQUELLE - B

1 lb ground chuck	1 lb can tomatoes
5 slices of bacon, cut in small pieces after browning	1/2 small jar stuffed olives, cut in pieces
1 small can mushrooms	Salt, pepper and cayenne to taste
3 tbsps olive oil	2 tsps ketchup
1 can tomato sauce	
1 large onion, chopped	

Put bacon in pan; add onions, pepper, olive oil, and ground beef. Cook till meat is done. Add rest of ingredients and simmer for about 1 hour. Add cooked elbow Spaquelle. Mix well.

RICE A LA CREOLE - B

1 cup chopped boiled ham
1 onion
1 cup boiled rice
1 cup tomatoes

2 cups fine, soft crumbs
2 tbsp butter or margarine
Celery salt
Salt and pepper to taste

Mix ingredients in the order given. Bake in a greased casserole dish for half an hour at 350°. This dish makes a good one dish meal or dinner for two.

SWEET AND SOUR MEATBALLS - B

For Meatballs:

3 lbs ground beef
4 eggs
1 tsp salt

1/2 tsp pepper
1 clove garlic minced

Mix; make into balls and brown. Add to sauce.

For Sauce:

4 small onions, diced
2 #2 cans tomatoes
2 cans mushrooms
2 cans tomato paste

1 paste can of vinegar (Tomato paste can to measure)
1 paste can sugar (Tomato paste can to measure)

Have the sauce simmering and drop in the meatballs.
The longer you simmer, the better. Serve over noodles, spaghetti, or rice.

The Ripest Fruit Fall First

CHAPTER V

"The Ripest Fruit Fall First"

(jellies, preserves, pickles, fruit salads, desserts, other fruit dishes, nuts)

Fruits, vegetables, and nuts were plentiful in early Louisiana and home canning and drying were a mainstay in every pantry, white and black. Families and friends would get together for "canning parties" and put up canned goods to last through the year. Family recipes were handed down from generation to generation and anything that could be canned, was. Along with the canned fruits and vegetables, there were dried fruits and nuts and home cured meats. There were smoke houses with plantations and even the not so affluent farmer would cure his meats.

In today's Louisiana, this way of life is almost extinct. It is becoming a lost art with freezers available to most households and commercial canned goods being so inexpensive. However, there are still many home canning recipes in use today and an abundance of fresh fruits and nuts for use in canning, salads, desserts, and breads.

These we will pass on in this chapter. Most of the recipes you won't find on the commercial shelves; at least, not the way they are here. Some are old; some have been updated and improved with time and manufactured products added.

PICTURE EXPLANATION

It was always fun to get the first fruits and nuts, having that first taste of the season. It was exciting to know that something good would come out of the kitchen from this harvest. Ethel's drawing shows the excitement of the girls with that first "pick" of the season.

GARLIC PICKLES - B

5 lbs cucumbers, sliced 1/4   1 1/2 cup slack lime
   inch thick   1 qt water

Mix lime and water. Pour over sliced cucumbers. Let stand for 24 hours, stirring several times. Wash carefully and drain. Add 1 quart vinegar, 4 1/2 cups sugar, 1 tablespoon salt, and 2 tablespoons pickling spices, letting stand 24 hours. Remove spices. Boil slowly for 30 minutes, covered. Put in jars with 1 clove garlic; fill with liquid and seal.

WATERMELON PICKLE - B

1/2 lg melon   1 bottle Lilly's lime
10 lb rind

Cover rind with cold water. Add lime and soak overnight. Rinse 2 times in cold water. Drain well and put in large pan in cold water. Cook till tender for about 1 hour.

2 qts water   1 box pickling spice (tie in bag)
10 lbs sugar   3 sticks cinnamon

Boil for 30 minutes. Add rind and cook about 1 hour.

PEANUT BRITTLE - B

1 1/2 cups sugar   2 cups raw peanuts
1/2 cup white karo   1 1/2 tsp soda
1/3 cup cold water

Mix sugar, water, karo, and bring to a boil. When boiling all over, add peanuts. Cook about 14 minutes and take off heat. Add soda quickly. Pour in well greased pan.

HOT PEPPER RELISH - W

24 hot peppers
3/4 qt vinegar (3 cups)
1 box brown sugar

2 tbsps salt
12 onions, ground

Grind pepper and cover with boiling water. Let stand 5 minutes; drain; cover again with boiling water and let stand 10 minutes. Drain and put all other ingredients and peppers in boiler. Cook till thick. When ingredients come to a boil, reduce heat to simmer and simmer an hour. Put in jars and seal.

PEAR RELISH (HOT) - W

6 pears
3 onions
3 bell peppers
6 to 8 hot peppers

2 tbsps salt
1 cup sugar
1 cup white vinegar

Peel pears and core; grind pears, onions, and peppers. Sprinkle with salt and let stand 2 hours. Drain. Bring sugar and vinegar to a boil and add vegetables. Bring to boil again and simmer 15 minutes. Seal in sterilized jars.

CANNED PEAR HALVES - W

Using cooking pears, peel, core, and half. Put in cold water and sprinkle with lemon juice so they won't darken. Make a medium syrup of 2 cups water to 1 cup sugar. Bring to a boil and put pear halves in syrup till they loose their firmness. Put pear halves in quart sterilized jars; add a few cloves to each jar and red or green food coloring. Fill jar with syrup. Seal and process in hot water bath, approximately 10 minutes.

PICKLED PEACHES - W

For every pound of peaches, use 1 cup water, 1/3 cup vinegar, 1 cup sugar, 1 small stick cinnamon, a few cloves, and a little ginger root. Peel peaches and drop in syrup of sugar, vinegar, and water. Add spices tied in bag and cook till peaches are clear and tender and syrup is like a preserved syrup. Pour syrup over peaches in sterilized jars and let cool. Seal and process for 20 minutes. Same recipe may be used for pears.

MAMA'S BREAD AND BUTTER PICKLES - W

Slice 12 cucumbers, thinly, 2 hot peppers, and 8 onions. Put in layers in vessel; add 1/2 cup salt, and cover with ice. Let stand for 2 to 3 hours. Drain and add 5 cups sugar, 5 cups vinegar, 1 1/4 teaspoon tumeric, 1/2 teaspoon ground cloves, 2 teaspoons mustard seed, and 1 teaspoon celery seed. Scald, do not boil, till rinds turn yellowish. Seal in sterilized jars and simmer in water bath for 10 minutes.

PICKLED OKRA - W

Make solution of 1 quart vinegar, 2 quarts water, 1 scant cup salt, 1 pea sized piece of alum. Bring to a boil and boil 3 to 4 minutes. Wash okra, cut into 2 1/2 inch pieces and trim not too close. Soak okra overnight in ice water in refrigerator. Drain and rinse. Pack in jar, alternating ends. In each jar, put a small red pepper, a strip of celery, and a strip of carrot. Do not pack too tight. Place jars in a shallow pan of hot water and fill jars with hot vinegar mixture. Clean outside top of jars, seal, and process in simmering water bath for 10 minutes.

VEGETABLE PEAR PICKLES - W

6 vegetable pears   1/4 cup salt
2 onions   1 1/4 cup sugar
1 1/2 qts cider vinegar   Long red peppers

Peel pears, using rubber gloves. Cut pears in half and slice. Put in bowl of cold water with ice and leave overnight. Do the same with onions and soak separately. Boil vinegar, salt, and sugar. Drain vegetable pears and onions and fill jars. Add a pepper to each jar. Pour hot liquid over pickles and seal in sterilized jars. Process in water bath for 10 minutes. Takes 6 weeks to make.

FRESH CRANBERRY SAUCE - W

1 qt cranberries (4 cups)   3 scant cups water

Boil for 10 minutes. Mash cranberries and add 2 cups sugar. Simmer for 50 minutes. Cool in refrigerator.

CRABAPPLE JELLY - W

Wash crabapples and put them in boiling pot with enough water to cover. Boil slowly till berries are tender. Mash berries on side of pot to bring out juice. Strain juice from berries. For each cup of juice, add 3/4 cup of sugar and boil rapidly to jelly stage. Pour into sterilized jelly jars, seal and process in boiling water bath for 6 minutes. Make sure bands are screwed tight when you seal caps. You can make plum jelly the same way.

OLD FASHIONED GLAZED FRUITS - B

1 tbsp lemon juice
1/4 cup molasses
1 tbsp butter or margarine

4 servings canned or fresh cooked
peaches, pineapple, pears, or
apricots

Combine lemon juice and molasses. Slowly bring to a boil and boil for 3 minutes, stirring constantly. Arrange fruit in well greased baking dish. Pour molasses mixture over fruit. Dot with butter. Place in broiler or bake in oven at 375° for 10 minutes, basting when needed. Serves 4.

FIG JAM - B

2 qts ripe figs
2 slices lemon

1 cup water
4 cups sugar

Wash and peel figs, and remove stems. Mash and add lemon and water. Cook until soft. Add sugar and cook until thick, stirring to prevent burning. Remove lemon and pour into clean, hot jars and seal. Makes 6 (1/2 pint) jars.

DILL PICKLES - W

1 gal dill pickles, drained and
   juice saved
Sliced cucumbers

4 to 5 lbs sugar
2 heads garlic
2 ozs tabasco, more if desired

Layer sliced pickles, sugar and garlic. Add juice and tabasco. Shake well by rotating jar (turning upside down until dissolved). Keep in refrigerator.

APPLESAUCE - B

Wash, core, and pare 8 cooking apples. Cook in covered pot with 1/2 cup of water and a pinch of salt. Cook until soft. While apples are hot, add 1/2 cup sugar. Let sit until sugar melts over apples. For more flavoring, add a rind of lemon, grated (or lemon juice), cinnamon, nutmeg, and a pinch of cloves to the sugar. For best results, keep lid tight on pot. The amount of sugar and water varies with the sweetness and juiciness of apples. Serve with lamb, turkey, chicken or it can be served alone as a dessert over ice cream.

GREEN TOMATO JAM - B

8 lbs green tomatoes	1 tbsp preserved ginger
6 lemons	6 lbs sugar

Remove any dark parts from tomatoes, wash and remove stems. Cover them with boiling water. Let them stand five minutes, then drain and slice them into a preserving kettle. Place a layer of the tomatoes, then a layer of sliced lemon, then the sugar with the ginger sprinkled over it. Let the mixture stand overnight. Drain and boil the syrup for 10 minutes. Skim, add the tomatoes and cook rapidly until they are clear. Pour into clean, hot jars and seal.

APRICOT ORANGE - B

25 to 30 (approximately) apricots	1/2 tsp salt
1/2 cup orange juice	1/2 tsp vanilla extract
Grated orange rind	1/2 tsp almond extract
1/4 cup white vinegar	1 cup finely chopped pecans
2 cups sugar	

In a large bowl, pour boiling water over apricots. Let sit for 1 minute in the water. Then plunge into cold water. Drain and peel. Take apricots and roll them in chopped pecans. Place gently in pint jars. Combine sugar, vinegar, orange juice, salt, almond and vanilla extract into a half quart saucepan. Bring to a boil on a high heat. Carefully pour syrup over apricots; cook on high for about 3 minutes. Remove from heat and serve with ice cream. If you prefer, place carefully into sterilized wide mouth jars, using a slotted spoon. Pour on syrup, working out bubbles by running a slender rubber spatula down sides of the jars. Seal. Makes 4 pints. MAKES A NICE CHRISTMAS GIFT!

PINEAPPLE APRICOT JAM - B

2 lbs dried apricots   3 1/4 cups sugar
2 cups crushed, fresh pineapple

Wash apricots. Cover with cold water. Heat slowly to boiling. Simmer until
soft. Add pineapple and sugar. Simmer slowly, stirring frequently until thick.
Place into sterilized jars.

APPLE BUTTER - B

4 qts sweet cider   Cinnamon
2 cups sugar   Cloves
2 1/2 qts quartered tart apples

Boil cider until it is reduced to 2 qts. Add peeled, quartered apples and cook
until very tender. Put through colander, add sugar and spices and cook until
thick, stirring to prevent burning. Pour into clean hot jars and seal. Makes
3 Pints.

ORANGE AND CARROT MARMALADE - B

1 lemon, juice and rind   6 carrots
3 oranges   4 cups sugar

Scrape and chop up carrots. In as little water as possible, cook carrots until
tender. Grate lemon rind. Slice the orange very thinly. Combine carrots, fruit,
and juice from lemon, measure and add sugar. Heat, stirring until sugar is
dissolved. Cook rapidly until thick and clear. Pour into clean hot glass jars
and seal with paraffin. Makes 6 (6 oz) jars.

PEAR CHUTNEY - W

4 cups pears, peeled and chopped
1 cup onion, chopped
2 cups vinegar
1 tsp salt

1 1/2 cup raisins
1 cup chopped bell pepper
2 cups sugar
2 cups celery, chopped

Put all but raisins in food processor. Chop and then add raisins, vinegar, salt, and sugar. Cook to 220° F. Seal in sterilized jars and process 10 minutes. Apples can be used instead of pears.

MAYHAW JELLY - W

The mayhaw is a "swamp" berry found growing close to water in Louisiana. It is difficult to obtain but there are ads in papers in early spring selling them. I fix this jelly like crabapple jelly. It is delicious!

PERSIMMON SALAD

Quarter the persimmons and peel skin backs from each quarter. Mix chopped green pepper with cottage cheese and fill middle of persimmon. Serve on lettuce leaf with french dressing or mayonnaise on top.

SUGARED WALNUTS - W

1 1/2 cup sugar
1/2 cup water
1 tsp white corn syrup

1/4 tsp salt
2 to 3 cups walnuts

Cook first four ingredients to a soft ball stage. Remove from heat and add nuts and stir till creamy.

PECAN COOKIES - W

Beat 1 egg white stiff. Fold in 1 tablespoon flour and 1 cup light brown sugar. Add 1 teaspoon vanilla and 2 cups chopped pecans. Drop on buttered cookie sheet with a teaspoon and cook at 250° for 25 to 30 minutes.

PEPPER JELLY (EXTRA HOT) - W

1 1/4 cup hot pepper
1/2 cup green or banana peppers
6 1/2 cups sugar

1 1/2 cup apple cider vinegar
1 bottle certo

Mix pepper, sugar and vinegar, cook to a full rolling boil. Take off fire. Let set 5 minutes. Stir in certo and seal with paraffin.

PEAR SALAD - W

Use either canned or ripe pears. Peel and halve, if ripe, sprinkle lemon juice on top. Place cold pear halves on lettuce leaf and sprinkle with grated sharp cheddar cheese. Put a teaspoon of mayonnaise on top.

PEACH SALAD - W

Peel and core fresh peaches or use canned peach halves. Put on lettuce leaf and stuff with cottage cheese. Sprinkle with sharp cheddar cheese. Pour on French dressing or dab with mayonnaise. Mango salad and pineapple salad can be made the same way.

PEACH-PECAN SOUFFLE SALAD - B

1 package (3 oz) peach
  flavored gelatin
2 tbsps lemon juice from
  grated lemon rind
1/2 cup salad dressing

1/4 tsp salt
1 1/2 cup diced peaches, drained
1 package (3 oz) cream cheese
  stored at room temperature
1/4 cup toasted, chopped pecans

Mix gelatin as directed on package, making sure gelatin is dissolved. Add lemon juice and grated rind, salad dressing and salt. Beat until well blended. You can use a hand mixer. Pour into freezing trays and chill in refrigerator until firm. Also chill bowl. Combine peaches, cream cheese and pecans until smooth. Turn gelatin into chilled bowl. Beat at high speed unil thick and fluffy. Fold in peach mixture. Pour into a 1 quart souffle mold. Chill until firm. Unmold on chilled plate. Serves 4.

STRAWBERRY CHEESE SALAD - B

1 1/2 cup cottage cheese
3 tbsps real or light mayonnaise
3/4 cup chopped pecans
Lettuce cups

Seedless green grapes
Sliced strawberries
Mint sprigs

Combine first four ingredients. Pile into lettuce cups. Garnish with grapes, sliced strawberries and mint sprigs. Serve with your favorite dressing.

SOUTHERN AMBROSIA SALAD - B

2 lg seedless tangerines
2 lg seedless oranges
1 cup seedless green grapes
1 cup small marshmallows
1 cup red cherries, dried

1 (8 oz) package cream cheese
   stored at room temperature
1 cup whipped cream
1 cup shredded coconut
1 cup pecans, chopped

Peel and section tangerines and oranges. Remove inner skins as well. Cut grapes in half. Mix whipped cream and cream cheese in a separate bowl and blend until smooth. Mix tangerines, oranges, grapes, marshmallows, cherries, coconuts, and pecans into creamed mixture. Fold well. Chill and sprinkle with mints. Serves 4 to 6.

WATERMELON PRESERVES - B

1 lb prepared watermelon rind
1 tbsp lime or salt
2 qts water

2 cups sugar
1/2 lemon, sliced thin
2 tbsps sliced preserved ginger

Pare the rind and remove the pink edge. Cut into 1 inch cubes and let stand overnight in solution of lime or salt and 1 quart water. Drain and rinse with cold water. Cover with boiling water and cook 15 minutes; drain again. Combine sugar and remaining 1 quart water and boil 5 more minutes. Add rind, lemon and ginger. Cook rapidly until rind is clean. Let stand in syrup overnight. Reheat to boiling; pour into sterile jars and seal. Makes 1 1/2 pints. Citron and unripe cantalope may be preserved in the same way.

DEEP DISH FRUIT SALAD - B

1/2 cup light mayonnaise
6 tsps lemon juice from grated
    lemon rind
2 tsps brown sugar
1 1/2 cups cantalope
1 cup honey dew melon, cubed
1 med peach, peeled and cubed
1 cup pineapple, chopped
    and drained

1 cup seedless grapes
1 cup fresh strawberries,
    halved
1 1/2 cup watermelon balls
Lettuce leaves
2 pts cream cheese, softened
6 fresh strawberries

Beat brown sugar with grated lemon and juice with a fork. Add mayonnaise and mix well. Let sit in refrigerator. Toss remaining ingredients. Beat cream cheese until fluffy. Then fold into fruit mixture. Line large salad bowl with lettuce leaves. Gently put fruit mixture on lettuce leaves and garnish with whole strawberries. Serve with mayonnaise dressing on top. Serves 6 to 8.

AMBROSIA

Oranges, seeded and white taken out
Coconut, fresh if available
Red and green cherries
Cut orange pulps into good bite size pieces and layer in a bowl.
Put a layer of coconut on top.
Put on a layer of oranges.
Put on another layer of coconut.
Sprinkle a little powdered sugar on top.
Put red and green cherries on top.
Refrigerate till ready to serve.
This can be done in individual desserts.

APPLE DUMPLINGS - B

2 cups sugar
2 cups water
1/4 tsp cinnamon
1/4 tsp nutmeg
1/4 cup butter
2 cups flour

1 tsp salt
2 tsps baking powder
3/4 cup shortening
1/2 cup milk
6 Rome apples

Make syrup of sugar, water, cinnamon, and nutmeg. Pare and core apples. Cut in eighths. Sift flour, salt, and baking powder. Cut in shortening. Add milk all at once and stir until moistened. Roll 1/4 inch thick and cut in 5 inch squares. Arrange 4 pieces of apple on each square and sprinkle generously with additional sugar, cinnamon, and nutmeg. Dot with butter. Fold corners to center and pinch edges together. Place 1 inch apart in greased pan. Pour over syrup. Bake in moderate oven (375°) for 35 minutes.

ORANGE NUT LOAF - B

1 med orange
1/2 cup dates, finely chopped
1 cup pecans, finely chopped
2 tbsps butter
1/2 cup orange juice
1 cup sugar

1 egg, slightly beaten
2 cups all purpose flour
1 tsp soda
1 tsp baking powder
1/2 tsp salt

Put orange through grinder and add dates, pecans, butter, orange juice, sugar, and eggs. Add dry ingredients and blend. Put in greased loaf pan at 350° for 60 to 70 minutes. Serve topped with whipped cream cheese.

BANANA NUT BREAD - B

3/4 cup sugar
1/3 cup soft vegetable shortening
2 eggs
2 tbsps orange juice
1 tbsp lemon juice
1 cup mashed bananas
  (2 large ones)

2 cups sifted all purpose flour
3 1/2 tsps baking powder
3 1/4 tsps salt
1/2 cup chopped nuts

Cream together the sugar and shortening. Add eggs and beat until light and fluffy. Blend in juices and mashed bananas. Sift together dry ingredients, gradually adding to banana mixture, stirring just until blended. Fold in nuts. Pour into a well greased 8 1/2 by 4 1/2 by 2 1/2 inch oven glass loaf pan. Let stand 20 minutes at room temperature. Bake 1 hour at 325° or until toothpick thrust into center comes out clean. Remove from pan to cooling rack. Serve thin. Cut with sharp knife to prevent crumbling.

NUT BREAD - B

2 cups all purpose flour
1/2 cup sugar
4 tsps baking powder
1 tsp salt

1 cup chopped pecans
1 egg, beaten
1 1/4 cups milk
4 tbsps melted oleo

Sift flour, sugar, baking powder, and salt. Add nuts. Combine eggs, milk, and oleo. Make well in dry ingredients and add egg mixture. Stir till flour is absorbed. Pour in greased loaf pan and bake 50 to 60 minutes at 350°.

PECAN ROLL - B

1 (7 1/2 oz) jar marshmallow cream
1 lb powdered sugar, sifted
1 tsp vanilla
1/3 tsp almond extract

1 lb Kraft caramels
5 cups pecans,
   chopped coarsely

Combine first 4 ingredients, kneading in the last of the sugar gradually. Shape in eight rolls, 1 inch in diameter. Wrap in waxed paper, and put in freezer overnight, or until candy is quite hard. Remove cellophane from caramels. Melt caramels with 2 tablespoons water in top of double boiler over boiling water. Remove from heat, but keep over hot water. Dip marshmallow rolls in caramel to cover, then roll in nuts, pressing nuts firmly into caramel with hands. Cool; store, covered, in a cool, dry place. Keeps for at least a month.

FRESH APPLE POUND CAKE - B

3 cups peeled, diced apples
1 1/2 cups corn oil
3 cups flour (use part to
   coat dates and nuts)
1 tsp salt
1/2 to 1 tsp soda
1 cup pecans

2 cups sugar
2 eggs, beaten
1 tsp baking powder
1 tsp cinnamon
1 to 2 tsp vanilla
1 cup chopped dates

Combine apple, sugar, corn oil, and eggs and mix well. Sift in dry ingredients. Add vanilla, nuts, and dates. Bake in greased, floured tube pan for 1 hour and 20 minutes at 325°.

FESTIVE PINEAPPLE CHERRY SALAD - B

1 cup pineapple
2 cakes cream cheese, softened
1 cup mayonnaise
1 cup whipping cream

1/3 cup powdered sugar
1 cup miniature marshmallows
1 small jar cherries

Soften cream cheese; add sugar, mayonnaise, and whipping cream, beaten stiff. Add pineapple, cherries, and marshmallows. Mix well and put in low pan with wax paper and freeze.

CREME DE MENTHE PEARS - W

1 (1 lb) can pear halves
1/2 cup sugar

2 lemon slices
1/4 cup creme de menthe

Drain pears, keeping 1 1/2 cups juice. Combine juice and sugar and cook till sugar dissolves. Add lemon slices. Boil 10 minutes till thick. Remove from heat and stir in creme de menthe. Pour over pears in bowl, cover, and let cool. Refrigerate 24 hours before serving.

TEA TIME TASSIES - W

Pastry: 1 (3 oz) package cream cheese
            1/2 cup butter or oleo
            1 cup sifted flour

Soften cheese and butter to room temperature and cream. Mix in flour and roll into balls the size of marbles. Press into little forms.

Filling: Beat together 1 tablespoon soft butter, 3/4 cup brown sugar, one egg, 1 teaspoon vanilla, and a dash of salt. Cover bottoms of forms with broken pecans. Put 1 teaspoon filling over pecans. Top with half pecan and bake at 325° for 25 minutes.

PROCESSOR OR BLENDER APPLESAUCE - W

6 med apples, cored, pared,
   and cubed
1/2 cup sugar
1/2 cup water

2 tbsps lemon juice
4 drops red food coloring
   (optional)

Put all ingredients in food processor or blender, cover, and blend till smooth. Serve chilled or warm, whichever you prefer. Heat in saucepan or microwave for short while.

PERSIMMON CAKE - W

3 cups all purpose flour
2 cups sugar
1 tsp soda
1 tsp cinnamon
1 cup vegetable oil
3 eggs, slightly beaten

1 1/2 cup persimmon pulp
(get persimmons in season
and freeze pulp till needed)
1 cup chopped pecans
Powdered sugar

Combine all ingredients and mix well. Pour into greased and floured Bundt pan. Bake at 325° for 1 hour till done. Remove from pan and dust top with powdered sugar.

FROZEN CRANBERRY SQUARES - W

2 (3 oz) packages cream cheese,
softened
3/4 cup mayonnaise
1 cup heavy cream, whipped
2 cups (1 lb) can jellied
cranberry sauce

1 (9 oz) cup crushed pineapple,
drained
1/2 cup chopped ripe olives
1/2 cup chopped celery

Blend cream cheese and mayonnaise. Fold in whipped cream. Cut cranberry sauce into half inch cubes and fold cranberry cubes, pineapple, olives, and celery into cream cheese mixture. Pour into tray and freeze. Cut in squares and serve on lettuce, topped with mayonnaise.

APPLESAUCE CAKE - W

1/2 cup shortening
1 cup sugar
2 cups sifted all purpose flour
1 tsp salt
1 tsp soda
1 tsp cinnamon

1/3 tsp nutmeg
1/3 tsp cloves
1/2 cup chopped nuts
1/2 cup seeded raisins
1 1/3 cup applesauce

Cream shortening and sugar. Sift dry ingredients. Dust raisins and nuts with some of flour mixture. Add remainder to first mixture, alternating with applesauce, mixing till smooth. Stir in raisins and nuts; pour mixture into loaf pan lined with waxed paper. Bake at 325° approximately 1 hour.

FRESH FRUIT AND VEGETABLE COMBOS FOR SALAD - W

Mix diced pineapple, fresh or canned, with diced cucumbers, French dressing or mayonnaise on lettuce.

Shredded cabbage, diced apples, and chopped pecans mixed with mayonnaise on lettuce.

Diced apples, sliced bananas, and chopped celery blended with mayonnaise over lettuce leaf.

Seedless grapes with cottage cheese, mixed with French dressing on lettuce leaf.

Orange and grapefruit sections on lettuce leaf, topped by French dressing.

Melon slices with cottage cheese and chives on lettuce, topped by mayonnaise.

KAT'S CRANBERRY SAUCE - W

For about 2 quarts, pick over and wash 3 pounds of cranberries and place in a roomy saucepan with 2 cups each of light brown and white sugar, the grated rind of 3 oranges, 1 cup orange juice, and 1 teaspoon cinnamon. Bring to a boil, stir and cover. Boil just till berries burst (4 to 5 minutes)- Sauce jells when cold.

CRANBERRY SALAD - W

1 lb cranberries   **1 1/2 cup water**
1 1/2 cup sugar

Cook till berries pop. Add 1 large package cherry jello and 36 small marshmallows. Heat till dissolved. Remove from fire and add 1 cup chopped nuts, 1 cup chopped celery, and 2 apples, grated. Pour in molds to congeal. Serve on lettuce, topped with mayonnaise.

Vegetable Man

CHAPTER VI

"Vegetable Man"

(vegetables, rice, potatoes, pastas,
salads, and dressings)

A familiar sight on streets of Louisiana towns in by gone years was the vegetable man. He had a horse and wagon and would go through the neighborhoods selling fresh fruits and vegetables. He usually made his rounds early in the morning when the produce looked appealingly "dew fresh." The housewife heard his call and would meet him on the street to make her selections.

As the years passed, the vegetable man changed to a truck and then simply disappeared from the street scene. He was replaced by the grocery store and produce shipped in from faraway places.

As the vegetable man went, so went the fresh, just picked fruits and vegetables of by gone days. The closest thing to the vegetable man today is the local farmers market, if your town is lucky enough to have one.

This chapter will include not only vegetables but also rice, pasta, salads and dressings.

PICTURE EXPLANATION

Ethel shows our little girls busy with the vegetable man. It was always a treat for them to visit with him and see all the fresh vegetables. Cook let them choose vegetables and fruit every once in a while.

As long as I can remember, we have stopped at Stelly's at Lebeau on the way to Baton Rouge, New Orleans and South Louisiana. As a child I called it "half way" and we never let Dad pass it by. I understand the first picture of Stelly's was taken in 1927 and it was in business at that time. The two founders have retired and their sons have taken over. If you happen that way at noon, try the plate lunches. They're delicious and quite economical. Their crayfish bisque in season is grand.

There's a friendly face at Stelly's and her name is Pie Hutchins and she has been with the restaurant some 25 years. She's a wonderful cook and won a ribbon for her sweet potato pie at the Yam Festival. Her recipe follows. You'll also find her homemade biscuit mix in our bread chapter.

Bibby

SWEET POTATO PIE - W

1 cup sweet potatoes (I use a 16 oz can)
Heat potatoes in boiler so as to have them hot to use
1 cup sugar
1 tablespoon margarine
1/2 cup cream (like Pet milk)
3 egg yolks (reserve the whites)
1/2 teaspoon salt
1 teaspoon nutmeg
1 teaspoon cinnamon
1 teaspoon vanilla

Mix together sugar and oleo–then add egg yolks, beat, then add the last 4 seasonings. Mix well, add 1/2 cup cream and mix. Set aside now in another bowl. Beat the 3 egg whites with a pinch of salt until stiff. Take a spoon and blend the whites into 1st mixture. Bake at 350 degrees for 30 to 40 minutes. Put in 2 9" crusts.

For topping:

Beat 4 egg whites till stiff. Add 1/4 cup sugar and beat till creamy. Put on tops of pies and bake in a 450 degree oven till golden brown. If you prefer, you may use strips of crusts and put criss cross on your pie instead of icing.

125

BASIC BEAN RECIPES - B

(White Beans, Navy Beans,
Pinto Beans, and Red Beans)

Some people soak their beans the night before to cut time for cooking. Others will wash beans and prepare for cooking. Either way is all right.

Once you have washed beans and removed any residue from them, place in a large pot with 3/4 teaspoon salt and cover beans with water. Let beans come to a rolling boil. Lower heat and put in seasoning. Cover with lid and continue to cook for one hour, stirring often. Some people will mash beans on the side of the pot as beans become tender to increase the thickness of the liquid. Others will take 2 to 3 tablespoons of flour and add water, beating until smooth, and pour into bean liquid to increase thickness.

RED BEANS AND RICE - W

2 lbs dried red beans
Hambone with ham
2 med onions, chopped
1 bunch green onions, chopped
1 cup chopped bell pepper

1 cup chopped parsley
2 cloves chopped garlic
Pepper, salt, cayenne, oregano,
  thyme, bay leaf

Sort and wash beans; cover with water and soak overnight. Drain well and add beans to water that already has hambone boiling. Add sautéd onions and bell peppers and parsley. Add garlic and other seasonings and cook on low heat till beans are mushy. Mash some of the beans on side of pot and taste for more seasoning. Must be spicy. If you wish, cook sausage in another skillet, slice in hunks and add to red beans. (Choose sausage from mild to hot, depending on your taste.) Serve red beans over rice. You can dice up onions and tomatoes and serve these fresh over the beans. Have tabasco on table. This makes a good company dish for a big crowd. Also great with broiled porkchops.

BLACK BEANS AND RICE - W

Take 1 pound black beans; sort, wash and soak them overnight. Drain next morning; cover with water and add 2 tablespoons oil, 1 small diced onion, 1 small diced pepper, 1 small diced tomato, bay leaf, oregano, cumin, salt, pepper, and red pepper. Cook slowly, covered till beans get mushy. Mash some on side and cook mixture till thick, adding a little wine vinegar, chili powder, and a dash of sugar. Add a little more oil and cook slowly. Serve over rice and top with onions. Pass the tabasco.

WHITE BEANS - B

4 cups white beans	Salt and pepper
4 to 6 lg ham hocks	1 tbsp parsley
1 onion	Tabasco to taste
1/2 tsp garlic cloves or powder	1 bay leaf

Place beans in a large stewing pot and cover with water. Bring to a rolling boil and then lower heat. Add onions, garlic, salt, pepper, parsley, and bay leaf. Cover with a tight lid and cook until tender for about 1 hour, stirring often. Remove bay leaf. You can add ham hocks along with beans or you can cook ham hocks in a separate pot. Add tabasco. Bring to a boil until tender then add to beans 20 minutes before beans are finished. This will add seasoning to your beans. This will work for red beans and sausage and navy beans.

FRIED SQUASH - B

2 lg yellow or white squash	Bread crumbs
A sprinkle of garlic powder	Salt and pepper to taste
Egg	

The best way to fry squash is to cut into about 4 inches in diameter. For best results dip into seasoned crumbs then dip into beaten egg. Dip once again into more crumbs. Fry in hot fat for about 5 minutes. Cook on both sides, then drain on brown paper bag. 2 to 4 servings.

ASPARAGUS WITH CHEESE - B

1 bunch asparagus
1/2 cup grated cheese
1 tsp salt

1 tbsp butter
1/8 tsp white pepper
1 clove fresh garlic

Smash garlic in a pot. Cut asparagus into bite size pieces. Add water and salt. Bring to a boil for ten minutes. Very lightly butter a baking dish and pour asparagus into dish. Sprinkle with cheese and pepper. Add pats of remaining butter. Bake in a moderate oven at 350°-400° until cheese and butter melts. Serves 4 to 6.

TURNIPS IN CREAM - B

1 lb white turnip bottoms
2 cups milk
4 tbsp flour

4 tbsp butter or margarine
Salt and pepper to taste

Wash and pare turnips, then cut into cubes. Use 1/2 cup water and steam until tender. Make a white sauce from the flour, butter, milk and seasonings. Pour sauce over turnip cubes and serve.

WHITE ONIONS AND POTATOES AUGRATIN - B

12 medium leek onions
6 new potatoes
1 cup medium white sauce
1/2 cup grated cheddar cheese

Bread crumbs
Sprinkle of garlic powder
Salt and pepper

Bring to a boil the leek onions in 1/2 cup of water. Wash and slice new potatoes. Do not peel. Drop the potatoes in with the onions. Arrange leek onions and potatoes in a greased baking dish, and pour the white sauce over them. Add the cheese and bread crumbs. Then season with garlic powder, salt and pepper. Bake at 350° for 15 minutes. Serves 4.

CABBAGE CASSEROLE - B

Medium head of cabbage
1/2 stick oleo or butter
7 slices American cheese,
  grated

1 can cream of mushroom soup
Tabasco, salt, and pepper to taste
1 small bag potato chips
1 small onion

Chop onion fine, saute in butter and add soup and cheese. Cook till cheese is melted. Boil quartered cabbage 10 minutes, drain and chop fine. Add to above mixture. Pour into a greased baking dish and sprinkle with crushed chips. Bake at 350° for 45 minutes.

AGGIE'S BAKED STUFFED POTATOES - B

12 fairly large white potatoes
1 cup green onions, chopped
1 cup bacon bits
1/2 carton sour cream

2 egg whites, beaten
Grated cheese to sprinkle on
  top of potatoes
Salt and pepper to taste

Bake potatoes in 400° oven till done. Stir in green onions, bacon bits and sour cream. Beat egg whites till foamy and add to mixture. Put cheese on top, season to taste, and bake at 350° till cheese is melted.

VEGETABLE ASPIC - W

2 cans string beans
2 cans petit pois
1 can carrots
6 hard boiled eggs
4 green onions, chopped
5 sprigs parsley
2 tsps french dressing

1 cup mayonnaise
8 or 10 stuffed olives
8 or 10 chopped sour salad pickles
1 jar pimento
3 packages gelatin
2 tsps chicken base
1 carton sour cream

Drain vegetables and mix these and other ingredients together. Dissolve gelatin in 1/2 cup cold water. When soft, heat over hot water. Season mixture to taste. Add gelatin to mixture and let congeal in refrigerator till hard.

CREOLE SWEET POTATOES - B

6 lg sweet potatoes
1 cup rich, brown stock
2 caramels

Grated nutmeg
White pepper
Celery salt

Preboil potatoes for 20 minutes, then peel skins and cut into halves. Lightly grease baking dish and sprinkle with celery salt, white pepper and nutmeg. Use stock from potatoes and add caramel. Pour over the potato halves. Bake in a hot oven of about 400-450° until slightly browned. Baste frequently with stock. Serve with fish. Makes 4 to 6 servings.

RICE A LA CREOLE - B

1 onion
Sliced cooked pork
1 tbsp fat
1 cup cooked rice
2 cups cooked tomatoes

Salt
Tabasco
Paprika
Bread crumbs

Chop onion and pork very fine. Add fat. Throw cooked rice in and stir well. Add tomatoes and seasoning. Mix well. Put into greased baking dish, cover with bread crumbs. Bake in hot oven at 400° for 15 minutes. Serves 6 to 8.

RICE CROQUETTES - B

1 1/2 cup cooked rice
1/4 tsp paprika
1 tbsp parsley flakes
1/2 tsp salt

1 cup milk
1 egg, slightly beaten
Bread Crumbs

Melt butter, blend parsley and salt together. Mix with flour and milk. Cook until thickened. Add paprika and rice. Cool. Shape into patties. Roll into crumbs, then in egg and again in crumbs. Fry in hot deep fat until golden brown. Drain on absorbent paper and use a sweet sauce or a gravy sauce over it. Makes about 6 patties.

OKRA SAUTE STYLE - B

1 lb fresh okra or 1 pack
  (10 oz) frozen okra
1/2 cup chopped green or
  red pepper

1/4 cup chopped green onions
2 tbsp butter or margarine
2 tbsp lemon juice

Steam okra with 1/2 cup salted water covered in large pot for 10 minutes until tender. Drain. Saute onions and green peppers in butter or margarine until soft, but not brown. Add lemon juice. Toss lightly with chopped okra. Serve over rice if desired. Makes 4 servings.

COLORFUL VEGETABLE SALAD - B

1 can (1 lb 4 ozs) red kidney
  beans, drained
1 can (1 lb) whole kernel corn,
  drained
1 can (1 lb) cut green beans,
  cooked and drained
1/2 cup light oil
2 tsps Worcestershire sauce

2 tsps cooking vinegar
1 tsp prepared mustard
3/4 tsp salt
1/2 tsp sugar
1/4 tsp garlic powder
1/4 cup chopped green peppers
1/4 cup chopped jalapenos
Sprinkle of salt and pepper

After draining vegetables, place all ingredients in a large bowl. Mix well. In a medium container combine the remaining ingredients. Mix well. Pour over vegetables. Cover and refrigerate for 2 hours or longer. Serve on lettuce lined salad plates. Serves 8.

FRESH VEGETABLE SALAD - B

3 med zucchinis
3 lg firm tomatoes
1 lg red sweet onion
2 ripe avocados
2 tbsps grated lemon rind
  juice from 2 lemons

2 tbsps chopped parsley
1/2 cup chopped celery and tops
1/2 cup salad oil
3 tbsps vinegar

In a large oblong serving dish, arrange tomatoes, zucchini, red onion, and avocados. Mix celery and tops with parsley. Sprinkle over tops of vegetables. In a jar squeeze lemon juice, grated lemon rind, salad oil, vinegar, salt and pepper. Shake well. Pour over vegetables. Chill. Makes 6 to 8 servings.

CABBAGE SLAW - W

1 lg head of cabbage, shredded
2 med onions, shredded

1 med bell pepper, shredded
3/4 cup sugar

Toss lightly; sprinkle sugar on top and set aside. Mix the following ingredients: 1 cup vinegar, 1 1/2 tsp salt. 1 tbsp sugar, 1 tsp dry mustard, 1 tsp celery seed. Bring to a boil. Remove from heat and add 1 cup salad oil. Let cool. Pour over cabbage and mix. Cover and refrigerate for 24 hours or longer. Improves with age.

CARROTS AND ZUCCHINI DELIGHT - B

2 lg carrots, diagonally sliced
2 med zucchinis, sliced
1/2 cup light olive oil
1/4 cup cider vinegar
Salt and pepper to taste

1/4 tsp dried tarragon leaves
1/4 tsp dried basil leaves
1/8 tsp dried oregano leaves
Lettuce

Cook carrots for 3 minutes in 1 cup of salted water. Add zucchini and cook 2 minutes more. Drain. Combine oil, vinegar and seasonings. Pour over hot vegetables. Cover and chill. Drain, reserving dressing. Serve vegetables on lettuce leaf with dressing. Makes 4 to 6 servings.

ASPARAGUS SALAD - W

2 lbs fresh asparagus, cooked
   and drained
1 clove garlic, minced
1/4 tsp salt

1/4 tsp pepper
1/2 cup lemon juice
3/4 cup salad oil (olive oil)

Mix minced garlic, oil, salt, pepper and lemon juice in a jar. Shake well, then refrigerate. Drain asparagus and place in a salad bowl. Pour mixture over asparagus. Return to refrigerator and chill for several hours. Yields 4 servings.

CREAMED STYLE COLE SLAW - B

2 cups green cabbage, shredded
2 cups red cabbage, shredded
1/2 cup sour cream
2 tsps lemon juice

1/2 cup chopped pecans
1/2 cup chopped onions
Salt and pepper to taste

Combine all ingredients in a large bowl and toss well. Cover and chill. Serves 6 to 8.

SIMPLE STUFFED MUSHROOMS - B

12 lg mushrooms
2 tbsps butter
1/4 cup chopped green peppers
1/4 cup chopped onion

1/4 cup seasoned bread crumbs
1 1/2 tbsps grated cheese
4 to 5 tbsps water

Clean mushrooms. Remove stems and baste mushroom tops with 1 tbsp melted butter in a skillet. Chop stems and saute in 2 tbsps butter. Add onion and green peppers and saute until tender. Add water. Simmer for 5 minutes. Stir in bread crumbs. Stuff mixture in mushroom tops. Sprinkle with cheese and place lid on skillet. Lower flame and steam for 20 minutes.

CARROT SALAD - B

8 carrots cut in cubes
2 tbsps olive oil
3/4 cup water
1/4 cup sugar

2 tbsps lemon juice
1/4 tsp celery salt
1/4 tsp parsley

Steam carrots in 3/4 cup water with olive oil for 5 minutes. Add sugar, lemon juice, celery salt and parsley. Stir 15 minutes longer. Set aside to cool and serve in spinach leaves. Salt and pepper to taste.

ENGLISH PEAS TOSSED SALAD - B

2 cans English peas, drained
1/2 cup olives, chopped
1/4 cup onion, chopped
1 tbsp soy sauce
Salt and pepper to taste

4 tbsps mayonnaise
3 hard cooked eggs
  (roundly sliced)
Lettuce

Heat peas for 5 minutes, then drain. In a large bowl add peas, olives, onion, soy sauce and salt and pepper to taste. Toss in mayonnaise. Arrange sliced hard cooked eggs on top. Sprinkle again with salt and pepper. Serve in lettuce leaves. Serves 6 to 8.

RICE STUFFING - B

1/2 cup rice or wild rice
1 qt boiling water
Salt and pepper
1/2 lb fresh mushrooms sauted
  in butter or margarine

1/2 tsp sage
1 tbsp melted fat
1 egg yolk, beaten

Cook rice in water for 25 minutes. Add remaining ingredients and blend well. You can use the seasoning that is suggested for bread stuffing with the combination accordingly. This will fill a 2 pound bird.

WATER CHESTNUT RICE - W

1/2 cup oleo
1 cup rice
1 cup diced onions
1 (4 oz) can mushrooms
1 (10 1/2 oz) can beef broth

1 cup boiling water to which 3
  bouillon cubes have been added
1 (6 oz) can water chestnuts
1/2 cup chopped green peppers
Tabasco, salt and pepper to taste

Brown rice in oleo; add onions and cook till wilted. Mix in mushroms, broth, bouillon water, pepper and water chestnuts. Cover and bake 45 minutes in 350° oven. Stir some while cooking.

KAT'S FESTIVE RICE - W

1 1/2 cups raw rice, parboiled for 5 minutes and drained
1 can cream of mushroom soup
1 can cream of celery soup
1 small jar of chopped pimentos
1/2 cup chopped celery
1/2 cup chopped bell pepper
1 bunch green onions, chopped
1 can water chestnuts, sliced
1 (11 oz.) can sliced mushrooms and juice
1 stick butter or oleo

Sauté chopped ingredients in butter and then add all other ingredients. Put in buttered casserole dish and bake at 300 to 350° for 2 1/2 hours, covered. Serves 6 to 8.

BROCCOLI AND RICE - B

Sauté a small, diced onion in 2 tablespoons oleo. Add 1 box chopped broccoli (not cooked) to 1 cup rice. Add sautéd onion. Add a can of cream of chicken soup, 1/2 cup milk, and 1/2 cup Cheese Whiz. Mix well and bake in buttered casserole dish about 20 minutes in 350° oven.

GREEN RICE - W

2 cups rice
2/3 cup chopped bell pepper
1 cup green onion, chopped
1/4 cup oil
1 1/2 tbsps Worcestershire sauce
4 cups beef or chicken bouillon made from 6 cubes & 4 cups water

Combine all ingredients and season to taste with salt, pepper, and cayenne. Bake without stirring in a 2 quart casserole dish with a tight fitting cover for 45 minutes at 350°.

COUNTRY FRIED POTATOES - W

Cover bottom of skillet with oil. Peel and slice potatoes and onions in layers in skillet. Cook, turning constantly as potatoes get brown and onions get limp. Cover and allow to cook down. Season with salt, pepper and paprika.

STUFFED ONIONS - W

4 lg yellow onions
1 lb ground beef
1 or 2 tomatoes
2 stalks celery

1 egg
1/4 tsp basil, oregano and tarragon
Paprika, salt, and pepper to taste

Scoop out onion middle, leaving 4 layers. Boil in salted water for 5 minutes. Mix other ingredients and stuff onions. Sprinkle each with basil and Worcestershire sauce. Top with pat of butter. Bake in 350° oven for 45 minutes to an hour.

HOT CHICKEN RICE SALAD - B

2 cups diced cooked chicken
2 cans cream of chicken soup
4 tsps diced onion
2 cups cooked rice
1 tsp salt
1 1/2 cup mayonnaise

6 tsps lemon juice
1 cup slivered blanched almonds
6 hard boiled eggs, sliced
2 cups diced celery
Rice Krispies

Combine all ingredients except cereal, in a well greased casserole dish. Top with crushed Rice Krispies and cook in 350˙ oven 20 to 30 minutes. Serve on lettuce with hot rolls and an olive for a luncheon.

COMPANY YAMS - B

5 yams, peeled and cooked
1/3 cup butter
3/4 cup light brown sugar
1/4 cup cinnamon

1 cup chopped pecans
1 can diced, drained pineapple
Package of marshmallows

Mash potatoes with a little butter and lemon juice. Bake approximately 15 to 20 minutes at 325°. Take out of oven and sprinkle with mixture of cinnamon, sugar and pecans. Top with marshmallows and bake till they melt.

CHRISTMAS YAMS - W

6 oranges
5 med sweet potatoes
Butter

Marshmallows
Cinnamon and nutmeg

Boil and mash potatoes. Halve oranges and scoop out pulps, saving juice. Add juice to mashed potatoes and a little cinnamon and nutmeg. Fill orange shells with mixture and top with marshmallows. Warm in 350° oven till marshmallows melt.

FRESH PURPLE HULL PEAS - W

2 slices bacon
1 small onion, chopped

1 hot pepper
4 cups peas

Fry bacon in heavy pot for a short while, keeping limp. Pour off some of grease and add water to pot, approximately 1/4 full. Add onion, hot pepper and peas, bringing to a boil. Season to taste. Turn heat down and cook slowly till done. Freezes well.

OKRA AND TOMATOES - W

Cut 2 pounds okra in small round slices, discarding both ends. Fry diced onions (2 medium ones) in small amount of oil in skillet. Add okra slices and cook till both begin to get soft. Add 1 can of diced Rotel tomatoes and 1 can of stewed tomatoes. Cover and cook mixture down and water off. Before covering, season to taste. When fresh tomatoes are in season, use them but you'll need to add hot pepper or pepper sauce to mixture. You may add cooked sausage to okra and tomatoes at this point. Freezes well.

YELLOW SQUASH CASSEROLE - W

2 or 3 lbs yellow squash, sliced in rounds	Italian bread crumbs
	Fresh grated parmesan cheese
1 med onion, diced	1 can cheddar cheese soup
1 med bell pepper, diced	1 can mushroom soup

Saute onions and peppers till soft and add sliced squash. Cook till tender and pour excess water out. Add cans of soup and a little milk. Season to taste. Pour in casserole dish and top with bread crumbs and cheese. Cook in 350° oven till heated thoroughly. Freezes well.

RICE SALAD - W

1/2 cup chopped onion	1 cup diced celery
1 tbsp vinegar	1/4 cup chopped bell pepper
2 tbsps oil	2 1/2 cups cooked, peeled shrimp
1/2 tsp curry powder	
1 1/2 cups cooked rice	1/4 cup mayonnaise

Combine onion, vinegar, oil and curry powder. Add rice and mix. Then add rest of ingredients. Chill for 2 hours before serving.

MIRLITON (VEGETABLE PEAR) SALAD - W

Boil vegetable pears in water till tender. Chill and then peel. Halve and take seeds out. Put pears on lettuce leaf and add sliced red onion. Top with Italian or vinaigrette dressing.

CAESAR SALAD - W

Mash a clove of garlic, 2 anchovies, 1/2 teaspoon capers with fork till smooth. Add 2 tablespoons oil, 1 tablespoon red wine vinegar, juice of lemon, tabasco, Worcestershire sauce, a little dry mustard and 1 coddled egg. Mix well. Pour over Romaine lettuce and lightly toss. Sprinkle parmesan cheese and croutons on top.

TARRAGON SALAD - W

1/2 cup vegetable oil
1/4 cup tarragon vinegar
1 tsp salt

1 tsp dry mustard
1/4 tsp white pepper

On torn Romaine leaves, place fresh, steamed asparagus, artichoke hearts, fresh mushrooms, a slice or 2 of onion, a few pimento stuffed olives, and a sliced hard boiled egg. Top with tarragon salad dressing.

MANDARIN ORANGES AND RED ONION SALAD - W

1 can of mandarin oranges or 4
   fresh regular oranges
1 red onion

Vinaigrette dressing
   (see recipes below)

Layer orange slices and onion slices on lettuce leaf. Dress with vinaigrette dressing.

Vinaigrette Dressing:

1/2 cup oil
3/4 cup red wine vinegar
1/2 cup water

1 tbsp basil
1 tsp tarragon
Salt, pepper and sugar to taste

GRANNY SMITH'S APPLE AND ROQUEFORT
or BLUE CHEESE SALAD - W

4 Granny Smith apples
8 ozs blue cheese or roquefort,
   crumbled

3 ozs any chopped nut

Mix crumbled cheese, peeled and sliced apples and nuts with a little mayonnaise. Serve on lettuce with a small amount of mayonnaise, paprika, cheese and nuts on top.

SCALLOPED CARROTS AND CELERY - B

3 cups diced cooked carrots   1 1/2 cups diced cooked celery
1/2 cup bread crumbs   1/2 cup grated cheese
2 cups medium white sauce

Combine cheese, crumbs, and white sauce. Fill a well-oiled baking dish with alternate layers of vegetables and white sauce. Cover, bake in moderate oven (375°F.) 30 minutes. 6 servings.

CAROLYN'S VEGETABLE SPECIAL - B

1 cup cracker crumbs   1/4 cup butter
3 eggs   1 cup milk
1 cup cheese   1/8 teaspoon pepper
1 can asparagus   1/2 teaspoon salt

Beat eggs slightly and add all other ingredients except butter + 1/3 cup 1/2 cup grated cheese cracker crumbs. Pour into buttered casserole, place remaining crumbs and butter on top. Bake in moderate oven.

CREOLE STYLE BEANS - B

1 quart green beans   3 slices bacon
Salt and pepper   6 potatoes

Wash beans. Remove strings. Fry bacon until crisp and brown. Add beans and sufficient boiling water to prevent burning. Cover. Cook slowly stirring occasionally, until tender. Season to taste. Pare potatoes. Place on top of beans. Steam until potatoes are tender. If desired a few slices of onion may be added. One-fourth pound diced ham may be substituted for the bacon. 6 servings.

STUFFED MIRLITONS - W

8 mirlitons (good size)
1 lb ground beef or cooked shrimp
1 green pepper, chopped
1 medium onion, chopped
1 tomato diced

Creole seasoning, tabasco,
   black pepper
Italian bread crumbs
Parmesan cheese

Boil mirlitons till done, but not too soft. Cool them and then halve, throw away the seed and scoop out insides to make boat. Sauté pepper, onion and ground beef in a little oil till beef is brown. Add tomato and insides of mirlitons and cook. Season with tabasco, pepper and creole seasoning. Fill boats with mixture and top with Italian bread crumbs and parmesan cheese. Cook in oven 350 degrees for 30 minutes.

Raw mirlitons are also good to use in place of cucumbers in a salad and used in place of water chestnuts in Chinese food.

Try to use freshly grated parmesan cheese if available.

GREEN BEAN SALAD - B

1 16 oz. can French style green
   beans drained
3 med onions cut into thin rings
1 cup finely chopped celery
1 8 1/2 oz. can peas drained
12 oz jar pimento strips drained

3/4 cup salad oil
1/4 cup vinegar
1 tsp salt
5 to 6 dashes hot sauce
1 tsp Worcestershire sauce

Combine green beans, onion rings, celery, peas and pimento. Combine remaining ingredients and pour over vegetable mixture. Refrigerate 2 to 3 hours. Serves 8 to 10.

OKRA SALAD - B

1 pkg frozen sm or fresh okra   Salt, pepper and vinegar
1 onion

Boil okra if frozen according to directions on package, if fresh drop cleaned okra in boiling hot water and boil until tender. Drain and add sliced onion, salt and pepper and vinegar to taste. Serve hot or cold.

ASPARAGUS SALAD - B

1 15 oz can green asparagus   1 cup finely chopped hard
2 tsps prepared mustard   cooked egg
1/4 cup mayonnaise   Pimento strips
1/4 cup finely chopped celery

Drain and chill asparagus spears on a salad plate. Blend mustard and mayonnaise; stir in celery and hard cooked eggs. Spoon over asparagus. Garnish with pimento. Yield: 4 servings.

SWEET POTATO PIE - B

1 cup mashed potatoes   1 tsp nutmeg
1 cup sugar   1 tsp cinnamon
1 tbsp margarine   3 egg yolks (save the whites)
1/2 cup cream (Pet or Carnation)   1 tsp vanilla
1/2 tsp salt

Mix sugar and margarine. Add egg yolks and blend well. Put the can of potatoes to heat on medium heat. Remove just the potatoes and add to mixture. Add cream and blend. Put in all seasoning and mix well. In a separate bowl take the 3 egg whites and a pinch of salt and beat till stiff. Take a spoon and fold them into potato mixture. Turn this mixture into 2 9" pie crusts. Bake in 350° oven for 30 to 35 minutes. Remove from oven and let cool for a few minutes.

PAPRIKA POTATOES - W

Peel and dice in cubes six whole white potatoes. Boil them a few minutes. (Do not overcook). Take out and drain. Melt oleo in skillet and sauté potato cubes till soft. Sprinkle paprika and salt and pepper over potatoes before serving.

OVEN BROWNED POTATOES - W

Wash and peel 6 white potatoes. Put a small amount of oil on a cookie sheet, and put fairly thick potato slices on sheet. Turn oven on 400° and bake one side till brown, turn potatoes over and bake on other side till brown. Salt and pepper before serving.

CHINESE FRIED RICE - B

1/4 cup salad oil
1/4 cup chopped scallions
2 cups diced cooked ham,
   pork or shrimp
2 2/3 cups Minute rice
4 eggs, scrambled in
   small pieces

2 cups chicken broth
2 cans (3 oz each) sliced
   mushrooms
2 cups cooked peas
2 teaspoons soy sauce

Heat oil in skillet. Sauté scallions, ham and rice in oil for about 5 minutes. Remove from heat. Stir in eggs.

Bring broth, mushrooms with liquid, peas and soy sauce to a boil. Stir into rice mixture. Cover and let stand 5 minutes. Stir to mix. Makes about 8 servings.

CABBAGE HOME STYLE - B

Cabbage usually takes a back seat when it comes to vegetable choices, but this recipe should make it a favorite in no time at all. It's an old Italian recipe and the bacon gives it a special flavor.

1 cabbage, shredded	1 tablespoon wine vinegar
1/2 cup bacon diced fine	Salt
2 1/2 cups water	Pepper

Saute the bacon gently until soft but not crisp. Add rest of ingredients, cover and cook over medium flame for 25 minutes, or until cabbage is tender. Stir occasionally and add more water if necessary. When cabbage is cooked there should not be more than a couple of tablespoons of liquid in the pan.

SPLIT PEAS WITH TOMATOES - B

1/4 cup chopped salt pork	1 teaspoon sugar
1/2 large onion	2 1/2 cups cooked split peas
1 cup cooked or canned tomatoes	Pepper to taste

Fry salt pork until light brown. Chop onion and add to salt pork. Cook until onion is tender. Stir in tomatoes, sugar cooked split peas and pepper. Heat. Serves 6.

PEPPERS WITH BUTTERED RICE - B

1 cup rice	2 tablespoons melted butter
2 green peppers chopped	or butter substitute
1 1/2 cups cold water	3/4 teaspoon salt
Parsley	

Wash rice. Place in shallow kettle. Add water and salt. Cover closely. Heat to boiling. Boil slowly until rice is tender. Let stand in covered container on back of stove or over low heat 15 minutes. Add chopped peppers to melted butter. Pour over hot rice. Mix by tossing lightly with 2 forks. Garnish with parsley. 6 servings.

EGGPLANT A LA CREOLE - B

1 large or 2 small eggplants
1 teaspoon celery salt
1/2 onion, grated
1 egg well beaten
Salt and pepper

1 tablespoon butter or
  butter substitute
1/2 cup bread crumbs
1 tablespoon chopped parsley

Boil eggplants until tender. Scoop out centers. Chop soft portions. Add remaining ingredients. Fry by tablespoonfuls on a hot oiled griddle browning well on both sides. If desired, 1/2 cup minced boiled ham or cold cooked chicken may be added. 8 servings.

JIMMY'S QUICK AND EASY MICROWAVE ONION - W

Peel and cut a large white or yellow onion lengthwise into 4 to 6 pieces. Add a few shakes of Greek or other seasoning. Place in a microwave dish or cup. Add 1 to 2 tablespoonfuls of Lea & Perrins, white wine, and Worcestershire sauce. Cover with plastic wrap and cook on high for 4 to 5 minutes.

COOKED GLOBE ARTICHOKES - W

Wash artichokes and drain. You may like to cut ends off leaves that stick. Place artichokes in saucepan and add water and salt. Boil 25 to 30 minutes. Water should be up to lower half of artichokes. To eat, pull off leaves and remove the base of the leaf with your teeth and discard top. When all leaves are removed, discard the choke (the hairy part over the heart). Eat the heart with a fork, dipping in sauce. Drain and serve with lemon, butter, and Worcestershire sauce.

For party hors d'oeuvres:

Open artichoke and remove choke. Combine mayonnaise and horseradish and put in middle of artichoke for guests to use as a dip with leaves.

ARTICHOKE CASSEROLE - W

3 cans artichoke hearts,
  cut in halves
2 1/2 lbs fried shrimp
3 (4 oz) cans mushroom pieces

2 1/2 cups cream sauce
2 tbsps butter
1/2 cup parmesan cheese

Make white sauce with 1 stick butter, 2 heaping tablespoons flour; add milk and 3/4 cup sherry, salt, and pepper. Add mushrooms. Grease casserole dish and dot with butter. Add artichoke hearts in layers. Cover with shrimp and pour white sauce and mushrooms over it. Cover with parmesan cheese and bake for 40 minutes at 350˚. Serves 9.

SAUERKRAUT SALAD - W

1 2 1/2 oz can kraut
1 lg chopped onion
2 chopped bell peppers

3/4 cup chopped celery
1 lg jar chopped pimento

Drain sauerkraut and cut fine. Add other chopped vegetables and cover with following mixture.

1/2 cup oil
1 cup sugar
2/3 cup cider vinegar

1/2 cup water
Dash of salt and pepper

Mix well and blend into sauerkraut mixture. Leave in refrigerator well covered for 1 or 2 days allowing it to marinate. Serve on lettuce leaf. Great with pork or ham and good for large crowds.

JERUSALEM ARTICHOKES - W

Wash, scrape, and place artichokes in cold water. Add a little salt and let come to a boil. Cover and boil about 30 minutes till tender. Season to taste and serve with melted butter.

TONI'S MARINATED VEGETABLES - W

1 cup pure vegetable oil
3/4 cup fresh lemon juice (about 4 lemons)
2 tbsps chopped parsley
1 tsp coarse ground black pepper
1 clove garlic, crushed or 1 tsp garlic powder
1 lg onion, thinly sliced
1 lb (3) zucchini squash or yellow squash, sliced
1 med cauliflower separated into flowerets
1 (14 oz) can artichoke hearts, drained and halved
1 tsp sugar
1/2 tsp salt

Combine oil, lemon juice, parsley, salt, sugar, pepper, and garlic in large screw top jar or plastic bowl with tight lid. Shake well. Pour over vegetables. Cover and marinate overnight in refrigerator. Turn vegetables at least once. When serving, remove vegetables with pierced spoon to drain liquid. The liquid can be stored in refrigerator for future use or salad dressing.

GREEN PEA CASSEROLE - W

1/2 stick margarine
1 med onion, chopped
1 can cream of mushroom
  soup
2 (No. 2) cans green peas,
  drained

2 hard boiled eggs, chopped
1 small can sliced water
  chestnuts
1 tsp Worcestershire sauce
1 tsp salt
1/2 tsp pepper

In large skillet, melt margarine and saute chopped onion until tender.   Mix all ingredients and put in baking dish. Put buttered bread crumbs on top. Heat 30 minutes before serving at 350°.

ASPARAGUS CASSEROLE - W

Boil fresh asparagus till tender. Be sure to wash them thoroughly first and cut off tough end. Layer asparagus in casserole dish and layer with sliced hard boiled eggs. Cover with a can of mushroom soup and cheddar cheese soup. Sprinkle seasoned bread crumbs and parmesan cheese over this.Cook in a 325° to 350° oven till warmed through.

ONIONS MORNAY - W

4 tbsps (1/2 stick) butter or
  margarine
2 lg sweet onions, coarsely
  chopped (4 cups)
2 cloves garlic, minced
1 can condensed cream of
  celery soup

1 cup milk
1/4 tsp seasoned pepper
1 can (1 lb) cut green beans,
  drained
2 (8 oz) pkgs sliced processed
  Swiss cheese

Melt butter or margarine in a large frying pan; stir in onions and garlic; cover. Cook 15 minutes and stir in soup, milk, and pepper. Heat, stirring several times, until bubbly. Make two layers each of beans, cheese slices, and sauce in a buttered 8 cup baking dish. Bake in moderate oven at 350° for 30 minutes or until bubbly hot.

ELLA'S GARDEN VEGETABLE MELANGE - W

1 1/2 cup carrots, chopped
1 cup parsnips, chopped
1 cup celery, chopped
1/2 lb mushrooms, sliced

2 cloves garlic, minced
3/4 cup chicken broth
1/2 cup white wine
1 tbsp margarine

Soak vegetables for 15 minutes and drain. Place in covered casserole dish in a 450° oven and cook for 1 hour. Makes 6 servings.

SWEET POTATO PONE - B

4 sweet potatoes (not too large)
3/4 cup sugar
3/4 cup brown sugar
1 egg

1/3 stick oleo
1/3 tsp baking powder
2/3 cup evaporated milk
1/3 tsp vanilla

Grate raw potatoes and mix with other ingredients, adding melted oleo last. Pour mixture in greased baking dish and bake approximately 25 to 30 minutes in a 350 to 375° oven.

RICE CASSEROLE - B

1 can Campbell onion soup
1 cup raw rice
1/2 stick oleo
1 small can water chestnuts

1 small can mushrooms
  (stems and pieces)
1 soup can of water

Melt butter in casserole dish. Add all ingredients and bake for 1 hour at 350°.

SALAD DRESSINGS

METHODIST DRESSING - W

Mix 1 pint mayonnaise, 1 1/2 pound sharp cheese, 1 chopped bell pepper, 5 green onions, sliced, 1/3 bottle chili sauce, garlic, salt, and pepper to taste. Blend all ingredients and keep in jar refrigerated. Good for all green salads.

BLEU CHEESE DRESSING - W

3 cups oil
1 cup white vinegar
1/4 chopped onion

Juice from half a lemon
1/2 lb bleu cheese, crumbled
Salt, pepper, and garlic

Mix all in blender or processor and store in refrigerator. If you wish to add mayonnaise, cut oil to 1 cup and mayonnaise to 2 cups.

THOUSAND ISLAND DRESSING - W

2 cups mayonnaise
2 boiled eggs

2 or 3 tbsps chili sauce
Sweet pickles to taste

Blend all together and store in refrigerator.

KAT'S FRENCH DRESSING - W

1 cup oil
1/2 cup cider vinegar
2 to 3 tbsps sugar
1/2 tsp salt

1/2 tsp paprika
1/2 tsp Coleman's dry mustard
1 clove garlic, chopped

Blend all ingredients together and keep in refrigerator.

ITALIAN DRESSING - W

3 cups oil
1 cup tarragon vinegar
2 tbsps anchovy paste
(optional)

2 tbsps capers
1/2 lemon, squeezed
1 tbsp Italian seasoning

Blend all ingredients and keep refrigerated.

SPINACH SALAD - W

1 lb spinach, washed and drained
1 small onion, cut in rings
4 slices crisp fried bacon
1 1/2 tbsps bacon drippings

1/3 cup olive oil
1/4 cup wine vinegar
2 hard boiled eggs, sliced
Salt and pepper to taste

Fry bacon and drain off all fat. Combine drippings, oil and vinegar and mix well. Place spinach leaves on salad plate and put onion slices, egg slices and crumbled bacon on top. Sprinkle with dressing.

SALLY'S CABBAGE AND ONION MARINADE - W

Shred a medium head of cabbage and slice onion and cover with 3/4 cups sugar. Combine 1 cup vinegar, 1 tablespoon sugar, 1 teaspoon salt, 1/2 teaspoon dry mustard, 1 teaspoon celery salt and 1/2 teaspoon pepper. Bring all to a boil. Add the oil and boil again. Pour over cabbage and onion; cover and refrigerate overnight. Serve on lettuce leaf.

Eatin High on the Hog

CHAPTER VII

Eatin' High on the Hog

(meats)

A typical Southern expression is the above, meaning you're eating well! Where the expression originated, we don't know. My father used it quite often.

It certainly is true of Louisiana cuisine and especially of cajun cuisine. The most famous pork recipe is the cochon-de-lait. Literally translated it means young suckling pig but the saying has come to mean a young pig cooked over an open fire. This custom started in the Mansura area where many French soldiers settled. They brought the custom from their homes in France. A couchon was, and still is, a big party and many Cajuns refer to it as "passez de bon temps" (pass a good time). It is still very prominent in south and central Louisiana towns. We'll start our chapter with the cochon recipe and will include other pork, beef, lamb, and veal recipes.

PICTURE EXPLANATION

Nothing was more fun than the cochon-de-lait. It was a party time for all, young and old. There were and still are chefs who specialize in this and no meal is more delectable. The girls are excitedly watching the cook while he is cooking the cochon, knowing good eating and fun is on the way.

Carl A. Ducoté

Preparing cochon-de-lait for 25 people.

50 lb. dressed pig, whole split from the throat, through chest and down belly to tail.

Mix generous portions of 2 parts salt and 1 part black pepper and rub liberally over entire surface.

Wrap whole pig in heavy gauge steel wire, such as reinforcement wire and tie securely with steel wire. Do not use galvanized wire. Fix hanging bridle on both ends of wire rack so that pig can be rotated.

Prepare bed of red hot coals using pecan or oak for stack. Have extra supply of wood to feed fire as necessary to maintain air temperature.

Hang wire rack with pig enclosed, a distance of 18 to 24 inches from the bed of coal and 6 inches off the ground.

Watch skin carefully for rapid discoloration, burning or bubbling during the first 1-3 hours of cooking. This is a sign that exterior is cooking too quickly. Adjust the distance from the fire as needed. After 3 hours a light even brownness indicates proper rate of cooking.

To avoid under cooked areas, turn the wire rack containing the pig every 15 minutes so that front and back cooks evenly. After 3 hours of cooking and turning with head and shoulders up, rotate the entire rack so that hams will be in the "up position".

Continue this procedure for a period of from 7-8 hours. During the last hour, raise the fire level to cause the skin to crackle. Check for degree of doneness by twisting a leg bone. If bone readily twists, then you will have outstanding cochon-de-lait.

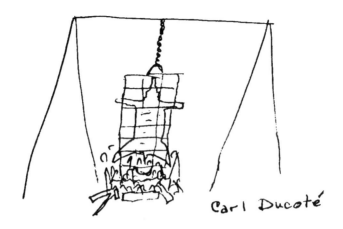

Carl Ducoté

Carl Ducoté is a native of Mansura, Louisiana, where the French soldiers, who had settled there, brought Cochon-de-lait custom from their homeland. It has grown thru the years into a Louisiana custom state-wide and is a real treat.

When you hear of a cochon-de-lait taking place, you know the group will "pass a good time".

Thanks to Carl for this authentic cochon recipe.

ROAST LOIN OF PORK - B

5 or 6 lbs pork loin
1 onion, sliced
4 garlic cloves

1/2 tsp thyme
1/2 cup red wine
Cajun seasoning and pepper

Cut little slivers in loin and insert garlic cloves. Season with thyme, cajun seasoning, and pepper. Put a little water in bottom of roasting pan and slice onion in pan. Place fat side up in roasting pan and cover. Roast for 30 minutes per pound (from 3 to 3 1/2 hours for a 6 lb roast) at 400°. After first hour, baste with wine and keep basting through cooking. In the last 45 minutes, add peeled sweet potatoes and layer in pan with roast. If more liquid is needed at this time, add a little more water. You may also add more sliced onion at same time as sweet potatoes, if you wish.

STUFFED PORK CHOPS - B

6 double pork chops
2 cups bread crumbs
3/4 tsp salt
1/4 tbsp minced parsley

1 tsp sage
1 tbsp grated onion
3 tbsps milk
Fat

Cut a pocket on the bone side of each chop. Combine next 7 ingredients and mix well. Stuff each chop with mixture. Brown chops in fat, season and add a little water. Bake in moderate oven at 350° for about one hour or until tender. Serves 6.

SMOTHERED PORK CHOPS - W

8 pork chops
Flour
Salt, pepper, cayenne, and
  paprika

1 onion, sliced
Minced garlic
Minced parsley

Put flour and seasoning in plastic bag and add chops one at a time to coat. Brown chops in a little oil in heavy skillet. Remove from skillet and drain. Pour off some of oil and add onions, garlic, and flour to make a brown roux. Make sure you brown flour, not burn. Add water to mixture and make gravy. Add chops and simmer, covered, for about an hour. Check to see if gravy is too thick and add water while cooking. Add parsley at very last. Serve with rice or grits or you can peel and slice red potatoes and add to skillet the last 30 minutes. An electric skillet is great for this dish.

PORK CHOPS AND VEGETABLES - B

4 to 6 pork chops
Flour
Seasoning

Vegetables, fresh or frozen
Canned mushroom soup or
  Lipton's cup a soup

Coat chops with flour and seasoning and brown in oil. Remove and drain. Add soup, water, and onion to skillet and smooth. Add chops and sliced carrots, potatoes, green beans, and rutabaga or turnips. Simmer mixture for approximately 45 minutes in covered skillet. If using frozen vegetables, use mixed vegetables or California vegetables and add in last 10 minutes of cooking.

PORK CHOPS SOUTHERN STYLE - B

Brown 8 pork chops seasoned with salt and red pepper in skillet. While browning, mix together in a bowl 2 tablespoons ketchup, 1 tablespoon Worcestershire sauce, 1 tablespoon dry mustard, 1 tablespoon lemon juice, 1 teaspoon salt, 1/4 teaspoon paprika, 1/8 teaspoon cayenne pepper, and 1 cup water. Pour the above mixture over the browned pork chops and simmer 30 to 45 minutes or until tender.

COUNTRY SPARERIBS AND BEANS - B

2 1/2 cups or 2 cans kidney
   beans, cooked
2 lg onions, chopped

3 lbs spareribs
Salt and pepper to taste
1 cup apple juice

Place a layer of beans in a greased baking dish. Season with some of the onions and salt and pepper. Repeat layers. Cut spareribs into serving size pieces. Place on top of beans. Season with salt and pepper. Pour apple juice over all. Cook, uncovered, in a moderate oven at 350° until spareribs are done for about 1 hour, making sure meat and beans are tender. Makes 4 to 5 servings.

HAM WITH ONION GRAVY - B

1 ham steak
2 cups sliced onions

1 cup sour cream
1/4 cup milk

Trim all but 1/4 inch of fat from ham. Put trimmed fat in black skillet. Pan broil steak over low heat until golden brown (3 to 4 minutes each side for fully cooked ham or 6 to 8 minutes each side for cook before eating type). Remove from pan. Pan fry sliced onions in pan drippings until tender and delicately browned. Stir in sour cream and milk. Heat thoroughly. Pour over ham steak on platter. Serves 4.

SOUTHERN SMOTHERED PORK CHOPS - B

4 to 6 medium center cut
   pork chops
2 tbsps fat or cooking oil

1/2 golden onion
1 tsp parsley
1/4 tsp garlic powder

In a skillet, heat fat or oil and add onion. Saute until onions are transparent. Season pork chops with salt, pepper, and garlic powder. Add pork chops to onions. Brown on both sides, making sure you do not burn the onions. If necessary, remove the onions. After browning, add 1/2 cup water, letting it come to a fast boil. Lower the fire and place a lid on the skillet. Simmer for 1/2 hour.

SAUSAGE AND RICE - B

1/2 lb smoked link sausage
1/2 cup bell pepper, chopped
1/4 cup celery, chopped
1/4 cup parsley
1/2 cup green onions and tops

1 can tomatoes
1 1/2 cup water
1 cup roux
1/2 cup grated cheese

Link sausage should be cut into 1/2 inch round pieces. Fry on a low flame in a skillet with about 2 tbsps oil until slightly browned. Put aside and drain on a paper towel. Add tomatoes and roux to drippings. Stir. Saute onions, celery and bell peppers in sausage drippings. Do not let them get hard or crisp. Add water and salt, bring to boil for about 1 1/2 minutes. Then add sausage, raw rice and green onions. With a tight lid, cook slowly until rice is done.

COUNTRY BEEF STEW - B

1 tbsp cooking oil
1 cup chopped onion
1 cup water
1 clove of garlic, mashed
2 tbsps cooking oil
2 1/2 lbs chuck round in cubes
1 cup beef broth or
    beef bouillon cubes
1 bay leaf

1/4 cup green pepper
1 tbsp Worcestershire sauce
6 peeled carrots, chopped up
6 peeled new potatoes,
    chopped in cubes
1 cup celery
1 tbsp flour
1/4 cup water

Melt fat in dutch oven or large kettle pot. Saute chopped onions and mashed garlic. Add more fat or oil and brown meat on all sides. Brown very slowly. (This gives you the rich dark color for gravy.) Add onion, garlic, beef broth cubes, 2 cups water, bay leaf, salt and pepper, and Worcestershire sauce. Bring to a boil; lower heat; simmer for 1 1/2 to 1 3/4 hours or until meat is almost tender. Add carrots, onions, and celery. Simmer 30 to 40 minutes longer or until vegetables and meat are tender. Vegetables may be cooked separately and added to the stew. Remove bay leaf. Thicken broth with 1 tablespoon flour mixed with 1/4 cup water. Mix paste till smooth. Makes 4 to 6 servings.

CREOLE STEAK - B

1/4 cup all purpose flour
2 tsps salt
2 tsps paprika
1/2 tsp pepper
1 (1 lb) round steak, cut into
  bite size pieces

1 onion, chopped
1 green onion, chopped
1/2 green pepper, chopped
3 tbsps salad oil
1/2 cup uncooked, regular rice
2 (16 oz) cans stewed tomatoes

Combine flour, salt, paprika,and pepper. Dredge steak in flour mixture. Saute onions and green peppers in hot oil. Remove from skillet. Brown meat in remaining oil in skillet and cover with onion mixture. Sprinkle with rice. Drain tomatoes, reserving liquid. Add enough water to tomato liquid to make 2 cups. Spoon tomatoes over rice and sprinkle with any remaining flour mixture.

LIVER AND ONIONS - B

1 lb veal liver (1/2 in. thick)
Salt and pepper to taste
1 lg onion

2 cups flour
2 tbsps cooking oil

Season liver and dip in flour. Heat oil in skillet. Pan fry liver on both sides until golden brown. Remove liver from skillet and fry onions in drippings, stirring constantly. Return liver to skillet, adding 1/2 cup water. Cover with tight lid and cook about 5 minutes longer. Do not overcook as liver will become tough.

OLD FASHION MEAT BALLS
AND GRAVY - B

2 lbs ground fresh beef
2 tbsps cooking oil
1/2 cup chopped onion
2 cloves of garlic, chopped
2 tsps parsley flakes

1 1/2 tsps salt
1/2 tsp pepper or salt and
  pepper to taste
Splashes of tabasco to taste
2 tbsps roux

Mix thoroughly beef with onions, garlic, parsley, salt, pepper and tabasco. Mix with fingers until ingredients are completely mixed with beef. Pinch meat and make balls about 2 inches in diameter. In a black skillet, add cooking oil and brown meat on all sides, but do not cook fully. Remove from skillet and drain off almost all fat. Leave enough fat to make roux. Then place meat balls in skillet and cover. Simmer for 1/2 hour or until center of meat is done. Makes 6 to 8 servings.

BARBARA'S SICILIAN MEAT BALLS AND SAUCE - W

2 lg can tomato paste
1 lg can tomatoes
3 cans water
2 tbsps Italian season
Olive oil
1/2 cup sugar

Salt and pepper to taste
2 med onions
8 to 10 cloves garlic
3 lbs hamburger meat
1 cup bread crumbs
2 cups flour

Mix meat, bread crumbs, 1 tbsp Italian seasons, 1 onion, chopped, and 3 cloves garlic, salt, and pepper. Make meat balls and roll in flour. Fry in hot oil. Set aside. In large pot, line bottom with olive oil. Cook onions and garlic and mix tomato paste, Italian season, salt, pepper, and sugar. Cook and stir until paste turns a dark red color about 15 or 20 minutes. Add tomatoes and water; bring to a boil. Reduce heat and add meat balls. Simmer about 1 to 2 hours. Let sit 2 to 4 hours before serving over pasta. Sauce may be used for lasagna. Just layer sharp cheese and lasagna pasta, and top with parmesan cheese. Bake 30 minutes.

KAT'S CREOLE DAUBE GLACE - W

1 cup finely shredded, cooked meat (can be roast beef, soup meat,
brisket, pork roast, veal roast or lamb roast)
20 stuffed olives
2 cans beef consomme
2 envelopes unflavored gelatin
1 bunch green onions, chopped
2 tbsps finely chopped parsley
3 cloves garlic, finely chopped
2 tbsps Worcestershire sauce
Tabasco, salt, and pepper to taste

Place olives in bottom of individual, lightly oiled molds and put chopped meat
on top. Heat 1 can consomme and dissolve gelatin in it. Add remaining can
of consomme, green onions, parsley, garlic, Worcestershire sauce, tabasco,
salt, and pepper. Pour over meat in mold. Refrigerate till hard.

SPICY POT ROAST - W

2 1/2 to 3 1/2 lbs boneless
  chuck roast
McCormick's Pot Roast Bag
1 can diced Rotel tomatoes
1 small can tomato sauce
1 chopped onion

1 chopped bell pepper (optional)
Mushrooms, canned or fresh
  (optional)
Salt, pepper, cajun seasonings,
  garlic powder to taste

Combine all sauce ingredients, including the seasoning from the pot roast
bag and 2/3 cup water. Put roast in bag and pour mixture over the roast. Turn
bag so mixture will cover both sides. Bake in 325° oven for 2 1/2 to 3 hours
or until roast has become very tender. Put slices of roast over freshly cooked
spaghetti and spoon sauce over roast. If roast is frozen, partially thaw, cut
water to 1/2 cup and cook at 300° for 3 1/2 to 4 hours.

BRISKET - W

6 to 8 lbs beef brisket
Jar of Italian salad dressing
Celery seed
Onion powder
Worcestershire sauce

Tabasco
Creole seasoning
Salt and pepper to taste
Hot barbecue sauce

Marinate brisket in Italian salad dressing in refrigerator overnight in roasting pan. Next morning, sprinkle with celery seed, onion powder, Worcestershire sauce, tabasco, creole seasoning, salt, and pepper. Cover and cook in 300° oven till tender, but not falling apart (approximately 6 hours). Uncover and pour barbecue sauce over roast and cook at 325° for additional 30 minutes. Let cool and refrigerate meat and juices overnight. Next day, scrape fat that has congealed on top off and throw away. Put back in oven and warm thoroughly. Slice meat and your juices have made the gravy.

BEEF POT ROAST - W

Use either 4 pounds beef shoulder or chuck roast. Season roast with lots of pepper, creole seasoning, and garlic powder. Lightly sprinkle flour on top (optional). Put quartered onions and some water in roasting pan and put in oven at 350° for approximately 2 1/2 to 3 hours till tender. Remove from oven and add canned gravy mix (or make your own). At this point, add peeled quartered potatoes, carrots, and small onions. If you have small potatoes, use the whole potato. Put pan back in oven, turn heat to 375° and cook till vegetables are done. Make sure gravy does not boil away while cooking, adding water as needed.

AGGIE'S SMOTHERED ROUND STEAK - B

2 to 3 lbs beef round steak
Salt, pepper, and flour
Potatoes
Onions

Worcestershire sauce,
   A1 sauce, and tabasco
Mushroom steak sauce or
   mushroom gravy

Cut steak in pieces and coat with flour seasoning mixture. Fry in oil in skillet and remove after browning. Pour off excess oil and add a little flour to crusts left in skillet. Brown flour and add water slowly to make gravy. Add dash of Worcestershire sauce, A-1, and tabasco. Slice potatoes and onion and add these and meat slices to gravy in skillet. Cook for 5 minutes and then add steak sauce or gravy to skillet. Cover and simmer till potatoes and meat are tender. This works well in an electric skillet.

SOUTHERN BARBECUE SAUCE - B

1 cup tomato juice
1/4 cup wine vinegar
2 tbsps firmly packed brown
   sugar
1 tbsp corn starch
1 tbsp instant minced onion

1 tbsp salad oil
1 tsp powdered mustard
1 tsp salt
1/2 tsp garlic powder
1/4 tsp ground red pepper

In a small sauce pan, combine all ingredients, bringing to a boil. Cook, stirring constantly until mixture thickens. Cook no more than 3 minutes. Use as basting sauce for barbecuing all meats. Yields about 1 1/2 cups.

OVEN POT ROAST WITH VEGETABLES - B

1 can 15 ounces tomato sauce
1 1/2 cup dry white wine
1/2 cup water
2 cloves garlic, minced
2 beef bouillon cubes, crumbled
1 bay leaf
1/2 tsp thyme
1/4 tsp pepper
5 lb. boneless beef rump roast

6 to 10 small whole white
   onions peeled
3 to 4 carrots, pared and
   thickly sliced
1/2 lb. fresh mushrooms
4 tbsp flour
1/4 cup cold water
Hot cooked noodles

In a 5 quart heavy saucepot mix together the tomato sauce, wine, 1/2 cup water, garlic, bouillon cubes, bay leaf, thyme and pepper. Cover roast in saucepan. Bake at 300° for 2 hours. Add onions, carrots, mushrooms, and bake until meat and vegetables are fork tender, for 1 hour longer. Remove roast and vegetables discarding bay leaf, to warm platter and keep warm. Use drippings from roast with flour and beat until smooth, return to stove and cook slowly gradually increasing heat, cooking until smooth and thick making sure you stir constantly. Serve meat and vegetables with noodles, pass gravy. Serve 8 to 10 servings.

OLD FASHIONED BEEF ROAST - W

The best cut of beef to use for this is a sirloin, eye of the round or rib roast but a rump may be used and cooked a little longer. To sear the roast, turn the oven at 500° and brown roast. Or, you may sear it on top of the stove, browning on all sides. This seals the juices inside the meat. Cook the roast in a slow oven, approximately at 300°. For a rare roast you will need to cook 18 to 20 minutes per pound. Meat thermometer should read 140°F. For a medium roast, cook approximately 25 minutes a pound. Meat thermometer should read 155° to 160°F. For a well done roast, cook 30 minutes per pound. Meat thermometer should read 165° to 170°F. Pour a little water in roasting pan with roast. Season meat after searing it and put in pan with water and halved onions. After roast is done, take drippings and add 2 tablespoons flour that have been browned in oil or oleo. Season well and make sure it is smooth. If gravy is not brown enough, add Kitchen Bouquet or add a can of brown gravy, beef gravy or mushroom gravy. Slice meat and serve gravy over slices and rice or mashed potatoes. Left over roast beef is great for hot roast beef open faced sandwiches on toast or hash on toast.

CORNED BEEF AND CABBAGE - W

4 or 5 lbs corned beef brisket	1 tsp dry mustard
Chopped onions	Few cloves
Dash of garlic powder	Peeled and quartered potatoes
Few peppercorns	Wedges of cabbage
1 or 2 bay leaves	Chunks of carrots

Place beef, onions, and seasoning in a large pot and cover with water. Bring to a boil, reduce heat and simmer approximately 3 hours till tender. Add potatoes and carrots and simmer another 20 minutes. Remove beef to platter, and add cabbage wedges to pot and turn heat up. Cook, uncovered, till cabbage is just getting tender but not limp. Serve with horseradish mustard sauce made by adding 1 tablespoon horseradish to 1/2 cup prepared mustard. Left over corned beef is wonderful in sandwiches with mayonnaise and thinly sliced onions on rye bread.

LUCILLE'S MEAT DISH - W

1 lb stew meat	1 can onion soup
1/4 cup Italian bread crumbs	1/2 tsp salt
2 tbsps all purpose flour	1 cup red wine

Cook at 350° for 3 hours in covered casserole dish.

SPAGHETTI & MEAT - B

1 lb ground chuck beef
5 slices bacon, cut in small
  pieces after browning
1 med can mushrooms
4 tbsps olive oil
1 can tomato sauce
1 lg onion, chopped

1 qt can tomatoes
1/2 small jar stuffed olives,
  cut in pieces
Salt, pepper, cayenne pepper
  to taste
2 tsps catsup

Put bacon in frying pan, brown and add onion and pepper. Then add olive oil and ground beef. Cook until blood is out of meat and add rest of ingredients. Simmer for about an hour until it has cooked down . Cook spaghetti and mix together.

MEAT BALLS AND SAUCE - W

1 lb ground beef
1 med onion, chopped
Dash of garlic salt
Italian bread crumbs
Worcestershire sauce

Tabasco
A-1 sauce
1 egg
Parmesan cheese
Salt and black pepper to taste

Mix all of above and make into small balls; fry.

Sauce:

1 can tomato sauce
1 can tomato paste
1 can tomato soup
1 chopped onion
1 chopped bell pepper

Worcestershire sauce
2 tbsps brown sugar
1 tbsp cider vinegar
Salt, pepper, and garlic
  salt to taste

Saute onions and peppers in a little oil. Add other ingredients and boil slowly. If too thick, add water. Put meat balls in and simmer for an hour or so.

PEPPER STEAK - B

Top round steak sliced 1 inch thick, **Sliced onions**
flour, salt, pepper, cayenne, **Green pepper sliced in strips**
soy sauce **Chinese brown gravy**

Best to use wok but can be cooked in a skillet.

Marinate meat in soy sauce. Cut in small strips and coat with flour, salt and pepper. Brown meat in a little oil (2 tbsps.), preferably peanut oil. Push aside and add onions and peppers and sauté slightly. Add soy sauce, marinade, brown gravy and meat. Heat mixture and serve over rice.

MAYETTA'S CHILI - B

Pass small condiment dishes of chopped onion, shredded cheese, and chopped jalapeno peppers.

5 slices bacon
8 ounces Italian style sausage links, sliced
1 1/2 pound beef chunk, diced
2 medium onions, chopped 1 cup
1 small green pepper, chopped 1/2 cup
1 clove garlic crushed
2 dried red chili peppers, seeded and crumbled
2 jalapeno peppers, seeded and chopped
1 to 1 1/2 tablespoons chili powder
1/2 teaspoon salt
1/2 teaspoon dried oregano crushed
2 1/2 cups water
1 12 ounce can tomato paste
1 16 ounce can pinto beans, drained

In a large saucepan or dutch oven cook bacon till crisp; drain and crumble. Set bacon aside. Brown sausage in same saucepan. Drain sausage, reserving 2 tablespoons drippings, set sausage aside. In reserved dripping, brown diced beef, onion, green pepper and garlic. Add bacon, sausage, chili peppers, jalapeno peppers, chili powder, salt and oregano. Stir in water and tomato paste. Bring to boil, simmer covered 1 1/2 hours, stirring occasionally. Stir in beans, simmer, covered 30 minutes more. Makes 8 servings.

QUICK BEEF PIE - W

1 can Franco American
   beef gravy
1 can cubed,cooked beef
1 can cubed, cooked potatoes
1/2 can cooked peas and
   diced carrots
1/2 cup minced celery

2 tbsps minced onion
1 small garlic, minced, or a
   shake of garlic powder
1/2 tsp Worcestershire
1/4 tsp tabasco
Dash black pepper
1 can packaged biscuit mix

In a 1 quart casserole dish, combine gravy, beef, vegetables, celery, onion, garlic, Worcestershire, and tabasco. Bake at 450° for 15 minutes. Prepare mix as directed and drop by spoonfuls on top of casserole. Bake for 15 minutes more. Note: Chicken pie can be made same way by using cream of chicken soup instead of gravy.

QUICK CHILI - W

1 tbsp shortening
1/2 cup chopped onion
1 lb ground beef
1 green bell pepper, chopped
1 (10 1/2 oz) can condensed
   tomato soup

1 tsp salt
4 to 6 tsps chili powder
1/4 tsp black pepper
1/2 tsp cayenne pepper
2 cans red kidney beans or just
   cooked red beans and liquor

Melt shortening in heavy skillet. Add onion and cook till brown. Add ground beef and brown. Stir frequently and break up lumps in beef. Add green pepper, tomato soup, salt, chili powder, peppers, and red beans. Heat thoroughly, turn heat down, and simmer 1/2 hour, adding water if needed. I usually make this chili after I have cooked a big pot of red beans so I can add them. Chili freezes well. Serves 6.

MAMA'S MOCK HOT TAMALE PIE - W

Cook grits according to directions for however many servings you need. Have chili hot on stove. Have grated sharp cheese and chopped onions ready. Spoon a good size helping in each bowl, spoon chili on top and sprinkle with grated cheese and onion. If you wish, you may put chopped lettuce and tomato on top of this at the last. Note: Now in the microwave days, I run bowl in to melt cheese before serving.

171

CHILI MEAT BALLS AND SAUCE - W

2 lbs ground beef
1/2 cup bread crumbs
1/2 cup tomato or V8 juice

1 egg, slightly beaten
2 tsps chili powder
Salt, pepper, and cayenne to taste

Combine all ingredients and make into meat balls. Brown meat balls and drain. Add to sauce and let simmer.

Sauce:

Saute chopped onion and green pepper till limp. Add a can of Rotel and a can of tomato sauce. Cook mixture down and add water if it gets too thick. Add 1 teaspoon chili powder and canned or just cooked red beans. Add meat balls and simmer. Serve over rice or spaghetti.

TAMALE PIE - W

1 lb ground beef
1/2 lb pork sausage or 2 lbs
  ground beef
1 lg onion, chopped
1 med green pepper, chopped
2 cans tomatoes or 1 can Rotel

1 can whole kernel corn
1 small can pitted black olives
1/2 cup yellow cornmeal
2 tsps chili powder
Salt, pepper, and cayenne to taste
Grated sharp cheddar cheese

Brown meats, onion, and pepper in skillet. Drain off fat and add remaining ingredients except cheese. Mix well and season to taste. Pour in baking dish, sprinkle with cheese, and bake in 350° oven for 40 minutes. If you prefer, make a topping of:

1 1/2 cups milk
1/2 cup cornmeal
2 beaten eggs

1 tbsp butter
1 cup grated cheese
Salt and pepper to taste

Heat milk and butter and seasoning and slowly stir in cornmeal; cook till thickened. Remove from heat and stir in eggs and cheese. Cover bottom with mixture and bake at 350° for 30 to 40 minutes.

BIBBY'S CHILI - W

2 lbs ground chuck
1 can tomato sauce
1 meduim onion chopped
1 medium green pepper,
  chopped
1 garlic clove chopped
7 or 8 tbs chili powder

2 tsp salt
2 tsp cumin
1 tsp oregano
1 tsp black pepper
2 or 3 tsp red pepper
4 or 5 sauce cans of water

Saute green peppers, onions, and ground beef till beef is brown. Add a can of tomato sauce and stir in with a can of water. Add chili powder, salt, cumin, oregano, paprika and red pepper, mix well. At this time, add red beans, either freshly cooked with their liquid or canned with juice. You may also add canned chili beans, if your prefer. Turn heat to low, add more water if needed, cover and simmer 30 to 40 minutes more.

SWEET AND PUNGENT PORK - B

Cut 1 1/2 pounds lean pork into 1/2 inch cubes. Cut 6 medium sized green peppers into 4 pieces. Prepare a batter by beating 2 eggs, 2 tablespoons flour, 1 tablespoon salt, and 1/2 teaspoon pepper together. Take 4 slices canned pineapples and cut each slice into 6 pieces. Mix the batter with pork until each piece is coated. Drop each piece into a preheated 10 inch frying pan containing 1/2 cup oil. Fry pork cubes, turning constantly, until both sides are brown. Remove oil from pan. Add green peppers and pineapple to the pork, together with the following seasonings:

1 1/2 tbsp Mee Boan (or Accent)
  in 1 cup water
1 tbsp corn starch
1 tbsp soy sauce

1/2 cup vinegar
1/2 cup sugar
1 tsp salt

Cook the mixture for about 5 minutes or until the juice thickens. Remove and serve. Serves 4.

FILET OF BEEF WITH CRAB MEAT - W

Buy separate filets or buy a beef tenderloin and cut your own. Have an inch and a quarter filet for each guest. Pan broil the filet according to each guest's choice. Make tags with toothpicks for rare, medium, and well done. Make a white sauce or Hollandaise sauce, whichever you prefer (see sauce section). Use 1 pound white crab meat, warmed. Cook the filets, top with crab meat and sauce. Garnish with parsley.

CABBAGE ROLLS - W

6 or 8 lg cabbage rolls

Cook approximately 2 to 3 minutes, dry and put on cookie sheet.

Ground beef filling:

1 lb ground beef
1 med chopped onion
1 med chopped green pepper
Chopped parsley

Salt, pepper, thyme, and
    cayenne
Cooked rice

Saute meat and vegetables. Add seasoning and rice. Put mixture on cabbage leaves. Roll each leaf and secure with a toothpick. Dot each roll with butter. Make a tomato sauce of 1 can of canned or fresh tomatoes, chopped onion, chopped green pepper, seasoning (salt, pepper, cayenne, sugar), flour or cornstarch to thicken. Cook till sauce thickens. Put cabbage leaves in greased casserole dish, top with tomato sauce, and bake at 350° for approximately 40 to 45 minutes. Note: Instead of ground beef, you can substitute cooked hot sausage, chopped left over ham, chopped left over corned beef or chopped left over roast.

STUFFED PEPPERS - W

Cut stem ends from large, green peppers and remove inside seeds and veins. Drop peppers in boiling water and cook, uncovered, till nearly tender. Drain them well and fill with any of the mixtures you use for cabbage rolls. Whole kernel corn may be used instead of rice, adding a little chili powder to the seasoning. Top peppers with seasoned bread crumbs and parmesan cheese. Put peppers in a pan of water (just enough to keep them from scorching) and bake in 350° oven for 15 minutes. Peppers and cabbage rolls may also be cooked in microwave for 5 to 7 minutes. Tomato sauce may be used with peppers in bottom of pan instead of water.

CALF LIVER IN WINE - B

1 1/2 lbs calf liver
3 tbsps butter
1 tsp minced parsley
1 tbsp chopped chives
1 tbsp minced celery
2 cloves
1 cup claret wine

3/4 tsp salt
1/4 tsp paprika
1 cup thinly sliced mushrooms
1 tbsp flour
12 slices toast

Slice the liver and cut into pieces, 2 x 2 inches. Melt the butter and when moderately hot, turn the pieces of liver in it until well coated with butter. Add parsley, chives, celery and cloves, heating the mixture. Put in wine, salt and paprika and cover. Simmer for 3 to 4 minutes. Remove the liver and add the mushrooms and simmer for another 3 minutes. Make paste with the flour and a small amount of water, stir until smooth. Add flour paste to the stock till the stock thickens. Replace the liver in the sauce. Heat and serve at once on toast. Serves 6.

NATCHITOCHES MEAT PIES - W

This little pie, along with the Christmas lights, has put the town of Natchitoches on the map nationally. Hundreds of thousands descend upon Natchitoches at the first of December for the "turning on of the lights." People sit on the riverbanks and enjoy this spectacle while they munch on the delicious meat pies sold in stands along the riverbank.

NATCHITOCHES MEAT PIES

Make a roux of 2 tablespoons flour and 1 tablespoon shortening. Add 1/2 pound ground beef, 1 1/2 pound ground pork, 1 large or 2 medium yellow onions, and 8 green onions, chopped, 5 or 6 sprigs of parsley, salt, black pepper, and cayenne pepper to taste. Cook thoroughly and cool before placing in dough.

Pastry:
Sift 4 cups flour with 2 teaspoons baking powder, 1/2 cup melted oleo or oil and 2 eggs. Add enough milk to make a stiff dough. Cut dough in circles and fill half of circle with meat mixture. Fold dough over, dampen edges with water and press closed with fork. Fry in deep hot fat till golden or bake in 350° oven for approximately 1/2 hour.

175

KIDNEY STEW A LA CREOLE - W & B

Veal, lamb, pork, or beef kidneys can be used. The secret is not to cook them too long for that will toughen them. Veal and lamb kidneys are preferred. Wash in cold water, skin, and cut in slices. Sprinkle them with mixture of flour, salt, and pepper and saute them in oil till brown. Add chopped onions, celery, and bell pepper. Pour off excess oil and add a little water and simmer for 5 minutes. Add fresh, diced tomatoes or a can of tomatoes, preferably Rotel. Also add salt and pepper at this time. Cover pan and simmer for 2 more minutes, stirring frequently. Good with rice or noodles.

VERVA'S HOGSHEAD CHEESE OR DAUBE - W

3 lbs pigs feet, head or hocks
2 veal, pork or beef steaks, with bone

Start meat in cold water and add onions, carrots, celery, peppercorns, and salt. Boil slowly till meat is done. Take meat out, separate from bones, and dice in small pieces. Take vegetables from pot and put meat back in with liquid. Add seasoning to taste (lots of tabasco or cayenne). When cool, divide in bowls and let jell.

BEEF STEW WITH DUMPLINGS - B

2 lbs beef cubes
1/8 lb salt pork
2 tbsps flour
2 cups water
Salt and pepper to taste

1/2 cup chopped green pepper
1 cup diced potatoes
1 cup peas
2 cloves garlic, chopped
1 recipe of dumplings

Cut salt pork in small cubes and fry until brown. Add floured beef cubes and brown well. Add 2 cups cold water and salt and pepper to taste. Add green peppers, diced potatoes, and cloves of garlic. Then cover with tight lid. Simmer for 1 1/2 hours. Add peas and drop in dumplings. Cover again with tight lid and steam for 15 minutes. Do not remove lid until dumplings are done. Serves 6 to 8.

No book on Louisiana would be complete without adding certain recipes. In the meat category, these include sweetbreads, calf brains, kidneys, liver, tongue, hogs head cheese and daube. For those of you who would like to try some of these recipes, we submit the following.

SWEETBREADS - W & B

Soak sweetbreads in cold water for a half an hour. While they are soaking fill a large pot about three fourths full with water and add chopped celery, parsley, onion, lemon juice (1 tablespoon), and salt and pepper. Bring water to a boil. Add the sweetbreads, and lower the heat. Simmer approximately 25 to 30 minutes. Drain them and put in cold water to harden. Be sure to save stock from pot. Drain sweetbreads and remove stir and membrane. Have plate of seasoned bread crumbs and another plate with a beaten egg and 2 tablespoons water. Dip sweetbreads in bread crumbs, egg mixture, and again in bread crumbs. Saute them in oleo till they are a dark brown. Serve them with white sauce (you can use sweetbread stock for liquid) or with canned cream of mushroom or cream of onion soup. Add a little wine to cream sauce and garnish with parsley.

CALF BRAINS AND EGGS - W & B

Soak and cook like sweetbreads. Make sure you remove membrane after first soaking and make sure you soak them again in cold water after cooking. Then drain and break into pieces. Add brains to eggs and beat in some diced onions, milk, salt, pepper, paprika, and tabasco. Scramble mixture. Serve on toast. Hog brains can be used instead of calf brains.

BEEF TONGUE - W & B

Place a fresh beef tongue in a kettle with sliced onions, celery, carrots, and parsley, barely covering the combination with boiling water. Add salt, peppercorns, and red pepper to mixture. Turn down heat and simmer till tender, approximately 2 1/2 to 3 hours, depending on the size of the tongue. Drain, and skin the tongue. Remove roots and slice. Serve with a mustard sauce made of 2 tablespoons powdered mustard, 1 teaspoon sugar, onion juice, a little oil, and vinegar. Tongue is delicious served this way and in cold tongue sandwiches.

VEAL CUTLETS - W

Choose cutlets 1/2 inch thick. Season with salt, pepper, and garlic powder. Dip them in seasoned bread or cracker crumbs, in a beaten egg/water mixture, and then back in crumbs. Brown cutlets in butter, then turn burner down and cook on low till done, approximately 1/2 hour. You can finish them in oven instead of on top of stove at 325°. Serve with juices poured over and garnish with lemon slices and parsley.

VEAL MADEIRA - W

Saute veal cutlets in a combination of butter and olive oil after you have floured, salted, and peppered them. Remove cutlets and keep warm. Make a sauce of beef broth, heavy cream, Madeira wine, and fresh mushrooms. Cook sauce for a few minutes and pour over cutlets just before serving.

VEAL WITH CRAB MEAT - W

Prepare cutlets just as for Veal Madeira. Saute cutlets till done, put aside, and keep warm. Make a sauce of 1 teaspoon creole mustard, 1/2 cup half & half, one tablespoon mayonnaise, 1 teaspoon horseradish, chopped green onions, and crab meat. Pour sauce over veal cutlets just before serving.

LEG OF LAMB - W

3 or 4 lb leg of lamb   **Lemon**
Bacon   **Salt, pepper, and garlic to taste**

Rub leg with oil and season with salt and pepper. Stick garlic slivers in lamb skin. Put bacon slices across top of leg and also thin lemon slices, securing with toothpick. Place lamb leg, fat side up, in roasting pan, elevated from juices. (Cooking lamb in drippings has a tendency to give it a strong taste.) Roast lamb 30 to 35 minutes a pound in preheated 300° oven. To serve lamb, place lamb on platter, add Worcestershire, tabasco, and water to juices and serve as a gravy next to lamb. Green rice or rice pilaf are excellent accompaniments to lamb. Lamb shoulder roast may be cooked in same way as leg of lamb.

BROILED LAMB CHOPS - W

Preheat broiler and place chops on broiling pan 2 to 3 inches from broiler after they have been seasoned with salt and pepper. Leave oven door a little ajar. Broil on one side till brown, take out, and turn and season on other side, then return to oven. Takes approximately 10 to 11 minutes to broil chops that are 3/4 inches thick.

LAMB OR BEEF CURRY - W

Cut up left over meat in cubes. Sauté green onion, bell pepper, celery, and meat in skillet till warmed through. Add a little flour, salt, and pepper to mixture after you have added a cup of tomato or V8 juice. Stir till thickened. Add curry powder and red pepper to taste. It is a strong seasoning and some don't like too much of a curry taste. Serve mixture on a bed of rice and top with chopped celery, tomatoes, pepper, green onions, hard boiled eggs, bacon bits, coconut, chutney, ripe olives, and anything else that appeals to you. Chicken, turkey or shrimp curry may be fixed the same way. With chicken or turkey, substitute cream of chicken soup for tomato juice and leave out flour, adding water to soup. With shrimp, use cream of shrimp soup, omitting tomato juice.

LAMB STEW - W

2 lbs lamb cubes or breast
  or shoulder
2 tbsps flour
2 tbsps fat
Salt and pepper to taste
Hot water

6 potatoes cut in cubes
6 carrots cut in cubes
3 onions, chopped
1 cup fresh peas
3 fresh tomatoes

Baste lamb with flour on both sides and brown well in hot fat. Season with salt and pepper to taste. Cover with water and simmer until nearly tender for about 1 to 1 1/2 hours. Add chopped vegetables, except the tomatoes, and cook 30 minutes longer or until vegetables are tender. Then add tomatoes and cook 10 to 15 minutes longer. Mix a flour paste by adding water to flour in a cup and mix until smooth. Then pour into liquid to achieve a slight thickness to liquid. Serves 6 to 8.

BEEF SALAD - B

1 1/4 cups diced, cold, cooked beef
1 small onion, sliced
1 1/4 cups diced, cold,
  cooked potatoes
Lettuce leaves
2 tsps chopped parsley

2 tbsps anchovies, chopped
2 tsps red wine vinegar
4 tbsps salad oil
Salt and pepper to taste
1 hard cooked egg

Mix meat, onion, and potatoes. Line serving bowl with lettuce leaves and place meat mixture in center. Combine remaining ingredients except egg and pour over mixture. Garnish with egg.

The Oyster Man

CHAPTER VIII

"Oyster Man"

(seafood)

Before the days of gasoline engines and motor trucks, oysters were brought to New Orleans In sailing luggers and oyster dealers flocked to the decks to purchase the delectable bivalves. They loaded barrels of oysters in their horse drawn wagons and went out in the streets selling them as nature produced, tightly encased in their shells—the purchaser had to open them. In later years, when ice was abundant, they carried opened oysters in tin pails swimming in their own juices and the housewife would bring her container to the wagon and purchase what she needed.

As the peddler roamed the streets he sang:

> Oyster man! Oyster man!
> Get your oysters from the Oyster Man!
> Bring out your pitcher, bring out your can
> Get your fresh oysters from the oyster man!

Some oyster men also carried fresh fish, shrimp, and crab and sold them in the same way. Because Louisiana waters abound in fresh seafood, this chapter will cover all of it from oysters to the now famous crawfish.

PICTURE EXPLANATION

The girls have heard the oyster man's call and they have been given the special privilege of taking the pail to the wagon and purchasing the oysters for the cook.

THE OYSTER LOAF - W

In New Orleans, there was a sandwich called the "Peace Maker" that got the name because late husbands would bring the hot loaf home to soothe angry wives. I have asked many natives but have not found out whether the sandwich is still used as a "Peace Maker." Whether or not, the Oyster Loaf is a delicious sandwich and well worth its praise. The following is the "Peace Maker." The top crust of a French bread loaf is cut out and the inside is taken out, creating a boat. The inside is buttered good and put in the oven to toast. The top is buttered and toasted, also. The bottom is then filled with "just fried," crisp oysters and garnished with lemons, and the top is replaced. If wrapped, it stays warm a long time. Serve with tartar sauce or cocktail sauce.

STUFFED FLOUNDER - B

1 cup boiled shrimp, chopped
1 lb crab meat, cooked
2 med celery stalks with
    leaves, chopped
1 lg clove garlic, chopped
1 can cream of mushroom
    soup, undiluted

1 cup Sauterne white wine
3 eggs, beaten
2 cups bread crumbs
1/2 lb butter

This recipe calls for 6 medium flounder cleaned, weighing about a pound each. Cutting down center of flounder and under fin, open and season with salt and pepper. In a large bowl, mix crab meat and shrimp and 1 cup bread crumbs. Beat eggs. Add to soup and mix well. Saute onions, celery, and garlic in butter until smooth and soft. Add soup and egg mixture. Cook for 15 to 20 minutes. Remove from heat and add shrimp, crab meat and bread crumbs. Add salt and pepper to taste. Mix well. If too thick, add warm water. Use a large Pyrex baking dish. Take a pat of butter or margarine to grease the baking dish. Stuff mixture in raw flounder in baking dish and place in oven at 250° and bake until meat flakes with a fork. Baste - with a mixture of 3 tablespoons of melted butter and lemon juice. Serve with green salad.

FISH SOUFFLE - B

1 cup fish	1/2 cup thick white sauce
3 eggs	Salt, pepper and paprika
1 tbsp lemon juice	to taste

Flake fish. Remove bones. Add white sauce, lemon juice and slightly beaten egg yolks. Season to taste. Stir lightly. Fold in stiffly beaten egg whites. Pour into well oiled deep baking dish or baking bowl. Set in pan of warm water. Bake in moderate oven at 400°. Serves 6. Pierce with a knife. If done, knife will come out clean.

FRIED SCALLOPS - B

1 cup dried bread crumbs	1 lb scallops
1 tsp salt	1 egg
1/2 tsp celery salt	2 tbsps water

Combine crumbs and seasoning. Dip scallops into crumbs, then into egg (diluted with water). Then dip into crumbs again. Saute or fry in hot oil in deep skillet at about 375°. Let cook for 4 to 5 minutes. Serve with tartar sauce. To make more, double recipe.

FISH CROQUETTES - B

2 cups fish	1 1/2 cups bread crumbs with
1 egg	butter or crackers, crumbled
3 tbsps water	1 tbsp chopped parsley
1 1/2 tbsps chopped onion	Salt, pepper, red pepper and
1/2 cup milk	celery salt to taste

Shred fish, remove bones. Add water and milk. Season to taste with salt, pepper, celery salt, onions, red pepper and parsley. Mix well and make patties, chill thoroughly. Dip into egg by using a little water (about 2 tbsps) with beaten egg. Roll into bread crumbs lightly. Let stand in refrigerator for 1 hour. Fry in deep fat at 385° until golden brown, drain on brown paper bag. Serves 8.

DEEP FRIED GARFISH AND BOILED POTATOES - B

3 1/2 cups potatoes, cut in cubes
1 cup garfish meat
2 tbsps butter
2 eggs
1/8 tsp salt

1/8 tsp black pepper
1/8 tsp red pepper
2 tbsps onions
1 clove garlic
1/2 cup water

Take garfish and scrape until you have 1 cup of white meat pulp. Combine meat and potatoes in 1/2 cup water and steam with tight lid for about 15 minutes. Cool and drain. Mash potatoes and meat and beat eggs. Add salt, pepper, onions, and garlic. Add butter and mix. Make balls about the size of a small meat ball. Fry in shallow fat until golden brown. Drain and serve hot. Serves 4. Double recipe to make larger servings.

SHRIMP IN MUSTARD SAUCE - B
(Louisiana Style)

1 1/2 lbs fresh shrimp, cooked or
    2 (5 3/4 ozs) canned shrimp
2 tbsps vinegar
1/3 cup salad oil
Salt and pepper to taste

2 tbsps prepared mustard
1 tsp paprika
2 green onions with tops
    finely chopped
1 celery heart, finely chopped

Clean shrimp. If using canned shrimp, drain and rinse. Combine remaining ingredients and pour over shrimp. Toss lightly and chill 2 hours. Serve on shredded lettuce or in scallop shells. Makes 6 servings.

SIMPLE CRAB SALAD - B

1 (16 1/2 oz) can crab meat
1 hard cooked egg
1 cup chopped celery
2 tbsps diced pimentos
1/2 cup chopped olives

1/3 cup mayonnaise
1 tbsp lemon juice
1/2 tsp salt
Black pepper to taste
Lettuce leaf

Flake crab. Dice egg and combine celery, pimentos, olives and mayonnaise. Blend and add lemon juice, salt, pepper and mix well. Serve in crisp lettuce leaf. Serves 4.

MARIE'S DEVILED OYSTERS - W

1 cup chopped onions
1 cup chopped celery

1 cup chopped peppers
2 tbsps butter or oleo

Boil the above in 1 cup water. Combine 1 pint oysters, chopped, 2 cups crushed crackers that have been soaked in milk and 1 tablespoon oil. Also add 2 tablespoons ketchup, 2 tablespoons Worcestershire, 1 teaspoon pepper, 1/4 teaspoon or more red pepper and salt to taste. Add 2 whole eggs, the boiled vegetables and a cup of chopped parsley. Mix all together well. Put in casserole dish with bread crumbs on top and bake 20 to 40 minutes at 300° till mixture thickens.

HEAVENLY FISH - W

4 nice size fish fillets
Butter or oleo
Flour, salt, and pepper
Milk
Green onions or shallots
3/4 carton sour cream, sour
   cream substitute or yogurt

Lemons
Parsley
Paprika
Carton of crab meat

Lightly flour and salt and pepper fish and brown in butter. Put in baking dish. Add more butter if necessary to skillet and saute 4 or 5 chopped onions. Do not brown. Blend in flour to thicken and slowly pour in milk to make a white sauce. Blend in sour cream and a little lemon juice and then add crab meat. Spoon sauce over fillets. Put thin slices of lemons on top and sprinkle with parsley and paprika. Top with grated mozzarella cheese. Bake at 350° for 30 minutes.

HELEN'S LARGE SHRIMP MOLD - W

Melt 1 (8 oz) package of Philadelphia cream cheese in 1 can of cream of tomato soup over low heat. Soften with 1 1/4 package of gelatin in 1/2 cup cold water. Dissolve in hot soup. Add 1 1/2 cups chopped celery, 1/2 cup chopped green onions, 1/2 cup chopped green peppers, 1 cup mayonnaise, and salt and pepper to taste. Add 1 1/2 pounds boiled shrimp, cut up. Place in oiled 6 1/2 cups ring mold and refrigerate till set.

OVEN FRIED FILLETS - B

2 lbs fish fillets
1 tsp salt
1 tsp pepper
1 tbsp paprika

1 cup milk
1 cup bread crumbs
4 tbsps butter or cooking oil

Cut into serving size pieces. Season with salt, pepper, and paprika. Dip fish in milk and roll in bread crumbs. Place in a well greased baking dish. Pour melted butter or cooking oil over fish. Place pan on the top rack in oven which should be set at 500° and bake for 10 to 12 minutes or until it flakes with a fork. Drain and serve hot on a platter, garnished with parsley.

BOILED CRAWFISH - W

15 lbs crawfish
6 lemons
4 onions
Salt, rocks or fine

Cayenne
3 heads garlic
Liquid or dry seafood boil

Wash in large tub of water and remove twigs, vegetation and dead crawfish. Purge crawfish by placing them in a strong salt water solution for about 5 minutes. Wash once more in plain water. Add to boiling water in large pot with unpeeled potatoes, onions, and ears of corn. Boil for 5 minutes after second boil starts. Turn off and let soak 25 to 30 minutes. Have lots of French bread to accompany it.

CRAWFISH PIE - W

1 lb crawfish
1 can evaporated milk, low fat
1/2 cup chopped green onions
1/2 cup chopped green peppers

1/2 cup chopped celery
Flour, salt, pepper, cayenne,
  pepper or tabasco
2 dashes Worcestershire sauce

Saute vegetables in 1 stick of oleo. Stir in flour to make roux. Add evaporated milk to make a thick white sauce. Add crawfish and seasoning. Add Worcestershire sauce. Bake in 350° oven in one large unbaked pie shell or 8 tart shells. Can substitute shrimp or crab meat.

SHRIMP COTTAGE CHEESE DIP - B

1/2 lb fresh, cooked shrimp or 1
   (5 oz) can of shrimp
1 cup creamed cottage cheese
3 tbsps chili sauce

1/2 tsp onion juice
1/2 tsp lemon juice
1/4 tsp Worcestershire sauce
4 tbsps milk (approximately)

Chop cleaned shrimp very fine. Combine with cottage cheese. Add seasonings and enough milk to make a creamy mixture. Add salt if desired. Pile into bowl.

LOUISIANA COCKTAIL SAUCE - B

1 1/2 tsps Worcestershire sauce
1/2 cup ketchup
4 tsps horseradish

4 tsps sweet pickle relish
1/2 cup chili sauce
Dash of tabasco sauce

Mix all ingredients and chill thoroughly. Yields about 1 cup.

CRAB CAKES - B

1 lb crab meat
1/2 cup chopped green peppers
4 tbsps mayonnaise
1 egg, beaten
2 tsps dijon mustard

1/2 cup chopped green onions
Hot sauce
Season to taste
Worcestershire sauce
Bread crumbs

Mix all ingredients together. Mixture should be not too dry and not too moist. Adjust with bread crumbs or mayonnaise. Fry in 1/2 inch of hot oil or broil till brown.

CRAWFISH A LA BILL - W

Brown 1 stick of oleo and 1 heaping kitchen spoon of flour to rich tan roux. Don't burn! Add 3 shakes of ketchup, 1 shake of chili sauce, and let this cook from a red to a brown color. Add 1/2 cup chopped celery, parsley, green onions, bell peppers and 2 1/2 cups water. Simmer until seasoning is tender; then add 2 packages or 2 pounds of crawfish tails and simmer again for about 5 minutes. Add salt, pepper and garlic to taste. Add 2 tablespoons of white wine, 2 teaspoons Lea & Perrins sauce and 1/2 cup evaporated milk. Let boil and adjust seasoning as needed. Serve over rice and put tabasco on table for those who prefer more seasoning.

SHRIMP MOUSSE - B

2 small cans of medium shrimp
1 can tomato bisque soup
1 (6 oz) package cream cheese, softened
1/2 cup minced onions or green onions (2 bunches)

1/2 cup celery, thinly sliced
1 cup mayonnaise
1 1/2 tbsp Knox unflavored gelatin
1 cup water
Parsley flakes to taste

Spray mold with Pam. Mix water and gelatin and let it sit to dissolve. Stir cream cheese and soup over low heat until well blended, but don't overcook. Add onions, shrimp, celery, gelatin and mayonnaise and stir. Pour into mold and refrigerate overnight. Unmold and serve with wheat thins or other crackers.

CREAMED SHRIMP - B

1 1/2 lbs boiled shrimp
2 cups white sauce (see sauce section)
1/2 tsp celery salt

1 tbsp minced pimentos
8 slices of bread, toasted on both sides

Shell and cream shrimp. Add white sauce, celery salt and pimentos. Heat to boiling and serve over toasted bread. Serves 6. You can add 3/4 cup sauteed mushrooms to shrimp mixture if you desire.

FRENCH FRIED SHRIMP - B

1 1/2 lbs boiled shrimp
1 pt milk
1 egg
Flour

Cornmeal or bread crumbs
1/8 tsp salt
Dash of pepper

Clean shrimp. Mix milk with eggs, and add whole shrimp and let stand for 3 minutes. Mix equal parts of flour and cornmeal or bread crumbs with seasoning salt. Coat shrimp well with mixture and cook in hot deep light cooking oil at 375° until brown. Shrimp will rise to the top of the cooking oil when done. Drain on brown paper bag. A brown paper bag helps keep the seasoning in the meat and will still absorb the oil.

PAN FRIED FISH - B

2 lbs fillets, steaks or pan
   dressed fish
1 tsp salt
1/8 tsp pepper

1 egg
1 tbsp milk or water
1 cup bread crumbs, cracker
   crumbs, or cornmeal and flour

Cut fish into serving size pieces and sprinkle both sides with salt and pepper. Beat egg slightly and add milk. If you want your fish to be hot, add 2 or 3 drops of tabasco sauce. Dip fish in egg batter and roll in bread crumbs. Heat shortening or cooking oil in a skillet until hot but not smoking. Brown fish on both sides or until golden brown. Cook about 10 minutes on each side depending on the thickness of the fish.

EGGPLANT STUFFED WITH CRAB MEAT - W

Boil eggplants till tender. Cool and cut top portion off lengthwise. Scoop out pulp. Mash in bowl. Sauté one large onion and one large pepper in oleo. Add to eggplant mixture. Add can of chopped Rotel tomatoes, a pound of crab meat, 2 eggs, beaten, 3 tablespoons chopped parsley and Italian bread crumbs. Season to taste. Mix well and stuff shells with mixture. Top with Parmesan and Romano cheese. Bake in 350° oven for 35 to 40 minutes. Can substitute crab meat with shrimp or crawfish instead.

OYSTERS BIENVILLE - W

1/3 cup butter
3 tbsps flour
1 clove garlic, minced
1 tbsp onion juice
1 1/2 tbsps Worcestershire
    sauce
1/3 tsp celery seed
1 small can stems and pieces
    mushrooms

1 can small shrimp
1 tbsp sherry
2 pts oysters
Parmesan cheese
Paprika
Salt to taste

Make sauce of first 6 ingredients. Add liquid from mushrooms and shrimp. Also add mushrooms, shrimp, and sherry. Slide oysters under broiler until edges curl. Pour off liquid. Sprinkle with Parmesan cheese and cover with sauce. Sprinkle with paprika. Slide back under broiler for 6 to 8 minutes until bubbly. Is also excellent over sauted fish fillets.

TROUT MEUNIERE - W

2 trout fillets
1 cup butter
1 tbsp parsley, chopped
1 tbsp green onions, chopped

2 tbsp lemon juice
Dash of tabasco and
    Worcestershire sauce

Mix flour, salt and pepper and lightly flour fillets. Fry in butter until golden brown. Trout can be broiled in butter rather than frying with flour. Make sauce from 1/2 cup butter, parsley, lemon juice, green onions, salt, pepper, tabasco and Worcestershire. Pour sauce over warm trout. Great dinner for two.

TROUT MARGUERY - W

2 trout fillets   5 green onions, chopped
2 tbsps olive oil

Put olive oil, green onions, and trout fillets in pan of 1/2 cup water. Bake in hot oven for approximately 12 minutes. Make a Hollandaise sauce (see sauce section). Add a dozen cooked shrimp, a chopped truffle, and 4 chopped mushrooms. Truffles can be omitted if not available. Season to taste. Pour over warm trout. Great dinner for two.

SHRIMP DE JOHNGE - W

12 peeled, boiled, good sized   Dash of garlic powder
  shrimp   Salt and pepper to taste
1/4 lb butter or oleo   1 tbsp chopped parsley
1 cup seasoned bread crumbs   1 tbsp lemon juice

Melt butter and add shrimp, mixed with above ingredients. Cook a few minutes and serve on toast points. Good dinner for two.

LIL'S BARBEQUED SHRIMP - W

6 lbs shrimp, large and deheaded   1 tbsp accent
9 sticks oleo   1/4 tsp rosemary
8 tbsps black pepper   1 tsp paprika
1/2 tbsp red pepper   1/4 tsp thyme

Wash and drain shrimp. In a skillet, melt butter and add dry ingredients. Place shrimp in a big, shallow pan and pour sauce over shrimp. Put oven on broil and broil on one side for 10 minutes. Then turn and broil for 10 minutes more. If shrimp are extra large, cook a little longer. Serves 6.

SHRIMP LOUIE - W

3 lbs cooked, cleaned shrimp
1 cup mayonnaise
1/3 cup bell pepper

1/3 cup green onions
1/3 cup chili sauce

Mix mayonnaise, pepper, onions, and chili sauce. Keep in refrigerator till salad is ready. Put shrimp on lettuce leaf and Louis sauce on top. Garnish with quartered, hard boiled eggs, bell peppers, and cucumbers. Serves 6.

SHRIMP REMOULADE - W

3/4 cup olive oil
6 tbsps white vinegar
3 tbsps creole mustard
2 tbsps paprika

4 chopped green onions
2 celery stalks, chopped
Salt, pepper,and horseradish
  to taste

Marinate sauce in refrigerator. Stir before pouring on boiled shrimp on a bed of shredded lettuce.

SAUTEED SOFT SHELL CRAB - W

Soak soft shell crabs in 1 cup milk and 2 beaten eggs for 30 minutes. Mix flour, salt, black pepper and cayenne pepper. Dredge crabs in flour mixture and sauté in 1 stick of melted oleo until golden brown.

CRAB EN BROCHETTE - W

1 lb fresh crab meat or 2 cans,
  drained
1 tsp green onions
1 jigger dry sherry

1 cup dry white bread crumbs
1 egg
1 tsp dry mustard
Salt and pepper to taste

Make balls the size of walnuts and wrap in half a slice of bacon, secured with a toothpick. Bake in oven till bacon is done. Serve with Hollandaise sauce (see sauce section).

CRAB MEAT RAVIGOTE - W

2 stalks celery, diced
3 green onions, diced

Handful of broken up parsley

Sauté the above in butter or oleo. Add 2 tablespoons flour and slowly add can of Carnation cream, stirring constantly. Beat 2 eggs and fold into mixture. Add 1 pound crab meat (fresh) or 2 cans crab meat. Season to taste with salt, pepper, red pepper or creole seasoning. Serve on toast or patty shells.

GOOGSIE'S CRAB MEAT RAVIGOTE - W

1 lb crab meat
1 cup mayonnaise
1 tsp dijon mustard
2 tbsps chopped parsley

1 tsp capers
1 tsp horseradish
Juice from lemon

Mix all ingredients and blend well. Add crab meat last. May be heated or served cold.

MARINATED BOILED CRABS - W

2 dozen boiled crabs
1 bottle Italian salad dressing
1 stalk celery, chopped
1 bell pepper, chopped

1/2 cup oil
1/3 cup chopped parsley
1/3 cup cider vinegar

Clean boiled crabs by removing top shell and deadman. Break crab body in half and crack crab claws. Marinate in refrigerator for 24 hours. Stir occasionally. Serve with crab or nut crackers and lots of napkins.

CRAB OR SHRIMP SALAD - W

1 lb crab meat or 1 lb cooked,
   peeled shrimp
1/2 cup chopped celery
1 cup mayonnaise

1 tsp dijon mustard
1 tsp capers
1 chopped, hard boiled egg
Lemon juice

Combine all ingredients and toss well to mix. Chill till serving time. Serve on lettuce leaf and garnish with tomato slices and bell pepper slices.

CRAWFISH SALAD - B

2 lbs crawfish tails, boiled
2 tbsps dry wine
1 tsp lemon juice from
   grated lemon rind
1/2 tsp mayonnaise

1/2 tsp tabasco
1/2 cup chopped onion
1/2 cup chopped green peppers
1/4 cup red pepper
Spinach, washed

Boil and remove shell from crawfish tails. Place in a large bowl. In another bowl add lemon juice and grated rind, mayonnaise, tabasco, onion, and peppers. Mix well. Pour in crawfish tails mixture. Mix well, add salt and pepper to taste. Spoon out on spinach leaves. Serves 4.

SIMPLE CRAB SALAD - B

1 (16 1/2 oz) can crab meat
1 hard boiled egg
1 cup chopped celery
2 tbsps diced pimentos
1/2 cup chopped olives

1/3 cup mayonnaise
1 tbsp lemon juice
1/2 tsp salt
Black pepper
Lettuce leaf

Flake crab. Dice egg. Combine celery, pimentos, olives, and mayonnaise. Blend lemon juice, salt, and pepper. Mix well all together. Serve in crisp lettuce leaf. Serves 4.

FRANCES' OYSTERS ROCKEFELLER - W

1 lg bunch green onions, chopped
1 lg bunch parsley, chopped

1/4 lb butter or oleo

Cook the above vegetables in butter slowly for approximately 15 minutes. Steam either 3 packages of frozen, chopped spinach or 1 large bunch fresh spinach. Puree in food processor. Add onions and parsley and puree. Add 1 tablespoon celery salt or seed, 3/4 tablespoon anchovy paste, 2 tablespoons Worcestershire, 2 to 3 tablespoons red hot, 1 tablespoon horseradish, 1 teaspoon basil, and 1 teaspoon marjoram. Bring all to a boil and remove from heat and add 1 teaspoon pechard bitters and 2 tablespoons absinthe or Pernod (can be found in a liquor store). Place whole oysters in shells or individual ramekins. Run oysters in oven till they curl. Top with mixture and then top that with bread crumbs. Run in hot oven (450°) for 8 to 10 minutes.

LIVER-SHRIMP SPREAD - B

1/2 cup ground, cooked chicken
  livers
1/2 cup ground, cooked shrimp
1/4 cup finely chopped onion

1/2 green pepper,
  finely chopped
Chili sauce to moisten

Mix ingredients to a smooth spread, using just enough chili sauce to bind mixtures.

LOUISIANA COCKTAIL SAUCE - B

1 1/2 tsp Worcestershire sauce
1/2 cup ketchup
4 tsp horseradish

4 tsp sweet pickle relish
1/2 cup chili sauce
Dash of tabasco sauce

Mix all ingredients and chill thoroughly. Makes about 1 cup.

TARTAR SAUCE - W

1 cup mayonnaise
1 tbsp sweet relish

1 tsp grated onion
Dash of tabasco

COCKTAIL SAUCE - W

1 cup ketchup
1 tbsp horseradish
1 tbsp Worcestershire sauce

1 tsp lemon juice
4 or 5 shakes of tabasco

BIBBY'S OYSTERS - W

(In individual baking shells)

1 stick oleo
4 chopped green onions
1 small bunch parsley, chopped
1 lg can mushroom pieces
1 can cocktail shrimp
1 clove chopped garlic
1/3 cup white wine

Oyster liquor from 3
  (3/4 pint) jars
1/3 cup milk
1 (8 oz) package grated sharp
  cheddar cheese
2 tbsps flour

Cook above till thick and pour over oysters in shells after oysters have been put in oven till curled. Top with Italian bread crumbs and parmesan cheese. Run in warm oven (325°) till warm.

OYSTER DRESSING - B

3 jars (12 oz) oysters
2 stalks chopped celery
1 lg chopped onion
4 chopped green onions
1 small bunch chopped parsley
1 med chopped bell pepper

1 loaf French bread
Creole seasoning, pepper, cayenne,
  basil and thyme to taste
Kellogg or Pepperidge Farm herb
  stuffing

Sauté above in 2 sticks butter or oleo. Drain oysters, saving liquid. Chop oysters. Soak bread and squeeze excess. Add to seasoning, stuffing, and liquid. Cook approximately 20 to 30 minutes. Do not stuff turkey with this, but serve as a separate side dish. Great with holiday turkey.

TUNA CASSEROLE - W

Melt 1 can mushroom soup, 1 cup Pet milk, and 1/2 pound cheese. Can use box macaroni and cheese mix instead of cheese and macaroni separately. Cook 1 box macaroni, 1/2 bell pepper, 1/2 can pimento, 1 small onion, 1 stick celery, salt, pepper, and 1 can tuna. Bake in oven for about 20 minutes at 350°.

CLARA'S SHRIMP AND MACARONI CASSEROLE - W

1/2 cup diced green pepper	1/4 tsp thyme
1/2 cup chopped onion	Dash garlic powder
2 tbsps butter or margarine	1 lb shrimp, cooked, shelled,
1 (10 3/4 oz) can condensed	and deveined
tomato soup	2 cups cooked, small shell
1/4 cup water	macaroni or noodles

Cook green pepper and onion in butter until tender. Add remaining ingredients. Spoon into buttered 1 1/2 quart casserole dish. Bake at 375° for 15 to 20 minutes or until hot and bubbling. Makes 4 servings.

JELLIED SALAD - W

6 hard boiled eggs	1/2 tsp Worcestershire sauce
1 can consomme	Salt and pepper to taste
2 cups water	Anchovy paste
2 envelopes gelatin	

Slice eggs in half. Mash yolks with small amount of anchovy paste and Worcestershire sauce. Stuff egg whites, add hot consomme and water.Put a little in mold to jell, then place eggs in mold, add more consomme, chill.

Sauce

1/2 # shrimp	1 hard boiled egg chopped
1 tbs green onion chopped	Anchovy paste to taste
1 tbs green pepper chopped	

Mix all and add 1 cup mayonnaise.

CRAWFISH SALAD - W

2 cups boiled crawfish diced
1 cup celery, chopped
2 hard cooked eggs, chopped
2 tbsps dill pickles chopped

1 tsp Worcestershire sauce
Mayonnaise
Salt
Pepper

Combine all ingredients thoroughly and mix with mayonnaise to desired consistency. Season, remembering that crawfish have already been seasoned in boiling.

FRIED FISH - B

2 lbs fish (fillets, steaks, or
  pan dressed)
1 tsp salt
Dash pepper
1 egg slightly beaten

1 tbsp milk or water
1 cup bread crumbs, cracker
  crumbs
Cornmeal or all purpose flour
Salad oil

Cut fish into serving size portions. Sprinkle both sides with salt and pepper. Combine egg and milk. Dip fish into egg mixture and roll in crumbs. Place fish in heavy skillet containing about 1/8 inch of hot salad oil. Fry at a moderate heat. When fish is brown on one side turn carefully and brown other side. Cooking time should be about 10 minutes, depending on the thickness of the fish. Drain on absorbent paper. Makes 6 servings.

SHRIMP IN SQUASH - B

2 pounds squash
3 tablespoons fat
1 tablespoon chopped onion
1 tablespoon curry powder
1/2 teaspoon salt
Dash of cayenne

2 tablespoons flour
1/4 cup undiluted evaporated
  milk or top milk
2 8 ounce cans shrimp cleaned
  or fresh shrimp
1/2 cup dry breadcrumbs

Split squash lengthwise and cook in boiling salted water for 5 minutes. Hollow out the center. Chop it and drain shells. Melt fat, add onions, curry, salt, cayenne, flour and milk. Stir well. When thickened add shrimp cut in small bits. Season to taste. Add chopped squash, stuff shells and sprinkle with crumbs. Brown in moderate oven at 350 degrees for 15 minutes. This dish serves 6.

SEA BURGERS - B

1 7 ounce can tuna (or lobster, or crab)
1/2 pound processed sharp cheese
1/4 cup minced onion
1/4 cup chopped sweet pickle
1/2 cup ketchup

1/4 cup mayonnaise
1 cup minced celery
2 teaspoons pepper
2 tablespoons minced pimento
12 burger buns

Drain seafood, flake with fork, removing any bones. Cut cheese into small chunks. Combine seafood, cheese, onions, pickle, ketchup, mayonnaise, celery, salt, pepper and pimento. Mix well, split burger buns crosswise without cutting all the way through and fill with seafood mixture. Wrap each in foil or stand with cut side up in a large casserole or roasting pan. Cover and bake at 350 degrees F. for 20 minutes. Serve immediately in foil or casserole. Makes 12 burgers.

PIQUANT HOT SHRIMP - B

1 bottle beer
1/4 cup chopped onion
1 teaspoon salt
Sprig of parsley
2 slices of lemon

1/2 bay leaf
1 1/2 pounds shrimp
2 tablespoons butter
2 tablespoons flour
1 can tomato sauce

Bring beer and seasonings to boil in saucepan. Add shrimp. Simmer five minutes. Strain liquid. Melt butter in separate pan, blend in flour. Gradually add tomato sauce, shrimp and liquid; bring to boil, stirring all the time. Serve on fluffy boiled rice. Makes four servings.

For a streamlined supper for pleasing an informal group, this is just the thing. Have a big tossed green salad with bleu cheese dressing and oven-toasted french bread.

MACARONI DINNER - W

1 (8 oz) package elbow macaroni, cooked and drained
1 (1 lb) can salmon, drained, boned, and broken up
1/2 cup chopped celery
1 small onion, grated
3 tbsps butter or margarine
3 tbsps flour
1 tsp dry mustard
2 1/2 cups milk
2 cups grated cheddar cheese
1 tsp Worcestershire sauce

Combine macaroni and salmon in an 8 cup baking dish. Sauté celery and onion in butter or margarine until soft in a medium size saucepan; stir in flour and mustard. Cook, stirring constantly, until bubbly. Stir in milk. Continue cooking and stirring until sauce thickens and boils 1 minute. Stir in 1 1/2 cups of the cheese and Worcestershire sauce till cheese melts. Stir into macaroni mixture; sprinkle remaining 1/2 cup cheese over top. Bake in moderate oven (350°) for 35 minutes or until bubbly hot.

GARFISH BOULETTES - B

1 cup garfish pulp (meat)
2 eggs
2 tbsps butter
3 1/2 cups potatoes cubed
1/8 tsp salt
1/8 tsp red pepper

Scrape garfish with spoon until you have obtained one cup white meat pulp. Combine fish and potatoes and cover with boiling water. Boil for about 15 minutes. Drain, mash, beat eggs and salt and pepper. Add melted butter and combine with potato fish mixture. Mix well. Shape into small balls. Fry in shallow fat until golden brown. Drain on absorbent paper. Serves 4.

OYSTER CLUB SANDWICH - B

1 pt oysters
12 slices bacon
1/2 cup flour
1/2 tsp salt

12 lettuce leaves
12 tomatoes
1/2 cup mayonnaise
18 slices buttered toast

Fry bacon and drain on absorbent paper. Drain oysters, roll in flour, seasoned with salt and pepper. Fry in bacon fat. When brown on one side, turn and brown on other side. Cooking time about 5 minutes. Drain on absorbent paper. Arrange lettuce, oysters, bacon, tomatoes and mayonnaise between three slices of toast. Fasten with toothpicks. Serves 6.

CREOLE OYSTER DRESSING - B

1 1/2 lb ground beef
1/2 lb ground pork
2 to 2 1/2 cups cooked rice
1 med onion chopped
3 to 4 shallots

1 bell pepper
1/4 cup parsley flakes
1 jar oyster
Salt and pepper

Grind or chop fine onions, shallots and bell pepper together. Set aside. Brown all ground beef and pork together, add all ground ingredients and parsley flakes. Cook on medium to low fire for one hour. Add rice and cook for 20 minutes. Add oysters and cook for 20 minutes longer. Salt and pepper to taste. Serves 6.

OYSTER PIE - B

2 unbaked pie crust shells
1 pt of oysters and oyster water
3 tbsps cooking oil
3 level tbsps flour
2 tbsps butter
3 tbsps chopped green onions

1 tbsp chopped parsley
1 tsp lemon juice
1 4 oz. can mushrooms and
liquid (stem & pieces)
Dash of tabasco pepper sauce
Salt and pepper to taste

Preheat oven to 350 degrees. In a saucepan make roux with cooking oil and flour. Over low heat, add oysters, oyster water, mushrooms and liquid. Stir constantly until blended and thickens. Add remaining ingredients and simmer for 5 minutes. Pour into pie crust shell and place second pie shell over filling. Seal edges and cut several slits in top. Bake on cookie sheet 45 minutes or until crust is brown.

FISH AU GRATIN - B

2 tsps butter
2 tbsps flour
1/2 tsp salt
2 cups milk

3/4 cup grated Swiss cheese
1 tbsp Lea & Perrins Sauce
2 cups flaked fish

Make a thin white sauce by melting butter in top of double boiler and blend with flour and salt. Stir in milk, gradually, and cook for 10 minutes. Add cheese and cook till melted. Stir in Lea & Perrins Sauce and flaked fish. Turn in 5 or 6 buttered ramekins and bake in moderate oven (350 degrees F.) till sauce is thick and browned on top.

We'll Kill the Old Red Rooster

CHAPTER IX

"We'll Kill the Old Red Rooster"

(fowl)

The above statement comes from the song, "She'll Be Coming Round the Mountain." However, in the South and very much of Louisiana, everyone had chickens. They were easy to raise and inexpensive. The hardest thing to do was to wring their necks and dress them. The more affluent left this job to their help; however, other housewives had to do the task themselves. The same went with turkeys, except the turkey's head had to be chopped off because the neck was too tough. The housewife felt a great deal of relief when the time came she could go to the grocery and buy a dressed chicken or turkey.

There was also much hunting in Louisiana for ducks, birds, and wild turkey. In the years following the Civil War, hunting wild game was a must for living and when the Acadians first settled in Louisiana, they lived off of hunting and fishing. Today, it is a popular sport and claims a huge number of enthusiastic participants. This chapter will deal with recipes for all of the above with emphasis placed on chicken dishes.

PICTURE EXPLANATION

The girls always followed the cook as she chased the rooster but as Ethel shows, when the cook finally catches the bird and is wringing its neck, the girls just can't watch!

AGGIE'S STUFFED CHICKEN BREASTS - B

8 chicken breasts, boneless
1/2 cup chopped green onions
  and bell peppers

1 lb ground beef
Cornbread made from scratch
Salt, pepper and cayenne to taste

Sauté green onions and bell peppers in oleo. Add ground beef and cook until done. Add cornbread to mixture and add seasonings. Make pocket in breasts and fill with stuffing mixture. Bake in 375° oven for 20 minutes. Be sure to put a little water in bottom of pan to keep from sticking.

Sauce:

1 lg can chopped mushrooms
3/4 cup minced onions

Make a white roux from 5 tablespoons oleo and flour and 1 1/2 cup heavy cream. Add mushrooms and onions to this. Pour over chicken breasts to serve.

SHERRIED ARTICHOKE CHICKEN - W

1 fryer, cut up
Salt, pepper, paprika, flour
6 tbsps butter
1 can (1 lb) artichoke hearts
1/4 lb sliced mushrooms

3 tbsps minced onions
2/3 cup chicken bouillon
2 tsps diced rosemary
1 cup sherry

Sprinkle chicken generously with salt, pepper, flour, and paprika last. Brown chicken in a little oil. Transfer chicken to casserole dish and arrange artichokes around chicken. Sauté onions and mushrooms in butter. Stir in chicken broth, sherry, and rosemary. Cook for a short while, stirring constantly. Pour over chicken and put slices of lemon over the top. Cover and cook at 350° for 1 to 1 1/2 hours. Baste while cooking.

CHEESY CHICKEN - W

6 chicken breasts
Flour, salt, pepper, paprika
Oil to cover bottom of skillet
2 tbsps butter
1/3 cup white wine

2/3 cup light cream
2 tbsps lemon juice
1/2 cup grated swiss or
  provolone cheese

Put chicken breasts in paper bag with dry ingredients and shake. Brown in oil. Add butter and white wine; cover and simmer till done, approximately 30 minutes. Remove chicken breasts and add to drippings a little cornstarch, cream, lemon juice and let thicken. Put chicken breasts in baking dish, pour mixture over top, sprinkle cheese over this and warm in 350° oven till cheese melts.

LIZ'S OVEN CHICKEN - W

Count on one quarter per person for this recipe but do have extra pieces just in case. Quarter chickens and brown in flour, salt, pepper, red pepper and paprika. Drain chicken and put in roasting pan or large casserole dish. Combine Worcestershire sauce, A-1 sauce, lemon juice and melted butter. Pour mixture over chicken pieces and bake at 350° till done, approximately 1 to 1 1/2 hours.

MUSHROOM ARTICHOKE CHICKEN - W

6 chicken breasts, skinned
1 (14 oz) can artichoke hearts
1 lg can mushrooms, stems
  and pieces
1 can cream of chicken soup

1 can cream of mushroom soup
1/3 cup white wine
1 cup Pepperidge Farm herb
  seasoning
Salt, pepper and cayenne to taste

Place artichokes, mushrooms, and chicken in buttered casserole dish. Pour soup that has been diluted with wine over combination. Cover with stuffing and dot with butter. Cover and bake 45 to 50 minutes at 350°. Remove cover and continue to cook till chicken is tender and brown.

CHICKEN ASPIC - W

2 envelopes unflavored gelatin
1/3 cup water
2 1/4 cups chicken broth (or
make from bouillon cubes)
3/4 cup mayonnaise
3 hard boiled eggs

1 tbsp chopped onions
1/2 cup chopped celery
1 tbsp chopped sweet pickles
1/2 tsp mustard
3 cups cooked chicken
Salt, pepper, and tabasco to taste

Sprinkle gelatin on cold water. Stir in hot chicken broth till gelatin dissolves. Turn 1 1/4 cups mixture into greased mold. Garnish with hard boiled eggs, asparagus, pimento or artichoke hearts and chill till set. Mix other ingredients into remaining gelatin and blend in blender or food processor. Pour over set gelatin and return to refrigerator till entire aspic is set. This is also delicious with tuna fish, ham, crabmeat, or salmon. With seafood, add lemon juice, dry mustard and more tabasco.

GUSTA'S STUFFED CHICKEN BREASTS - W

10 chicken breasts
3/4 cup flour
1 1/4 tsps salt

3/4 tsp paprika
1 1/4 cups oleo
Cayenne

In breasts a little split along bone line. For stuffing, toss and blend 5 cups dry bread cubes, 2 1/2 tablespoons chopped onions, 1 1/4 teaspoons salt, 3/4 teaspoon poultry seasoning, 5 tablespoons melted oleo, 3/4 cup hot water, and pepper to taste. Stuff chickens (in pocket). Cook in slow oven at 325° for 45 minutes. Drizzle butter on top just before you put in oven. After 45 minutes, turn breasts over and bake 30 to 40 minutes longer, after you sprinkle chopped parsley over top. For sauce, you could make same sauce as "Aggie's Chicken Breasts".

CHICKEN PINEAPPLE BOAT - B

2 1/2 cups (13 ozs) cubed,
  cooked chicken
1 16 oz can pineapple chunks
  in own juice,
chilled and drained
1 cup green pepper strips,
  chilled

1/2 cup sliced pecans, walnuts,
  or almonds, chilled
Lettuce leaves
3/4 cup salad dressing

Broil chicken, remove skin and bones. Cut meat in cubes. You can use canned chicken. Make sure it is drained. In salad bowl, arrange chicken, pineapple, green pepper and nuts on top of lettuce leaves. Add salad dressing and toss lightly. Makes 4 servings.

CHICKEN SAUCE PIQUANT - B & W

Make a roux with flour and oil and then add 3 large chopped onions to brown. Add a large can of tomatoes and a small can of tomato paste and let this cook down. Add chicken that has been seasoned; cover and cook slowly till chicken leaves bone. Taste sauce for seasoning and at this time, add garlic powder, cayenne pepper and salt and pepper, if needed. Just before serving, add a can of small peas and mushrooms. Serve over cooked rice.

BAKED TURKEY - W

Follow timing instructions on turkey wrappings. Wash cavity and pat dry with paper towel. Salt and pepper the cavity and rub oil on outside of turkey. Put a little water in bottom of pan and bake covered in roasting pan at 325° for approximate time according to pounds (25 minutes a pound). The last 30 to 45 minutes, take cover off so top can brown. Have neck and giblets in same pan for cooking. Remove turkey to platter and take a little of drippings and brown with flour. Add this back to pan and cook with juices so browning will take place. Leave giblets and neck in gravy, adding more water if needed.

Wild game should not be cooked right after being killed. And it should not be hung too long. Depending on the temperature and the way you are storing the game, you should keep it for one to four days. White flesh game should be cooked longer and not too fast. To take away the too-wild taste of wild game soak them over night in salt water in proportion of 1 teaspoon salt to 1 quart water. Rabbits may be cut up and covered with brine, and kept in a cool place for several days. Rabbit prepared this way is extremely tender and has a fine flavor. Other wines can be used as well.

BRUNSWICK STEW - B & W

4 pounds chicken
1/4 cup butter
1/2 cup chopped onions
2 cups tomatoes
1 cup boiling water
6 cloves

Few grains cayenne
3 cups lima beans
3 cups corn
Salt
2 tsps Worcestershire sauce
1 cup toasted bread crumbs

Saute chicken parts in butter until light brown. Remove chicken and brown onions. In a large stewing pan, place chicken, onions, tomatoes, water, cloves and cayenne. Simmer these until the chicken is nearly tender. Add the lima beans and corn and simmer until vegetables are tender. Season with salt, Worcestershire sauce and bread crumbs. Serves eight.

BROILED PIGEONS - B

6 pigeons
8 slices bacon
6 orange slices
Parsley, minced

6 lemon wedges
Salt and pepper
Toast

Season birds inside and out with salt and pepper and rub skins well with butter. Wrap each pigeon in a slice of bacon. Top with an orange slice and secure with toothpicks. Broil for 25 minutes, turning often. Remove bacon and orange slices and serve on toast with wedges of lemon and parsley. Serves 6.

211

BRO'S BAKED DUCK - W

Make sure ducks are plucked good and cavity is clean. Salt and pepper inside and outside and stuff cavities with sections of oranges and onions. Turnips may be added also, if desired. Put bacon slices over duck breasts and put approximately 1/2 inch water in bottom of pan. Cook at 350° till tender when pierced with fork. Remove duck and make a roux from drippings for gravy. If you wish an orange sauce with ducks, add orange juice and orange marmalade to a little cornstarch to thicken.

QUAIL ON TOAST - W

Dredge quail with flour, salt, and pepper. Brown quail in oil that has covered the bottom of the skillet. Take quail out and pour off excess oil, if any. Return quail to pot and add a little hot water. Cover pot and steam slowly, adding a little more water when necessary. When birds are done, place on toast and pour some of the pan gravy over them. Garnish with parsley and white grapes.

GUINEA HAM FRICASSEE - B

1 Guinea ham	2 tbsps flour
4 slices bacon	Salt and pepper to taste

Clean ham and cut into serving pieces. Fry bacon to extract fat and sauté pieces of fowl in fat until brown. Add the flour, stirring until thoroughly mixed. Add 2 cups hot water, salt, and pepper and stir until gravy boils. Cover and simmer until tender about 1 1/2 hours.

STEWED CHICKEN AND DROP DUMPLINGS - B

1 stewing chicken
1 small onion
Salt and pepper to taste
1 cup sifted flour
2 tsps baking powder

1/2 tsp salt
Sprig of parsley, minced
Celery
1/2 cup milk

Clean chicken and remove fat. Cut into serving size pieces. Place in a stewing pot and cover with salted water. Add onion and pepper and cook until tender, approximately 2 1/2 to 3 hours. Mix flour, baking powder, salt, minced parsley, celery, and milk to a thick batter and drop from spoon into boiling chicken broth. Cover tightly and cook for 20 minutes without raising lid. Place chicken on platter and surround it with dumplings. Serves 6 to 8.

YOUNG FRIED TURKEY - B

1 young turkey
2 tsps salt
2 eggs

2 tbsps water
Bread crumbs

Cut turkey into serving size pieces. Season with salt and seasoning and steam until almost tender. Cool. Just before serving, use bread crumbs, crushed fine. Roll turkey into crumbs, then dip into eggs beaten with water. Roll again in the crumbs. Fry in hot, deep fat until golden brown for about 10 to 12 minutes or longer if not tender. You can also do this with cooked turkey. Do not fry long, only long enough to brown the bread crumbs. Serve with sauce.

LOUISIANA HERB BAKED CHICKEN - B

1 (2 1/2 to 3 lbs) fryer
1 tsp garlic powder
1 tsp white vinegar
1/3 cup butter or margarine,
    melted

1/3 cup dry white wine
1/2 tsp basil leaf, crumbled
Salt and pepper to taste

Heat oven to 400°. Wash chicken. Cut in half or serving size pieces. Sprinkle with garlic powder and vinegar. Combine melted butter and wine. Add basil, salt and pepper. Place in a roasting pan. Brush with butter/wine sauce. Bake 1 1/2 to 2 hours or until tender. Brush with sauce several times during baking for a moist, flavorful chicken. Serves 4 to 6.

ROAST CHICKEN - B

1 (3 1/2 to 6 lbs) roasting chicken   1 tbsp parsley flakes
1 tsp brown sage   Salt and pepper to taste
1 tsp paprika   1/4 cup lemon juice

Preheat oven to 350°. Wash and dry chicken with paper towel. Rub chicken inside and out with sage. Sprinkle with salt, pepper, parsley flakes and papilka. Sprinkle with lemon juice outside and inside. Cover and let sit for 1 hour or longer in refrigerator. Place in a baking dish and cover. Bake for 45 minutes. Then uncover and continue baking for 10 to 15 minutes or longer until chicken is tender. Serves 6 to 8.

RABBIT STEW - B

3/4 cup mushrooms   1 cup stock or broth
1 rabbit   1 stalk parsley
4 strips bacon   1/2 tsp ground thyme
1 1/2 stalks celery   Salt and pepper to taste
1 cup white wine   Flour

Cube as much of rabbit as you can. Crisp cut up bacon in a sauce pan. Remove and place rabbit into the bacon fat and brown well. Dredge with flour and add bacon, stock, wine and seasonings to taste. Cook for 20 minutes. Add mushrooms and simmer all together until meat is done through. Thicken gravy with flour if necessary.

DUCK A LA CREOLE - B

2 tbsps fat
1 tbsp flour
2 tbsps chopped pork
Salt, pepper and paprika to taste
2 tbsps minced onions
2 tbsps chopped green peppers
2 tbsps chopped hot red peppers

1/2 cup chopped celery
1 tbsp chopped parsley or
  parsley flakes
1 1/2 cups consomme
1 whole clove
1/2 tsp mace
2 cups diced, cooked duck

Melt fat and add flour. Stir in chopped pork. Season with paprika, salt, pepper, onions, green and red peppers, celery, and parsley. Stir for 2 minutes and add the consomme, clove and mace. Simmer for 1 hour. Strain the broth and stir in diced, cooked duck. Heat thoroughly and serve with rice or potatoes. Add favorite sauce or gravy.

TURKEY AMANDINE - B

3 packages cornbread mix
1 lb mushrooms, sliced
6 tbsps butter, margarine,
  or oil
3/4 cup flour
3 tsps salt
1/4 tsp pepper
1/2 tsp thyme, crumbled

2 qts turkey broth or chicken
  broth
5 cups turkey, cooked and cut
  up in serving sizes
3/4 cup dry sherry
1 cup blanched almonds,
  toasted

Prepare cornbread according to directions on package or use left over cornbread. Sauté mushrooms in cooking oil, butter, or margarine. Cook 5 minutes until tender. Add flour, salt, pepper, and thyme. Mix well. Gradually add turkey or chicken broth. Cook until sauce thickens and simmer for 5 minutes, stirring constantly. Add turkey and sherry. Heat well. Add seasoning to taste. Add salt, pepper, and almonds.

FRIED CHICKEN ON THE SOUTH SIDE - B

1 frying chicken (2 1/2 to 3 lbs)
1 tsp grated lemon rind
2/3 cup pure vegetable oil
1/3 cup lemon juice
1/4 tsp pepper
1/2 tsp Worcestershire sauce

1 cup sifted all purpose flour
1 tsp salt
1 tsp paprika
1/2 cup butter or margarine
1 1/2 cups milk
1 cup light cream

Place chicken in shallow dish. Combine lemon rind, juice, oil, pepper, and Worcestershire sauce. Marinate for 2 hours or overnight. Drain chicken. Place flour, salt, pepper, and paprika in a brown paper bag. Shake chicken until well coated. Save the rest for making gravy. Melt butter in large skillet over medium heat. Saute chicken about 30 to 40 minutes until tender and golden brown. Drain and keep warm. Pour off drippings. Leave chips in skillet but remove drippings. Return 3 tablespoons of drippings into skillet. Stir one fourth of flour mixture in with drippings. Slowly add milk, stirring constantly until thickened and bubbly on a medium heat. Turn heat down and stir in cream. Taste before adding more seasonings. Add chicken to gravy or serve separately over rice or potatoes. Makes 4 to 5 servings.

ROAST DUCKLING WITH PEACH SAUCE - B

1 (4 to 5 lbs) duckling, quartered
1 cup water
1/3 cup sugar
3 tbsps cornstarch
1/2 tsp salt
2 tsps grated orange rind

1/2 cup orange juice
1 tbsp lemon juice
2 packages (10 ozs) frozen
  peach slices, slightly thawed
  or canned peaches can be used

Place duckling on rack in roasting pan. Roast at 350° for 2 1/2 hours or until tender. Transfer duck to platter and keep warm. Pour off all fat from roasting pan. Add 1 cup water to pan, heat and stir, to dissolve all brown particles. Combine sugar, cornstarch, salt, and orange rind in sauce pan, gradually stirring in stock from roasting pan and orange and lemon juices. Add peaches. Cook on medium heat, stirring constantly until mixture thickens and comes to a boil. Serve warm over duckling. Serves 4.

Duck and goose can be cooked the same way. Around Christmas, you can find fresh goose and duck in your supermarkets. Goose, like duck, is fatty. Fat should be removed on both the inside and under the skin of the birds before serving. They can be cooked stuffed or unstuffed with your favorite dressings.

CHICKEN LIVERS AND GIZZARD - B

1 lb chicken livers
1 lb chicken gizzards
1 onion, chopped
1/2 green pepper

1/3 tsp salt and pepper
1/2 cup cooking oil
3 to 4 tbsps flour

Wash chicken livers and gizzards and season with salt and pepper. Place cooking oil in skillet until hot. With extra flour, flour chicken livers and gizzards,then place in hot cooking oil until lightly browned. Take out of skillet and drain. Pour off most of the cooking oil and make a roux with remaining flour. Place onions and bell peppers in roux, then add 1 cup water. Place liver and gizzards into roux and cook about 15 minutes. Serve over rice.

COUNTRY FRIED TAME DUCK - B

1 3/4 lbs ready to cook duckling
1 cup flour
2 tsps salt
1/3 tsp white pepper
1/3 tsp red pepper

2 tbsps paprika
1/4 cup butter
4 tbsps shortening
1/4 cup water

Wash and clean duckling and cut into serving size pieces. Rinse in cold water and drain. Mix flour, salt, pepper, and paprika in a paper sack. Shake 2 to 3 pieces of duckling in the sack at a time to coat thoroughly. Heat the butter and 4 tbsps shortening in a heavy skillet to make a layer of fat 1/4 inch deep. With kitchen tongs, place duckling in hot shortening, skin side down. Brown and turn. Remove most of the shortening except for 2 tablespoons. Add water and cover tightly. Reduce heat and cook slowly or bake in an oven at 350° until tender.

BRUNCH OR SUPPER QUAIL - W

6 quails
1 med chopped onion
2 cups water

Flour, salt, and pepper
Oil
1 can mushroom stems & pieces

Salt, pepper, and flour quail and brown in oil in skillet. Add water, chopped onion, mushrooms, and cover tightly. Let simmer till quail is tender. Serve on toast with pan liquid and garnish with parsley. Also good for doves.

ROAST WILD DUCK - B

Salt, clean, dress duck well on both sides, inside and out, and place 1/4 large onion in cavity of each. For each duck cut 1 medium clove garlic in half and one tabasco pepper in half.

Make slit in each side of duck near wing. In right side slit, insert 1/2 clove garlic, in left side slit, insert 1/2 tabasco pepper. Make incision in inner sides of legs near groin and in right side insert 1/2 tabasco pepper, in left side slit insert 1/2 clove garlic. Put duck in hot oven and brown for about 20 minutes. Then lower oven temperature adding small amount of water, cook duck for 2 hours. For ducks 6 months or older place a small piece of bacon on each side of breast bone to keep moist.

CHICKEN BREASTS IN CREAM - B

2 whole chicken breasts
  about two pounds
3 tsps fat
1/3 cup chopped onion
1 small clove garlic, minced
3/4 cup chicken broth

3/4 cup cream
1 1/2 tsps salt
1/4 tsp black pepper
2 tsps Worcestershire sauce
1/4 cup cooking sherry
  (optional)

Heat oven to 300° F. Cut chicken breasts in two making four serving pieces. Brown the breasts in the fat until golden brown. Heat onions, garlic, broth, cream, seasonings and sherry in saucepan. Place the chicken in roaster and pour sauce over them. Cover and bake for two hours. Uncover and bake for 15 to 20 minutes more. Remove chicken from pan, keeping it warm while making gravy from drippings. Serves four.

FRIED RABBIT - B

1 young rabbit
1/2 cup flour
2 tsps salt

1/8 tsp paprika
1/2 cup drippings
Red pepper to taste

Wash rabbit, dry thoroughly, and cut into serving size pieces. Dredge with flour to which seasoning has been added. Heat drippings in frying pan. Place the rabbit in fat, which is hot but not smoking. Cook to a golden brown on all sides. Reduce heat and cook slowly about 35 to 45 minutes, depending on the size of the rabbit. Serve as is or with cream gravy.

CYNTHIA'S BREADED ALLIGATOR - W

1 egg
1 1/2 c milk
1/4 c flour
1/4 tsp chili powder

1/4 tsp cajun spice
2 to 4 drops tabasco
2 tbsps oleo

Beat egg, add milk, flour, seasonings and margarine. Whip together really well. Slice alligator 1/2 inch thick and season with cajun spice. Place alligator into mixture, let set for an hour or two. Pass in flour and place in hot oil. Cook till golden brown.
(Cynthia Schroeder is from South Louisiana and this is an authentic cajun recipe.)

SESAME BAKED CHICKEN - B

2/3 cup fine cracker crumbs
1/4 cup toasted sesame seed
1 2 1/2 to 3 pound ready to
  cook broiler fryer, cut up

1/2 6 ounce can (1/3 cup)
  evaporated milk
1/2 cup butter or margarine,
  melted

Combine cracker crumbs and toasted sesame seed. Dip chicken pieces in evaporated milk, then roll in cracker mixture. Pour melted butter into 11 1/2 x 7 1/2 x 7 1/2 inch baking dish. Place chicken in dish, cover, and cook in a moderate oven (350°) for 1 1/2 hours or till done. Remove to warm serving platter; garnish with parsley. Makes 3 or 4 servings.

* To toast sesame seed, place in a shallow ungreased baking pan. Heat in a moderate oven 350° for 10 minutes stirring once or twice.

CHICKEN GRILLED WITH BRUSH ON GARLIC - B

1/2 cup butter (1 stick)
1/4 cup lemon juice
1 tbsp (1/2 envelope) garlic salad
  dressing mix

2 fryers, quartered

Melt butter and blend in lemon juice and salad dressing mix. Brush chicken with seasoned butter. Place on grill, cut side down, 5 to 6 inches from coals. Cook about 1 hour, turning and brushing with seasoning butter about every 10 minutes. Serves 6.

BARBEQUED COON - B

Marinate coon in sauce consisting of 1 bay leaf, 3 cloves garlic, 1/2 cup lemon juice, 1/2 cup wine, 1/2 cup beer, and 1/2 teaspoon tabasco. Wash and clean coon. Cut into serving pieces. Place in a large pot of water with 1/2 cup vinegar and salt. Bring to a boil for 1 hour, making sure it is a slow boil. Marinate with remaining ingredients for 2 days so seasoning can go all through meat. Add onion, salt and pepper to taste and boil again on the third day for 1 1/2 hours. Place on open pit and baste with favorite barbecue sauce. Cook until tender.

COON AND SWEET POTATOES - B

Cut up coon and boil for 1 hour. Season with 1 clove, salt and pepper to taste, 6 yams, 1/2 stick margarine, 1/2 teaspoon cinnamon, 1/2 teaspoon nutmeg, and 1 teaspoon vanilla. Place boiled coon with seasoning into a large, greased baking dish. In another pot, put cut up yams and other ingredients. Steam for 10 minutes. When tender, take out and pour over coon. Cover and place in 350° oven and cook for 45 minutes or until coon is tender.

CHICKEN LIVERS AND BACON - B

1 1/2 lbs chicken livers
1 lb bacon
Flour

Onions
Green peppers
Salt and pepper to taste

Sauté bacon but do not let get crisp. Remove from frying pan and drain off excess fat. Pour off all but 2 tablespoons of fat. Season the liver and roll it in flour. Season again with salt, pepper, bacon, chopped onions, and chopped green peppers. Sauté in drippings at reduced heat for 5 to 8 minutes until browned on both sides. Remove from skillet and drain. Add 1/2 cup water to make light gravy; cover and let steam for about 5 minutes. Serve over fried liver.

CHICKEN FRICASSEE - B

1 3 lb chicken, cut up
1 cup flour
Salt, pepper, paprika and
  cayenne to taste

1 cup chopped onions
1 cup chopped peppers
1 cup chopped celery
1 cup chopped parsley

Use heavy kettle and fill bottom with oil. Salt, pepper and flour chicken. Brown chicken in oil and drain on paper towel. Sauté vegetables in oil till limp. Add a little flour to thicken and brown with oil in kettle. Add water slowly to make gravy. Add chicken again, cover and simmer till very tender. Serve over rice. Makes 4 servings. This recipe was a favorite dish in the Reconstruction days.

RABBIT OR SQUIRREL SAUCE PIQUANTE - W

Cut up meat, season, and brown in heavy pot with hot oil. Remove meat when well browned and add flour to make a roux. Add chopped onion, bell peppers, celery, and garlic. Add 1 can tomato sauce and water so mixture is not too thick. Cook till vegetables are soft. Add rabbits or squirrels at this time. Cover and cook over low heat till tender, approximately 1 to 1 1/2 hours. Serve over rice.

Eks! Eks! Tres Pour Oun Dima!

CHAPTER X

"Eks! Eks! Tres Pour Oun Dima!"

(eggs, cheese)

In Louisiana of the 1880's, an egg man roamed the streets, carrying his basket of fresh eggs and selling them from neighborhood to neighborhood. Because quite a few people had "laying" hens and eggs were cheap, they were added to many recipes. Egg dishes were popular then and still are.

Eggs are almost a necessity in Louisiana cooking and recipes range from creole eggs for brunch to supper quiche. They are also key ingredients in most recipes. Many plantations made a form of cheese with clabbered milk. In the 1800's the imported and Yankee cheeses were hard to come by but they have now become a part of many southern recipes. The recipes in this chapter will focus primarily on egg and cheese as the main ingredients.

Picture explanation

The girls have been given a dime each so they can buy their own egg. Naturally, they have to search long and hard before they decide on the "just right" egg that the cook will fix "just for them."

TOMATOES AND EGGS - B

1 small onion
2 cups tomatoes, skins removed
1/2 cup chopped celery
1/4 cup parsley flakes

Salt and pepper to taste
6 eggs
1 tbsp butter or margarine
Toast

In a shallow pan, melt butter and add chopped onion, celery, parsley flakes, and tomatoes. Sauté very slowly for 8 to 10 minutes. Add salt and pepper. Then reduce heat and cook. Break the eggs and slip them on top of the mixture of tomatoes, being careful not to break the yolks. Cook slowly until the white of the eggs are set. Poke with a fork and let the yolks mingle with the tomato mixture and the whites. The mixture should be soft. Serve over buttered toast.

EGGS AND PORK CHOPS - B

6 eggs
3 med. pork chops, removed from
   bone and cut into small pieces

Salt and pepper to taste
1/4 cup bell pepper, chopped
1 tbsp cooking oil

Sauté cut pork chops in cooking oil until chops are white in color. Do not brown. Remove from heat. Add bell pepper to meat. In a separate bowl, beat eggs and add salt and pepper. Return skillet to stove with pork chops. Pour eggs over meat and stir constantly until eggs are cooked to softness. Reduce heat very low. Place a lid on top and cook 1 to 2 minutes longer. Serve with green vegetable of your choice. Makes 4 to 6 servings.

MUSHROOM AND VEGETABLE OMELET - B

1/4 cup olives
1/4 cup mushrooms
1 tsp salt
1/4 tsp white pepper
1 med tomato, peeled
1 small green pepper

1/2 cup onion
1 tsp parsley flakes
1/4 cup chopped celery
4 eggs
1 tbsp butter or margarine

Chop the olives, mushrooms, onions, parsley flakes, celery, and green pepper. Place in a large bowl. In a saucepan with butter, add mixture and season with salt and pepper. Cook for 2 to 3 minutes. Beat the eggs, then put in the omelet pan and, as soon as they begin to cook, add the chopped vegetables. Finish as you would a plain omelet. Serves 4.

EGG AND CHEESE BAKE - B

2 tbsps cooking oil or butter
1/4 cup green onion tops
1 cup grated cheese

Splash of tabasco
1 cup cream
Salt and white pepper to taste

Baste the bottom and sides of baking dish with cooking oil, sprinkle a layer of cheese and break the eggs on the cheese. Be careful not to break the yolks. Pour a small part of the cream over the eggs, then more cheese. Season with salt, white pepper, and tabasco. Then bake in a slow oven at 250° until the eggs are set, but not hard. If you don't like the yolk firm, prick with a fork and let run. Serve in baking dish. Makes 4 to 6 servings.

DEVILED EGGS - B

For side dishes, use hard boiled eggs. Cool and cut in half, either lengthwise or crosswise. Mash the yolks and season with salt, pepper, 1/2 cup mayonnaise, and 1 tablespoon vinegar. You can add soft minced ham. Refill the whites with the mixture, pressing down to pack the whites. Cover with wax paper and place in refrigerator. Serve with molasses; as a substitute for salad; or serve as an appetizer.

CHEESE CROQUETTES - B

3 tbsps butter
1/3 cup flour
1/4 tsp salt
1/4 tsp paprika

1 cup milk
2 egg yolks, slightly beaten
1 1/2 cups cubed cheese

Melt butter and blend in flour and add seasonings and milk. Cook until thickened, stirring constantly. Add to egg yolks. When well mixed, add cheese. Cool and shape into balls. Fry balls in hot deep fat at 380° until browned. Makes 12 croquettes.

EGGS AND TOMATOES - B

6 small tomatoes
2 tbsps butter or margarine
Salt and pepper to taste

6 eggs
1/2 cup green onions

Blanch tomatoes in hot water. Peel tomatoes and cut up into small bite size pieces. Season to taste. In a separate bowl, beat eggs and add salt and pepper. Add green onions, and chopped up tomatoes to eggs. Place in a hot skillet with melted butter or margarine. Fry like scrambled eggs. Serve on top of crisp toast.

POACHED EGGS WITH SHRIMP - B

2 cups water
1/2 tsp salt

2 eggs
1/2 tsp vinegar

Heat water until it simmers in a shallow pan. Add salt and vinegar. If you like the yolk unbroken, crack eggs gently into simmering water. Let cook for 3 to 5 minutes or until white is firm and film has formed over the yolk. Remove egg with spatula, drain and serve on toast. Saute 2 cups shelled, boiled shrimp in 1/2 teaspoon butter or margarine. Add salt and pepper to taste. Saute for 10 minutes. Top eggs with shrimp.

CHEESE AND SAUSAGE BALLS - W

(For Brunch or cocktails)

This recipe calls for 3 cups Bisquick, 1 lb hot sausage, 10 ozs sharp cheddar cheese, grated, and cayenne pepper to taste. Mix all ingredients together to form into balls and bake in 350° oven till browned and cooked through. Bake 30 minutes longer if frozen before.

BAKED EGGS - W

Line muffin tin with bacon slices. Broil for 5 minutes in oven till bacon is partially cooked. Drain off grease; break egg in each tin and top with dash of tabasco, salt, and pepper. Turn oven on bake and bake till eggs set in middle. Serve on toast or English muffins.

CREPES AMANDINE - W

Use basic crepe recipe from this chapter.

For filling:

3/4 cups Miracle Whip Salad
  dressing
3 tbsps flour
1 1/2 cups milk
1 cup grated Swiss cheese
2 cups cooked, chopped chicken

1 cup chopped celery
3/4 cup almonds
2 tbsps chopped pimento
2 tbsps chopped green onions
Salt, pepper, and paprika to taste

Add milk to flour and salad dressing and cook slowly till thick. Add cheese and melt. Then add rest of ingredients. Fill each crepe with 1/4 cup of mixture and roll up. Put in casserole dish and pour rest of mixture, to which a little milk has been added, over crepes. Bake in 350° oven for approximately 20 minutes.

RED BEET EGGS - W

2 cans small whole beets
1 cup cider vinegar
1/2 cup sugar

1 tsp salt
6 hard boiled eggs, shelled

Drain beets and reserve liquid. Put drained beets in 1 1/2 quart jars. Measure reserved liquid. If necessary, add enough water to measure 1 cup. Combine beet liquid, vinegar, sugar, and salt and bring to a boil. Pour over beets, then refrigerate, tightly covered for 16 to 20 hours. Next day, remove beets from jar; put in eggs; refrigerate for 20 hours. Refrigerate beets in another container, covered. Make a salad with fresh lettuce or romaine, topped with 2 or 3 beets, halved, sliced onions, and a hard boiled egg, cut in half. Sprinkle bleu cheese over top and pour Italian or dijon salad dressing over top.

CHEESE CASSEROLE - W

2 (4 oz) cans green chilies
1 lb Monterey Jack cheese,
  grated
1 lb sharp cheese, grated
4 egg whites
4 egg yolks

2/3 cup evaporated milk
1 tbsp flour
1/2 tsp salt
1/4 tsp pepper
2 tomatoes, sliced
Tabasco to taste

Preheat oven to 325°. Remove seeds from chilies and dice. Combine chilies and cheeses. Put mixture in buttered, shallow 2 quart casserole dish. At high speed, beat egg whites till stiff peaks form. In another bowl, beat egg yolks, milk, flour, and seasonings. Pour mixture over cheese mixture and gently mix. Bake for 30 minutes and remove from oven. Arrange tomatoes around top. Bake 30 minutes longer till knife comes out clean. Garnish with chilies.

MAMA'S EGG SALAD DRESSING - W

Use 1 hard boiled egg for each 2 people. Mash egg yellows with a little cider vinegar to soften and a pinch of sugar. Add salt and pepper. Then add mayonnaise to desired consistency. Use Romaine green leaf lettuce or spinach for your green bed. Spoon dressing on top and generously sprinkle green onions and chopped egg whites over dressing. A real hit!

CREOLE EGGS - W

This recipe calls for 12 hard boiled eggs, 1 large can stewed tomatoes, 2 bell peppers, and 1 large, diced onion. Sauté onion and pepper in 2 tablespoons oleo till done. Add tomatoes, a dash of chili powder, dash of red pepper, and 1 tablespoon Lea & Perrins sauce. Make a white sauce and combine with tomato/pepper sauce and pour over quartered eggs in casserole dish. Spread bread crumbs on top and bake in 300° oven till warm through.

CREAMED EGGS - W

Make patty shells or use Pepperidge
   Farm patty shells
1 cup cooked ham, cut in
   small pieces
2 tbsps butter
1/2 cup chopped green pepper

1/2 cup chopped green onions
1 1/2 tbsps flour
1 1/2 to 2 cups evaporated milk
6 hard boiled eggs, sliced
Can of asparagus, cut in 1
   inch pieces

Bake patty shells. Sauté onions and peppers. Add ham and cook mixture a few minutes. Add flour and stir till smooth. Stir in milk slowly. Add asparagus and eggs and heat complete mixture. Serve in patty shells.

CAROLYN'S SCRAMBLED EGGS WITH MUSHROOMS - B

4 tbsps butter
1 1/2 cups sliced mushrooms
1 1/2 tsps flour
4 tbsps finely chopped onions

5 eggs, slightly beaten
1/2 tsp salt
Pinch of cayenne pepper

Melt the butter in a skillet. Dust the mushrooms with flour and put in the skillet with the onion. Cook and stir 4 to 5 minutes until the mushrooms darken and become soft. Lower the heat. Stir in the eggs, salt, and cayenne pepper and cook; continue to stir until desired texture is achieved and eggs are creamy and set.

CAROLYN'S SCRAMBLED EGGS CREOLE - B

These flavorful eggs are especially good with warm tortillas.

2 tbsps butter
4 tbsps finely chopped onions
1 cup tomatoes, peeled,
   seeded and chopped fine
1 tsp sugar

1/2 tsp salt
1/4 tsp freshly ground pepper
5 eggs slightly beaten
4 tbsps freshly grated
   parmesan cheese

Melt the butter in a skillet and cook the onions over medium heat until soft. Add the tomatoes, sugar, salt and pepper and cook 5 minutes. Stir in eggs. Cook over low heat, stirring as the eggs set until they are creamy. Sprinkle with the cheese. Serves 4.

BASIC CREPE BATTER - W

1 cup flour
1/3 tsp salt
3 eggs, beaten

2 tbsp butter, melted
1 1/2 cup milk

Stir flour and salt together. Blend eggs, milk and butter and add to flour mixture, beating till smooth. It is good to let batter stand at room temperature for one hour. Use batter to cook thin pancakes.
Crepes freeze well up to 4 months and filled crepes keep well up to 2 months.

TURKEY-BROCCOLI-MUSHROOM CREPES - W

2 tbsps oleo
1/3 cup chopped green onions
1 can cream of mushroom or
   chicken soup
1 can mushroom stems & pieces
1 pkg frozen chopped broccoli
2 cups cooked and cut up parsley

1 cup sour cream or light sour
   cream
1 tsp salt
1/3 tea pepper
1 tsp Worcestershire sauce
1 tsp dijon mustard

Cook broccoli till done. Sauté onion in skillet and add remainder of ingredients, including drained broccoli. Stir to blend. Fill crepe with about 3 tbsp mixture. Roll crepe and arrange in oven proof dish, seam side down. Top with slivered almonds and grated provolone cheese. Cook at 375° for 10 minutes.

HAM AND SPINACH CREPES - W

Follow basic crepe recipe

2 cups cut up ham
Can mushrooms, stems & pieces
Can cream of mushroom soup
Can cheddar cheese soup

1 pkg chopped spinach
1 tsp creole mustard
Salt, pepper and cajun
  seasoning

Cook spinach and drain. Warm soups in saucepan and add all other ingredients. Stuff like for turkey crepes and top with grated sharp cheddar cheese. Cook the same time and temp.

SEAFOOD CREPES - W

1 chopped green pepper
1 can mushrooms stems & pieces
3 chopped green onions
1 lb cooked shrimp
Salt and pepper

1 lb cooked crabmeat
1 can cream of shrimp soup
1/4 cup milk
1/4 cup white wine

Follow directions as for turkey and ham crepes, saute vegetables. and add rest of ingredients. Stuff like other crepes, top with grated swiss cheese and slivered almonds.

CRABMEAT CREPES - W

2 tbsps oleo or oil
3 tbsps flour
3/4 cup milk
1/2 cup white wine
1/3 cup diced green onion

1 can mushrooms, stems
& pieces
1 lb crab meat, fresh, frozen
or canned

Melt oleo and blend in flour. Gradually stir in milk, wine, salt and pepper to make white sauce. Sauté onions, mushrooms, and crabmeat and add to sauce. Fill crepes and bake in oven 375 degrees for 10 minutes.

CRABMEAT QUICHE - W

1 lb crabmeat
Chopped green onions
Chopped parsley
Can mushrooms
1/2 stick oleo
1/2 cup evaporated milk

2 eggs
1/3 cup white wine
1/2 cup grated Gruyere cheese
1/2 cup parmesan cheese
Unbaked pie shell

Bake pie shell slightly and put to the side. Sauté onion, parsley, mushroom in oleo. Beat eggs and add milk to mixture. Add a little flour, salt and pepper to thicken. When mixture becomes thick, add crabmeat and pour into pie shell. Sprinkle with cheese and bake in 350 degree oven for 30 to 40 minutes. You may substitute shrimp or crawfish for crab.

CHEESE CUSTARD - W

6 slices bacon
2 cups half & half
4 green onions

6 eggs
2 cups grated Swiss cheese
Salt, pepper and cayenne

Cut bacon in 1 inch pieces and sauté till almost crisp. Remove and drain on paper toweling. Scald cream in small saucepan. Beat eggs with seasoning and chopped green onions. Stir in cream and pour 1/2 mixture in casserole. Top with swiss cheese and more egg mixture. Top with bacon and bake in moderate oven (350°) 20 minutes till set.

Preparing perfect hard boiled eggs requires placing a layer of eggs in a saucepan and covering with enough water to come at least one inch above eggs. Then cover pan and bring water to a boil. Turn off heat and let eggs stand for 15 to 16 minutes.

STUFFED EGGS - W

Onion Pickle Stuffing: Halve and peel eggs and remove yellows. In a bowl, mash yellows, adding a little white vinegar. Chop green onions and add them, pickle relish (either sweet or dill) and a few shakes tabasco. Add mayonnaise for desired consistency and stuff egg whites. Sprinkle with paprika.

Curry Stuffing: Add grated onion, sweet relish, a little tabasco, a little chutney, mayonnaise, and curry powder. Top with chopped peanuts.

Bacon Cheese Stuffing: Add crumbled bacon, chopped green onions, and grated sharp cheddar cheese to chopped yellows. Soften with sour cream. Top with paprika.

Pimento Olive Stuffing: Add chopped pimento stuffed olives, chopped parsley, mayonnaise, and a little yellow mustard to egg yellows. Top with olive slices and paprika.

Mexican Stuffing: Add chopped, seeded jalapeno peppers, Cheese Whiz, chopped onions, and chili powder to yellows. Top with small jalapeno slices.

SHRIMP QUICHE - W

Needed for this recipe is 1 (4 oz) package of Swiss cheese, 4 ounces shredded Gruyere cheese, 1 tablespoon flour, 3 eggs, 1 cup half & half, 1/2 teaspoon mustard, pinch of salt, 1/4 teaspoon Worcestershire sauce, black pepper, 1 cup diced shrimp, and pastry for pie shells. Line tart shells or muffin tins with pastry. Mix cheeses and flour and line pastry with this layer, a shrimp layer, and another cheese layer. Beat eggs and milk with other ingredients. Pour over cheese mixture. Bake at 375° to 400° for 30 minutes or until middle is firm.

TINY VEGETABLE QUICHES - W

Make pie dough and put in small tart shells. For filling:

Broccoli: 1 package chopped broccoli
        1/2 lb swiss cheese, shredded
        1 cup half & half
        3 eggs
        Dash of salt, pepper, and cayenne

Bake at 400° for 25 minutes till middle is set.

Spinach: Substitute 1 package chopped spinach for broccoli.

Artichoke Hearts: Chop can of artichokes and
                  substitute these for broccoli.

Asparagus: Chop can of asparagus and substitute
      these for artichoke hearts.

Cauliflower: Chop fresh or frozen cauliflower and substitute these for
              asparagus.

CHEESE RICE RING - B

2 tbsps chopped onions
1 green pepper, chopped
2 tbsps butter
1 1/2 cups cooked tomatoes

3 1/2 cups cooked rice
1/4 tsp salt
Dash pepper
1 1/2 cups grated sharp cheese

Cook onions and green pepper in butter until tender. Add tomatoes and rice. Cook slowly until rice has absorbed liquid. Add seasonings and cheese. Pack into buttered ring mold. Unmold onto serving plate and fill with scrambled eggs. Serves 6.

HOMEMADE CUP CHEESE - B

4 qts thick, sour milk
1 tsp salt

3 tbsps butter

Cut through milk several times with long, sharp knife. Then heat slowly to 90° or scald until curd is very dry. Remove from heat and place in a wet cheesecloth bag. Press under a heavy weight 12 to 24 hours or until cheese dries. Force through a cheese sieve or grate fine. Place in a wooden bowl, cover with a heavy cloth and keep in a warm place 3 to 7 days or until soft and ripe, stirring occasionally. Then place in a skillet and cook, stirring constantly until smooth. Add salt and butter and mix well. Pour into cups or bowls. Makes 3 cups. Jars can be used as well. This is good for a Christmas gift basket.

CHEESE FONDUE - B

5 eggs, separated
1 1/4 cup milk
2 cups soft bread crumbs

3/4 tsp salt
1/2 tsp dry mustard
1/2 lb American cheese, shredded

Beat egg yolks and add next 5 ingredients as listed. Fold in stiffly beaten egg whites. Pour into buttered custard cups. Place in pan of hot water and bake in slow oven at 325° until firm. Unmold and serve at once. Serves 8.

CHEESE AND GRITS - B

2 cups cooked grits
2/3 cup grated cheese
2 eggs
3/4 tsp salt

Dash pepper
2 tsps chopped pimento
2 tbsps chopped parsley
1 cup milk

Combine ingredients. Pour into buttered individual baking dishes. Place in pan of hot water and bake in slow oven at 325° for 30 minutes. Serves 6.

EGGS AND SAUSAGE - B

6 eggs
2 cups cut round pork sausage
1/2 cup chopped green peppers
1/3 cup onions

2 tbsps butter or margarine
Salt and pepper to taste
4 tbsps milk
1 tbsp butter or margarine

Beat eggs in large bowl. Add milk, salt, and pepper. Put to the side. Sauté onions and green peppers in 1 tablespoon of butter. Add pork sausage and stir for about 5 minutes on medium flame. Scramble eggs in 2 tablespoons butter. Place scramble eggs in center of platter and arrange sausage mixture all around. Garnish with parsley. Serves 4 to 6. Serve hot.

BROUILLADE'S TRUFFLES - W

Put 12 beaten eggs in casserole dish with the bottom covered with 1 teaspoon olive oil. Grate small can of truffles and mix with eggs and season with salt and pepper. Let marinate half day in refrigerator. Put in skillet on low heat till mixture thickens. Pour in casserole dish and keep in oven on 225° till serving time.

HOT CHEESE CANAPES - W

White bread slices, without crust   1 cup mayonnaise
Slice of cold assorted meats   Tabasco
   or fish   1/2 cup shredded cheese

Cut bread in small squares. Put a piece of meat on each square and top with cheese/mayonnaise mixture. Broil till bubbly. Good with canned corned beef, ham, turkey, chicken, tuna or salmon. With turkey and chicken, use provolone cheese. With the rest, use sharp cheddar cheese.

Many of our egg and cheese recipes you will find under the Brunch section.

CREPE BATTER RECIPE - W

1 cup all purpose flour   Dash of salt
3 eggs   2 tbsps vegetable oil
1 1/3 cups milk

Beat milk and eggs. Add salt to flour and sift into egg mixture. Add the oil and blend thoroughly, mashing any lumps. Allow mixture to stand an hour; if batter becomes too thick, add a little milk. Pour 1 to 2 tablespoons of batter in center of hot, lightly greased skillet or crepe pan. Tilt to spread batter to edges. Cook till top is dry. Turn over and cook 10 to 15 seconds on other side. Makes 12.

CHEESE BALLS - W

Horseradish: **1 (8 oz) package cream cheese, softened**
1/2 tsp horseradish
1/4 tsp celery salt or seed
1/2 cup chopped dried beef
1/2 cup chopped parsley

Blend cheese till smooth. Add other ingredients, mixing till well blended. Shape mixture into balls and wrap in wax paper. Refrigerate overnight. When firm, reshape and roll in parsley. Cover and refrigerate till serving time.

Blue Cheese: **1 (8 oz) package cream cheese, softened**
1 (4 oz) package blue cheese, crumbled
1/4 tsp dry mustard
1/2 tsp mayonnaise
Dash of tabasco

Blend cheeses with mixer till smooth. Add mustard, mayonnaise, and tabasco. Shape cheese mixture into balls. Wrap with waxed paper and refrigerate overnight. Next day, roll in sesame seeds.

Small Cheese Balls: **1 1/2 lbs sharp cheddar cheese**
1 small can chopped pimentos
Worcestershire sauce
Mayonnaise
Tabasco
Ground pecans or peanuts

Blend cheese and pimentos in food processor. Add Worcestershire and tabasco and soften with mayonnaise to hold mixture together. Form into small balls; roll in pecans or peanuts; harden in refrigerator. You can roll these in paprika; put a clove in one and two little parsley leaves in other, to make apple instead of rolling in nuts.

CHEESE SOUFFLE - W

4 slices bread buttered, leave
  crust on and cut into cubes
2 cups sharp cheese
1 tsp salt

1 tsp dry mustard
4 well beaten eggs
2 1/2 cups milk
Tabasco

Line buttered casserole with two slices of buttered bread cubes. Sprinkle 1 cup cheese, 1/2 salt, 1/2 mustard over that. Add rest of bread cubes, cheese and seasonings. Mix well beaten eggs with milk and tabasco. Pour over all. Let stand in refrigerator overnight. Take our casserole 1 1/2 hours to reach room temperature. Bake in 350° oven for 1 hour. Serve immediately. Serves 6.

LUNCHEON CUSTARD - W

Serve with a tomato or mushroom sauce to add distinction to this mild custard.

4 eggs, slightly beaten
1 cup milk
1/2 tsp salt
1/8 tsp freshly ground pepper

Pinch of cayenne pepper
1 tbsp minced onions
1 cup tomato sauce or
  mushroom sauce

Preheat the oven to 350˚. Butter four 1 cup molds and place them in the oven in shallow pan with 1 inch of hot water. Combine the eggs, milk, salt, pepper, cayenne pepper and onion. Divide the mixture among the molds and bake 25 to 30 minutes until set. Serve with a sauce. Makes 4 servings.

Tomato Sauce:

2 tbsps olive oil
3/4 cup tomato paste
2 1/2 cup peeled and chopped
  fresh tomatoes or canned
  tomatoes

1 carrot grated or 1 tsp sugar
1/2 tsp freshly ground pepper
1 tbsp basil, crumbled
5 tbsps butter
Salt to taste

Heat the oil in a heavy bottom sauce pan. Stir in tomato paste, tomatoes, carrot, pepper and basil. Simmer for 30 minutes. If the sauce is too thick, add a little water. Cook for 15 minutes more and then stir in butter and salt.

Bel Calas Tout Chaud

CHAPTER XI

"Bel Calas Tout Chaud"

(Breads, cakes, pie, cookies)

In the New Orleans of the 1800's, there were black women who were street vendors and their specialities were calas (pronounced col' ahs). They were out early in the morning so the man of the house could have calas with the morning coffee. The pastry was carried on their heads in a large wooden bowl covered by another, to keep them warm. They also carried a pint size shaker of confectioners sugar to sprinkle on the calas when they were sold.

In the same era came the coffee stands in the Quarter. Rose Nicaud was the most famous of these black women and she "bought" her freedom by selling her cafe-au-lait (coffee with whole milk in equal portions). Rose's place was the "in" place for members of first New Orleans families, rice and sugar planters and steamboat and railroad men.

From these women came our still famous Louisiana coffee houses. This chapter deals with breads and cakes and such famous recipes as calas, shortnin' bread and custard pies.

PICTURE EXPLANATION

The girls are intrigued by the "calas lady" and especially by what is in the bowl balanced gracefully on her head. They would wait, not so patiently, with the cook for the calas to start the day off right!

CALAS TOUT CHAUD - B

1 cup sugar
1 cup boiled rice
2 tsps baking powder

2 eggs, separated
2 cups flour

Mix the yolks of the eggs with sugar, flour, baking powder, and rice. Beat the egg whites till fluffy and add to mixture. Drop mixture by spoonfuls into deep, hot grease. They will come out golden brown, light, and delectable. Drain on paper towel and sprinkle with powdered or granulated sugar. Serve hot.

HOW TO SEASON FLOWERPOTS
FOR BAKING - B

Have you ever tried baking bread in a crockery flowerpot? Proper seasoning for baking in a flowerpot is very important. First, soak new flowerpots for 1 hour in warm water. Dry completely and coat inside heavily and completely with cooking oil. Bake in a 325°F oven for 30 minutes, coating with oil several times. Grease and flour or spray with a prepared oil or no stick coating before baking. The more you use your pots, the less chance of sticking will occur. Most common breads can be used, but yeast breads are best and work well in clay pots. Try a variety of pot sizes for different white breads, potato bread and whole wheat bread. It looks good in a country setting of a table and you can use other size clay flowerpots for cheeses or butter.

BIBBY'S HOLIDAY DRESSING - W

3 tbsps oleo or butter
2 med chopped bell peppers
2 med chopped yellow onions
4 stalks chopped celery
4 chopped green onions
4 or 5 sprigs chopped parsley
2 boxes Jiffy cornbread mix

2 boxes Kellogg's Herb
  seasoned croutons
1 chopped, hard boiled egg
1 egg
Drippings from meat or chicken
  bouillon cubes
Salt, pepper, & red pepper to taste

Make cornbread the day before and let sit. In oleo or butter, sauté peppers, onions, celery, and green onions till slightly limp. In large mixing bowl, combine crumbled cornbread and croutons. Add sauteed vegetables and chopped hard boiled egg to above and toss lightly. Then add the whole egg and mix. Add 2 cups of drippings or 2 cups of hot bouillon made with 3 chicken bouillon cubes. Mix in liquid to make a moist but not juicy dressing. If too dry, add more juice; if too moist, add bread crumbs. Season to taste with salt, pepper, and red pepper. Put in baking dish and cover with top or foil and bake at 300° till warmed through, approximately 20 to 30 minutes. If gravy is made in time, put it on top of dressing before putting dressing in oven. If not, add it on top after taking dressing from oven.

REFRIGERATOR ROLLS - B & W

2 cakes yeast
1/2 cup lukewarm water
7 1/2 cups sifted flour
3/4 cup shortening
1 cup boiling water or
  scalded milk

2 eggs, beaten
3/4 cup sugar
2 tsps salt
1 cup cold water

Combine shortening and boiling water, stirring until shortening is melted. Combine egg, sugar, and salt. Beat in cold water. Soften yeast in lukewarm water. Combine the 3 mixtures and add flour. Cover and chill overnight. Shape and let rise. Bake as for standard rolls. Makes 36.

BREAD - B & W

Melt 4 tablespoons Crisco and put aside to cool. Mix 1 cup buttermilk, 1 1/2 teaspoons salt, 4 tablespoons sugar, 1/2 teaspoon soda, 1 teaspoon baking powder, and 1 dissolved yeast cake in 1 cup lukewarm water. Mix together and add 4 1/2 cups flour and shortening. Put in warm place till rises to double size. Work in 1/2 cup flour. Put in 2 well greased loaf pans, cover with cloth and let rise to top of pans. Bake for 40 minutes at 350°.

YEAST CORN BREAD - B

1/2 cake yeast
1/4 cup lukewarm water
1/2 cup corn meal
1 3/4 cups boiling water

1 1/2 tsps salt
2 tbsps sugar
1 tbsp shortening
2 3/4 to 3 cups sifted flour

In a large bowl, soften yeast cake in lukewarm water. Cook corn meal in water for 10 minutes. Add salt, sugar, and shortening. Cool until lukewarm, stirring occasionally to prevent a film. When cool, add softened yeast and beat well. Add flour and mix well. Knead, using as little flour on board as possible. Put into a greased bowl and let rise until almost double in bulk. Knead down and let rise again. Shape into loaves, place in pan, and let rise until it has almost doubled in bulk. Bake as for standard white bread. Makes 2 loaves.

MEXICAN CORN BREAD - W

Beat 2 eggs slightly. Add 1 cup sour cream, 1/2 cup salad oil, and 1 cup cream style corn. Stir together 1 1/2 cups white meal, 1 teaspoon salt, and 3 teaspoons baking powder. Add to first mixture and fold in 1/2 tablespoon minced hot peppers. Grease baking pan and heat it. Pour in 1/2 mixture, sprinkle with 1/2 cup grated sharp cheese, and put rest of batter on top. Sprinkle 1/2 cup grated sharp cheese over mixture. Bake for 1 hour at 350°.

TOP OF THE STOVE
FRIED CORN BREAD - B

1 1/2 cups corn meal
2 cups sifted flour
3 tsps baking powder
1 tbsp sugar

1 tsp salt
2 cups boiling water
1 1/2 cups milk
2 eggs, beaten

Mix all dry ingredients together, then sift. Beat eggs and add milk and water. Add a little dry ingredients into milk mixture, slowly beating as you add it, until all have been mixed. With 1 tablespoon cooking oil in frying pan, scoop out large serving spoons of batter and fry on both sides until golden brown. Serve hot with anything. Best with syrup.

MEXICAN CORNBREAD - B & W

1 cup yellow corn meal
1/4 cup flour
2 eggs, beaten
1 cup sweet milk
1/2 tsp soda
3/4 tsp salt

1 can cream style corn
1/2 lb ground beef
1 med onion, chopped
1/2 cup bacon drippings
2 Jalapeno peppers
1/2 cup grated cheese

Combine meal, flour, salt, soda, and milk. Add corn, and bacon drippings. Brown meat and drain. Chop onion, Jalapeno peppers, and grated cheese. Set aside. Cover bottom of skillet with small amount of oil. Sprinkle with a little meal and heat. Pour in 1/2 of the batter. Sprinkle cheese, meat, onion, and peppers. Add rest of the batter. Bake for 45 to 50 minutes in 350° oven.

PIE'S HOMEMADE BISCUIT MIX - W

6 cups all purpose flour
3 tablespoons baking powders
1 tablespoon salt

1 cup crisco (I use Butter
Flavor)

In a large bowl put all ingredients, and with your hands mix together until it forms fine particles. Store in a tight container and use as needed. Makes about 7 cups.

To make biscuits:

Use desired amount of mix. Mix with ice water or milk and mix till a soft dough. Drop on floured board and roll and put down on an ungreased sheet. Bake at 450 degrees for 12 to 15 minutes or until golden brown.

From Pie Hutchins

BROWN SUGAR BREAD - B

3/4 cup sugar
2 cups flour
2 tsps baking powder
1/4 tsp salt
1/2 cup brown sugar

2 tbsps butter or butter
    substitute
1 egg, well beaten
3/4 cup milk
1/3 tsp cinnamon

Cream sugar and 1 tablespoon butter. Add egg and milk; mix well. Add flour which has been sifted, measured, and sifted again with baking powder and salt. Pour into well oiled pan and sprinkle with brown sugar. Sprinkle with cinnamon and dot with butter. Bake in hot oven at 435°.

COUNTRY FRIED CAKES - B & W

1 cup light cream
2 beaten eggs
1/2 tsp salt

1 tbsp sugar
2 cups sifted enriched flour
1/2 cup butter

Combine cream, eggs, sugar, and salt; mix well. Add flour to make a soft dough and turn out on a floured board. Dot dough with butter and with the hand, work into the dough. The butter should be firm, but not hard. Chill dough in refrigerator for 1 hour, then roll out 1/8 inch thick. Cut in any desired shape, making a 1/2 inch gash through the center of each. Fry in deep fat (370°F). Drain on brown paper bag and roll in brown and white sugar while still hot. Makes about 36.

FIG BREAD - B

1 egg
1/2 cup brown sugar
1 cup buttermilk
1 cup sifted flour
1 tsp baking soda
1/2 tsp salt
1 cup rolled oats (quick or
   old fashioned, uncooked)

1 cup chopped, dried figs
2 cups chopped nuts or pecans
2 tbsps chopped orange peel
1/4 cup melted butter or
   margarine

Beat egg until light; add sugar, gradually beating until fluffy. Add buttermilk. Sift together flour, soda, and salt and add egg mixture, stirring lightly until combined. Fold in rolled oats, figs, nuts, and orange peel. Lightly stir in melted butter or margarine. Bake in greased waxed paper lined bread pan (1 lb size) in oven at 350° for about 1 hour. Touch in middle with toothpick to see if done. If toothpick comes out clean, bread is done. Cool. Slice, then serve with favorite spread or use this suggested glaze over it. Glaze: 1 cup confectioner's sugar and 1 1/2 tablespoon orange juice. Poke holes in bread and pour over it.

ICING

ICING FOR TWO PIES - B & W
MERINGUE

Put 4 or 5 egg whites in a bowl with a pinch of salt. Beat till stiff. Add 1/4 cup sugar and continue to beat till smooth. Divide this on the 2 pies and bake at 450° for 5 to 8 minutes or until golden brown. Remove and let cool. Enjoy.

CARAMEL ICING - W

2 cups brown sugar
1 cup granulated sugar
1/8 tsp baking soda

3/4 cup cream
1 egg white

Combine sugar, soda, and cream. Cook, stirring constantly to 238° or until a small amount forms a soft ball when dropped into cold water. Cool to lukewarm without stirring, but until creamy. Add unbeaten egg white and beat until enough to spread. Will frost 3 (8 inch) layers.

DIVINTY ICING - B & W

1 1/2 cups sugar
6 tbsps water
1/8 tsp cream of tartar

2 egg whites, stiffly beaten
1 tbsp vanilla

Combine sugar, water and cream of tartar. Cook without stirring to 238°F or until a small amount forms a soft ball when dropped into cold water. Pour 1/3 of the syrup in a fine stream over stiffly beaten egg whites while beating constantly. Cook remainder of syrup to 248° F or until a small amount forms a firm ball when dropped into cold water. Remove from heat and pour 1/2 of the remaining syrup in a fine stream into the icing mixture while heating constantly. Cook remaining syrup to 268°F or to the hard ball stage. Remove from heat and pour the last of the syrup in a fine stream into the icing, heating thoroughly. Add flavoring and heat mixture until thick enough to spread. Covers 2 (9 inch) layers.

COCONUT CREAM FROSTING - B

1 cup heavy cream
1/2 tsp vanilla

3 tsps confectioner's sugar, sifted
1 cup grated coconut

Whip cream until stiff. Add vanilla and fold in sugar. Spread between layers and over top of cake. Sprinkle with coconut. Will frost 2 (8 inch) layers.

UNCOOKED CHOCOLATE FROSTING - W

1 egg white, beaten
1/2 cup butter
3 ozs chocolate squares
1/4 tsp salt

3 cups confectioner's sugar, sifted
5 tbsps cream or evaporated milk
1 tsp vanilla

Heat butter and chocolate over hot water until chocolate is melted. Stir until smooth; then add salt, sugar, and cream, beating until smooth and blended. Stir in beaten egg white and flavoring and beat until cool and thick enough to spread. Will cover 2 (9 x 9 inch) layers.

CAKES

VANILLA COCONUT PECAN CAKE - B

2 cups sugar
2 sticks butter or oleo
1 (12 oz) package vanilla wafers
1/2 cup milk

1 (7 oz) package Angel flake
  coconut
1 cup chopped pecans
6 eggs

Preheat oven to 300°. Heavily grease a tube pan. Cream butter and sugar until really fluffy and add eggs one at a time and beat between each egg. Mix crushed wafers; add milk, coconut, and pecans to batter. Mix well. Bake for 90 minutes. Let cool at least 1 hour.

SALLY'S COFFEE CAKE - W

Cream 2 sticks oleo with 2 cups sugar. Add 2 eggs, one at a time and beat well. Add 2 cups sifted flour, 1 1/2 teaspoons baking powder, and 1 teaspoon salt to egg/sugar mixture. Fold in 1 teaspoon vanilla and 1/2 pint sour cream by hand. Grease bundt pan with Crisco and flour lightly.

1 cup chopped pecans
1 tsp cinnamon

4 tsps sugar

Put part of dough in pan, sprinkle filling over, and put remainder of dough on top of filling. Cook at 350° for 1 hour. Cool upright in pan. Can sprinkle powdered sugar over coffee cake after removing from pan.

BISHOPS CAKE - W

1/2 lb butter

2 cups sugar

Cream ingredients well and add 5 whole eggs, one at a time and beat. Add 1 tablespoon lemon juice and 1 teaspoon vanilla. Add 2 cups sifted cake flour. Put in lined and greased angel food cake pan and bake for 1 hour and 20 minutes in slow oven at 250°.

COCONUT CAKE - W

1 Duncan Hines yellow cake mix
2 packages frozen coconut
2 cups sugar

1 small carton sour cream
2 tbsps water (more if dry)

Prepare cake according to package in 13 x 9 inch pan. Combine remaining ingredients. Pierce cake with fork in several places. Ice cake with coconut mixture and refrigerate.

PATTY'S CAKE - W

1 package Duncan Hines yellow
  cake mix
1 package lemon jello
4 eggs

1/2 cup Wesson oil
3/4 cup apricot nectar
1 tsp vanilla

Put all together in mixer and beat well.

Icing:

1 1/2 cup powdered sugar
Apricot nectar

1 tsp lemon juice

Ice cake while hot. Bake in oven at 325 to 350° for 40 to 50 minutes.

SOUR CREAM LEMON PECAN CAKE - B & W

3 cups sugar
1 cup softened oleo
6 eggs, separated
2 ozs lemon extract
Small carton sour cream

3 cups flour
1/4 tsp soda
1/4 tsp salt
1 1/2 cups chopped pecans

Cream sugar and oleo. Add egg yolks, well beaten, lemon extract, and small carton of sour cream. Mix. Then add flour, soda, salt, and mix. Fold in 6 egg whites, stiffly beaten, and pecans. Bake in greased and floured pan for 1 to 1 1/2 hours at 325°. Remove while hot.

SOUR CREAM POUND CAKE - B

Cream 3 cups sugar and 2 blocks oleo. Separate six eggs. Add one yolk at a time, beating constantly. Sift together 3 cups flour (not cake flour) and 1/4 teaspoon soda. Add alternately 1 1/2 pints sour cream and 1 teaspoon lemon extract. Beat egg whites stiffly and fold in. Put in well greased, floured pan. Bake at 300° for 1 hour and 10 minutes.

Icing:

Mix 2 cups powdered sugar and enough whiskey to dissolve sugar. Let cake stand 5 minutes in pan from oven. Then pour icing over this.

POUND CAKE - B

8 eggs, separated
2 2/3 cups sugar
1 lb butter (no substitute)

3 1/2 cups sifted cake flour
1/2 cup coffee cream
1 tsp vanilla

Separate eggs. Measure sugar and set aside. Beat egg whites till soft peaks form, gradually adding 6 tablespoons sugar. Continue to beat till stiff. Refrigerate till needed. In large bowl, cream butter, gradually adding remaining sugar. Beat in well beaten egg yolks. Sift flour 3 times and add alternately with cream and vanilla. Beat till mixture is very light (about 10 minutes at low speed). Fold in egg whites by hand. Pour in lightly greased 10 inch tube pan at least 4 inches deep. Bake at 300° for 1 3/4 hours. Loosen around edges with spatula and put on serving plate. Serves 15 to 18 slices.

BUTTERMILK POUND CAKE - B

3 cups sugar
3 cups flour
1 cup shortening
2 sticks oleo

1 cup buttermilk
6 eggs, separated
1/2 tsp salt
2 tsps lemon extract

Blend sugar and oleo. Add egg yolks, one at a time. Add flavoring. Sift dry ingredients and add alternately with milk. Beat egg whites till stiff and fold into batter. Pour into greased, floured pans. Bake at 300° for 1 hour.

FRESH STRAWBERRY CAKE - W

1 box Duncan Hines white
   cake mix
1 box jello
1/2 cup mashed strawberries

1 cup cooking oil
4 eggs
1/2 cup water or milk

Bake in medium oven (350°).

Icing:

1 box powdered sugar
1 stick oleo

1/2 cup mashed strawberries

CHOCOLATE CAKE - W

1 cup oleo
2 1/2 cups sugar
2 eggs, beaten
3 cups flour
1/2 tsp salt

2 tbsps cocoa
2 tbsps vanilla
2 cups buttermilk
2 tsps soda

Cream oleo and sugar, adding eggs one at a time. Beat well; add milk and dry ingredients alternately. Bake in 4 greased, floured pans at 350° for 25 minutes.

Chocolate Frosting:

3 cups sugar
1/2 cup cocoa
1/4 lb oleo

3/4 cup sweet milk
1 tsp vanilla

Mix cocoa and sugar in saucepan; add milk and stir till dissolved. Let come to a boil. Cover pot and boil hard for 1 minute. Remove from stove and add vanilla and butter. Let cool. Beat until right consistency to spread.

COCONUT CAKE - B

3 cups sifted cake flour
3 tsps baking powder
1/4 tsp salt
1 cup shortening

2 cups sugar
1 tsp vanilla
4 eggs, separated
1 cup milk

Sift flour, baking powder, and salt together. Cream shortening with sugar and vanilla until fluffy. Add beaten egg yolks and beat thoroughly. Add sifted dry ingredients and milk alternately in small amount, beating well after each addition. Beat egg whites until stiff, but not dry. Fold into batter. Pour into greased pans and bake in 375° oven for 30 minutes. Makes 3 (9 inch) layers. Spread lemon or orange filling between layers. Cover top and sides of cake with seven minute icing and sprinkle generously with coconut.

SPICE CAKE - B

2 cups sifted flour
1/4 tsp salt
1 tsp baking soda
2 tsps cinnamon
1 tsp cloves

1/2 tsp nutmeg
1/2 cup shortening
2 cups brown sugar
3 eggs, separated
1 cup thick sour cream

Sift flour, salt, soda, and spices together 3 times. Cream shortening with sugar until fluffy. Add beaten egg yolks and beat thoroughly. Add sifted dry ingredients and cream alternately in small amounts, beating well after each addition. Beat egg whites until stiff, but not dry, and fold into batter. Pour into greased pan and bake in moderate oven at 350° for 40 to 50 minutes. Makes 1 (9 x 9 inch) cake.

ONE BOWL CAKE - B

2 1/4 cups sifted cake flour
1 1/2 cups sugar
3 tsps baking powder
1 tsp salt

1/2 cup softened shortening
1 cup milk
1 1/2 tsps flavoring, vanilla
2 eggs (1/3 to 1/2 cup)

Sift flour, sugar, baking powder, and salt together. Add shortening and a little over half of milk mixed with flavoring. Beat vigorously with spoon for 2 minutes (or 2 minutes with mixer at medium speed). Add remaining milk and unbeaten eggs. Beat 2 minutes with spoon (150 strokes per minute) or with mixer for 2 minutes. Turn batter into prepared pans. Bake at 350° for 25 to 30 minutes. Makes 2 (9 inch) layers.

SOUR MILK CHOCOLATE CAKE - B

2 cups sifted cake flour
1 tsp baking soda
1/2 tsp salt
1/2 cup shortening
1 1/2 cups sugar

1 tsp vanilla
3 eggs, separated
2 ozs chocolate, melted
1 cup sour milk

Sift flour, soda, and salt together. Cream sugar, shortening until fluffy. Add vanilla and beaten egg yolks and beat thoroughly. Stir in chocolate. Add sifted dry ingredients and milk, alternately in small amounts, beating well after each addition. Fold in stiffly beaten egg whites. Pour into greased pans and bake in 350° oven for 30 to 35 minutes. Makes 2 (9 inch) layers.

COUNTRY WHITE BUTTER CAKE - B

1 cup butter
2 cups sugar
1 tsp vanilla
3 cups sifted cake flour

1 cup milk
2 tsps baking powder
7 egg whites

Cream butter and sugar. Add vanilla. Sift flour with baking powder; add alternately with milk, beating well after each addition of flour. Beat egg whites until stiff, but not dry, and fold into cake batter. Bake in 3 greased 9 inch cake pans in slow oven (325°) for 35 minutes. Turn out on cake racks. When cool, frost with 7 minute frosting.

OLD FASHIONED POUND CAKE - B

1 cup butter
1 cup sugar
5 well beaten eggs
2 cups sifted cake flour

1/4 tsp mace
1 tbsp brandy or 1 tsp
   lemon extract

Cream butter thoroughly; add sugar gradually and continue beating well till light and fluffy. Add well beaten eggs and then beat about 10 minutes on electric mixer at moderate speed. Blend in flour, mace,and brandy using low speed. Pour into greased 9 1/2 x 5 1/2 x 2 3/4 inch loaf pan. Bake in slow oven at 325° for 1 hour and 15 minutes.

COUNTRY LEMONADE CREAM CAKE - B & W

3/4 cup sugar
1/3 cup butter
2 eggs
1 tsp frozen concentrated
   lemonade

1 1/2 cups sifted cake flour
2 tsps baking powder
1/3 tsp salt
1/2 cup milk

Sift sugar; cream butter and sugar together and beat until they are very light. Beat in eggs, one at a time. Add concentrate of lemonade. Resift flour with baking powder and salt. Add sifted dry ingredients to the batter alternately with the milk. Line 2 (8 inch) cake pans with wax paper. Pour batter in them and bake in moderate oven (375°) about 25 minutes. Cool the layers.

Lemonade Filling:

2 tbsps butter or margarine
1/4 cup sugar
3 tbsps flour
1/4 tsp salt

3/4 cup milk or warm water
2 egg yolks
3 tbsps frozen concentrate for
   lemonade

Melt butter and add sugar, flour, and salt. Stir in milk gradually and cook over boiling water until thickened. Add slightly beaten egg yolks mixed with concentrate lemonade and cook 1 minute longer. Cool before putting between cake layers. Put cake together and sift powdered sugar over the top. VERY, VERY GOOD!

SOUR CREAM SPICE CAKE - B

1/4 cup shortening
1 cup brown sugar
1 egg
3/4 cup thick sour cream
1 3/4 cups cake flour, sifted

1/4 tsp baking soda
2 tsps baking powder
1/8 tsp salt
1/4 tsp cloves
2 tsps cinnamon

Cream shortening. Add sugar gradually. Add egg and beat well. Add sour cream. Sift flour with baking soda, baking powder, salt, cloves, and cinnamon. Add 2 tablespoons of dry ingredients to the creamed mixture. Beat thoroughly. Add dry ingredients to the first mixture, beating well. Pour into a well greased and floured pan 8 x 12 x 2 inches. Bake in 350° oven for 30 minutes. Spread confectioner's sugar icing on top and sides. Serve with cold peaches or ice cream.

COFFEE CAKE - B & W

1 cake yeast
1/4 cup lukewarm water
1 cup scalded milk
2 cups (approximately) sifted flour
1 egg, beaten

2/3 cup sugar
3/4 tsp salt
4 tbsps shortening
Sugar and cinnamon

Soften yeast in warm water. Cool milk and add yeast and half the flour. Beat well and let rise until very light. Add egg, sugar, salt, and melted shortening. Mix thoroughly and add remaining flour. Let rise until almost double in bulk. Pour into shallow greased pan. When light, sprinkle thickly with sugar and cinnamon. Bake in hot oven at 400° for 20 to 25 minutes. Serve hot. Makes 1 (9 inch) cake.

SPICED TEA CAKES - B

3/4 cup shortening
2 eggs, well beaten
3/4 cup milk
1 cup sugar
1 2/3 cups sifted cake flour
1 1/2 tsps baking powder

1/4 tsp salt
1 tsp lemon extract
1/4 tsp vanilla extract
1/4 tsp nutmeg, cinnamon, cloves
Coconut

Mix all dry ingredients together. Sift flour, baking powder, salt, and sugar together. In a large mixing bowl, cream shortening and add beaten eggs, milk, extracts, and spices. Then add dry ingredients a little at a time, mixing well. Fill greased cupcake pans 2/3 full. Bake in hot oven at 400° for 15 to 20 minutes. Sprinkle with coconut just before cakes are done. Let cool. Makes about 2 dozen.

ANGEL FOOD CAKE
LEMON JELLO DESSERT - B & W

1 angel food cake (made or boxed)
1 cup sugar
2 cups milk
2 egg yolks, beaten
1 small package lemon jello
2 egg whites, beaten

1 pt whipping cream, beaten
1 med can crushed pineapple, drained
1 cup chopped pecans
1 small bottle Maraschino cherries

Cook sugar, milk, egg yolks in double boiler until creamy. Dissolve jello in creamy mixture while still hot. Fold in beaten egg whites. Place in refrigerator. When it begins to sit, fold in whipped cream, pineapples, pecans, and cherries. Break cake into walnut size pieces and layer in oblong pan. Cover with mixture. Add another layer of cake. End with mixture on top. Freeze overnight.

SOUR CREAM POUND CAKE - B

1 cup butter or oleo
3 cups sugar
6 eggs, separated
1/4 tsp soda

3 cups flour
1/2 pt sour cream
1 tsp lemon extract

Cream butter and sugar; add egg yolks, one at a time, beating well. Add soda to flour, alternating with sour cream. Fold in beaten egg whites. Bake at 300° for 1 1/2 hours.

NANNIE'S PINEAPPLE UPSIDE DOWN CAKE - W

1 cup butter
2 cups sugar
4 eggs
3 cups flour

1 cup milk
2 tsps baking powder
1/2 tsp salt

Mix all together and have ready to pour in the following mixture. Take 1 cup brown sugar and melt in iron skillet. Add 2/3 stick butter and 4 tablespoons whipping cream or undiluted evaporated milk. Stir till smooth and add 1 large can of crushed pineapple. Pour cake batter into mixture and bake in slow oven of 350° for about 30 minutes.

FIG CAKE CLEMENTINE - B & W

Silver Part: 2 cups sugar
2/3 cup butter
2/3 cup sweet milk
8 egg whites
3 tsps baking powder, sifted with 3 cups flour

Stir sugar and butter to a cream and add milk and flour. Then add the white of eggs. Place in 2 long cake tins. Bake in a slow moderate, preheated oven until done.

Gold Part: 1 cup sugar
3/4 cup butter
1/2 cup sweet milk
1 1/2 tsp baking powder

Sift baking powder in a little more than 1 1/2 cups flour, 7 egg yolks, thoroughly beaten, 1 whole egg, and 1 teaspoon allspice. Stir sugar and butter to a cream; add milk and flour. Add eggs, after beating together, and cinnamon. Place in long cake tin. Halve a pound of figs and sprinkle with flour and spread them on batter. Pour remainder of batter over this. Bake in slow oven at moderate heat until done. Cool and remove from pans. Place gold between silver and cover with frosting.

CHOCOLATE CHIP POUND CAKE - W

1 box yellow cake mix
1 cup sour cream
4 eggs
1 package vanilla pudding mix

1/2 cup oil
1/2 cup water
1 (6 oz) package chocolate chips
1 German chocolate bar, grated

Mix everything well, except chips and grated bar. Add chocolates and put in well greased pan. Bake at 350° for 50 to 60 minutes.

PIES

DEEP DISH FRUIT PIE - B

This is an easy dish to prepare at last minutes' notice of company coming. Any canned fruit can be used, peaches, apples, cherries, blueberries, etc.

Batter:

1 cup sifted flour	**1/4 tsp baking powder**
1/4 cup sugar	**1/2 cup milk**
1 egg	**1/4 tsp vanilla extract**

Beat egg and sugar; mix until smooth. Beat in milk, adding baking powder to flour. Add a little at a time until all flour is mixed into batter. Add vanilla and mix well. Grease side and bottom of pyrex deep dish and pour batter in. In a saucepan on top of stove, pour in 1 large can of your favorite fruit (peaches, apples, etc.), 1/2 stick margarine, 1/4 cup sugar and 1/4 teaspoon lemon juice. Bring to a rolling boil. Pour over batter. Bake in hot oven (375 to 400°) for 30-45 minutes until batter browns to a golden color. Serve with ice cream on top.

SOUR CREAM PIE - B & W

2 cups sugar	**2 tsps cinnamon**
2 (1/2 pt) cartons sour cream	**1 tsp cloves**
5 egg yolks	**1 1/2 cups raisins**

Use egg whites for meringue. Cook all together slowly. Stir while cooking. Put in baked pie shell and cover with meringue and brown at 425°. Makes 2 small or 1 large pie.

CHESS PIE - B & W

4 eggs	**3 tbsps buttermilk***
1 1/2 cups sugar	**Pinch of nutmeg**
1/4 lb butter	**1/2 tsp vanilla**
2 tbsps yellow corn meal	

Cream butter and sugar and add beaten eggs, corn meal, buttermilk, nutmeg, and vanilla. Pour in unbaked pie crust and bake at 300° till custard is firm.
*Make buttermilk by adding 1 tablespoon lemon juice to 1/3 cup milk.

RUBY'S CUSTARD PIE - W

2 cups sugar
1/2 cup flour
6 egg yellows
1/2 cup butter
1 pt milk

Pinch of salt
1 tsp vanilla
1 tsp butter
Flavoring

Cook in double boiler or Presto cooker. Heat milk in double boiler. Mix sugar, flour and beat in egg yolks. Add little milk before you add eggs. Put in Presto and stir till thick. Add butter before taking off fire. Add vanilla after taking off fire. Beat with Mixmaster. For chocolate pie: put 2 squares melted chocolate in wax paper and melt in double boiler. Add to sugar, flour, and eggs. Bake pastry at 300°. For meringue, bake in 400° oven for 8 to 10 minutes.

PECAN PIE - B & W

Unbaked pie shell
2 eggs, slightly beaten
1 cup Karo syrup
1/8 tsp salt

1 tsp vanilla
1 cup sugar
2 tbsps oil
1 cup nuts

After fixing crust, mix ingredients together, adding pecans last. Pour into pastry shell and bake in hot oven (400°) for 15 minutes. Reduce heat to moderate oven (350°) and bake 30 to 35 minutes longer. Filling should appear slightly less set in center than at outer edges.

PEACHEESY PIE - B

2/3 cup shortening
2 cups sifted self rising flour

6 to 7 tbsps peach syrup
2 tbsps butter

Preheat oven to 425°. Cut shortening into flour until size of peas. Sprinkle peach syrup over mixture, stirring until dough holds together. Roll out half of dough on floured surface to 1/8 inch thickness. Fit into 9 inch piepan. Fill with peach mixture. Dot with butter. Cover with cheesecake topping. Roll out remaining dough. Cut into circles. Brush with peach syrup. Arrange on topping. Bake at 425° for 10 minutes. Cover edge with foil. Bake at 350° for 30 to 35 minutes until deep golden brown.

PEACHES 'N CHEESECAKE FILLING - B

1 (1 lb, 13 ozs) can cling
   peach slices
1/2 cup plus 1/3 cup sugar
2 tbsps corn starch
2 tbsps corn syrup
2 tsps pumpkin pie spice

2 tsps vanilla extract
2 eggs, slightly beaten
1 tbsp lemon juice
1 (3 oz) package cream cheese
1/2 cup dairy sour cream

Peach Mixture:

Drain peaches; reserve syrup. Combine peach slices, 1/2 cup sugar, corn starch, corn syrup, pumpkin pie spice and vanilla.

Cheesecake Topping:

Combine eggs, 1/3 cup sugar, lemon juice, and 2 tablespoons peach syrup in small saucepan. Cook, stirring constantly, until thick. Soften cream cheese. Blend in sour cream. Add hot mixture; beat smooth.

APPLE PIE THE OLD FASHION WAY - B

6 apples
1 cup sugar
1/4 tsp salt
2 tbsps flour

1 tbsp butter
1/2 tsp nutmeg
1/4 tsp mace
1/2 cup seedless raisins

Use a 9 inch pie pan to bake pie in. Make your favorite pie crust recipe. Pare and slice apple. Sift dry ingredients together. Mix with apples. Line pie pan with pastry. Fill with apple mixture; dot with butter and cover with a top pastry. Scallop edges with a fork. Poke holes on the top with fork to permit pie to bubble. Bake in very hot oven (450°) for 15 minutes. Reduce heat to 350° and bake 45 minutes longer.

CHERRY CHEESE PIE - W

1 (9 inch) graham cracker crumb crust
1 (8 oz) package cream cheese, softened
1 (14 oz) can Eagle Brand sweetened condensed milk

1/2 cup lemon juice
1 tsp vanilla extract
1 (12 oz) can Comstock cherry pie filling, chilled

Combine soft cream cheese in large bowl. Add condensed milk; mix. Add lemon juice and vanilla extract and mix well. Place mixture in pie shell and add cherry pie filling on top of mixture. Chill in refrigerator for 1 to 1 1/2 hours.

BUTTERSCOTCH PIE - W

1 cup brown sugar
2 tbsps flour
1 cup cold water

3 egg yolks, beaten
2 tbsps margarine
1/2 tsp vanilla

Blend sugar, flour, and water and cook till thick. Add beaten egg yolks, melted margarine, and vanilla; simmer. Pour into baked pie shell and top with meringue of 3 egg whites and 6 tablespoons sugar, beaten till stiff. Bake at 400° for 8 to 10 minutes till meringue browns.

MOLASSES PIE - B & W

1 cup sugar molasses
1/2 cup sugar
2 tbsps butter (more, if needed)

Pinch of salt
3 slightly beaten eggs
1 tsp vanilla

Mix all ingredients and cook in unbaked pie shell for 10 minutes. Reduce heat to 350° and cook for 30 minutes longer or until it is cooked through.

AGGIE'S CHOCOLATE PIE - B

Heat 1 1/2 cups milk slowly in double boiler so as not to burn. Pour into mixture of 1 cup cocoa, 1 cup sugar, 1/2 cup flour, and 1 teaspoon vanilla. Stir till well mixed. Cook till thick, stirring all the time. Pour into baked pie shell; cover with meringue and bake in 350° oven till top is brown. Make meringue with 2 egg whites and 4 tablespoons sugar, beating till thick and fluffy.

FRUIT COBBLER - W

1 stick oleo
2 cups biscuit mix
2 tbsps sugar

2/3 cup light cream
1/3 cup milk
Fresh or canned fruit

Put oleo in baking pan. Heat oven to 375° and melt oleo in pan. Prepare biscuit mix with sugar, milk, and cream. Spread batter over butter, but do not blend. Mix fruit with 1/3 cup sugar and layer over batter. Do not blend. Bake in oven 30 to 40 minutes or until crust is browned and cake is done through. Serve warm with whipped topping or ice cream.

MA' TATE'S JAM CAKE - W

Cream 1/2 cup oleo, 1 cup sugar, 2 eggs, and 3/4 cup buttermilk. Sift flour and spices and add to creamed mixture. Mix 3 cups flour, 1/2 teaspoon salt, 1 teaspoon soda, 1 teaspoon cinnamon, 1/2 teaspoon cloves, 1/2 teaspoon nutmeg, 1 teaspoon vanilla, and 1/2 teaspoon lemon juice. Mix in with 1/4 cup flour the following: 1 cup chopped nuts, 1 cup chopped raisins, 1 cup jam or jelly, and 1 cup preserves. Bake in 2 or 3 layers. Ice between layers and top and sides. Icing consists of 1 cup milk and 2 cups sugar, boiled to a soft boiled stage. Put on layers while still warm to make cake juicy. Save 1/3 of icing mixture to cool and heat for icing top and sides.

270

COOKIES

PECAN STICK COOKIES - B

1 cup shortening
1 cup sugar
1 egg yolk
1 tsp vanilla
1 tsp nutmeg

1/2 tsp cinnamon
2 cups sifted flour
1 egg white
1 cup chopped pecans
1/2 cup lemon, peeled and grated

Cream shortening and sugar together. Add egg yolk and vanilla, nutmeg, cinnamon, and flour. Mix well. Spread in a pyrex greased baking dish about 1/4 inch thick dough. Beat egg white and brush over dough. Sprinkle with pecans or you can add them to dough. Bake for 30 to 35 minutes at 300°. Cut while warm in skinny strips. Remove while cooling. Makes 75 sticks.

SOFT SOUTHERN MOLASSES COOKIES - B

3 cups flour, sifted
1/4 tsp salt
1/2 tsp baking soda
1 3/4 baking powder
1/2 tsp raisins
1/2 tsp nutmeg

1 cup chopped pecans
1 1/2 tsps cinnamon
1/2 cup melted shortening
1 egg, beaten
1 cup molasses
2 tbsps warm water

Combine all dry ingredients, sifted together. In another large bowl, beat egg, molasses, warm water, and melted shortening; mix well. Then add dry ingredients to mixture, beating well. Let stand for 10 minutes at room temperature. Roll out on a floured cutting board. Cut in any angle you please, but make them cookie size. Bake in a hot oven (400°) for 15 to 20 minutes. Makes 4 dozen.

LEMON SUGAR COOKIES - B

2 eggs
1 cup water
1 tbsp milk
1/2 tsp lemon extract

2 1/4 cups sifted flour
2 tsps baking powder
1/2 cup shortening or butter
1/4 tsp salt

Cream shortening and sugar together, adding eggs and lemon extract. Then add sifted ingredients and add milk. Roll and cut and put on cookie sheet. Bake at 375° for 12 minutes. Sprinkle with powdered sugar. Makes 2 1/2 dozen cookies.

OLD FASHION VANILLA WAFERS - B

1/3 cup butter, softened
1 cup sugar
1 egg, beaten
1/4 cup milk

1 tbsp vanilla extract
2 cups sifted cake flour
2 tsps baking powder
1/2 tsp salt

Cream butter and sugar. Combine eggs, milk, and vanilla. Mix all dry ingredients together (flour, baking powder, salt) by alternating liquid to dry mixture. Mix until mixture is a cream. Place very thinly on greased cookie sheet. Bake at 325° until browned for 20 minutes. Makes 30(2 inch) cookies.

SUGAR PECAN CRISPS - W

3/4 cup butter
2/3 cup sugar
1 egg
1 tsp vanilla

1/4 tsp salt
1 3/4 cups sifted, all purpose
   flour
1/2 cup chopped pecans

Cream butter and sugar. Beat in egg, vanilla, and salt. Gradually stir in flour. Shape dough into 2 rolls, each 1 1/2 inch in diameter and 6 inches long. Roll in 1/4 cup pecans to coat. Wrap in waxed paper and chill. Cut into slices 1/4 inch thick. Place on ungreased cookie sheet and bake in moderate oven (350°) for 15 to 17 minutes till light brown. Makes 4 dozen.

6 LAYER SQUARES - W

1 stick oleo
1 cup graham cracker crumbs
1 can coconut

1 (6 oz) package chocolate chips
1 can Eagle brand milk
1 cup pecans, chopped

Put in a 9 x 12 pan in layers, melting butter first. Bake at 325° for about 35 minutes.

CRACKER TORTE - W

Beat 3 egg whites with 1 teaspoon cream tartar until dry. Add 1 cup sugar and 1 teaspoon vanilla. Crumble 16 saltine crackers and add 1 cup pecans or almonds. Bake for 20 minutes at 375° in an ungreased 9 x 9 pan. When cool, add 2 tablespoons pineapple preserves. Whip 1/2 pint cream and spread over. Sprinkle 1 package frozen coconut over and chill or freeze. Will keep in deep freezer as long as you want to leave it.

LIZZIES - W

1 1/2 cups flour
1/4 cup butter
1/2 cup brown sugar
2 eggs
1 1/2 tsps soda
1 1/2 tsps cinnamon
1/2 tsp nutmeg

1/2 tsp cloves
1 lb raisins
1/2 cup bourbon
1 lb pecans (2 1/4 cups)
1/2 lb citron, diced
1 lb cherries, cut

Cream butter and beat in sugar. Add eggs and beat well. Sift soda, flour, and spices. Add to butter mixture. Add bourbon and raisins. Add nuts and fruit. Drop by teaspoonfuls on a greased cookie sheet. Bake at 325° for 15 minutes. Cool and store. These freeze well. Note: May drop a bit of extra booze over them after they have cooled.

OLD FASHIONED BREAD PUDDING - B & W

7 slices bread or stale
    French Bread
3 cups sweet milk
2 tbsps butter

Raisins (optional)
3 eggs
1/2 cups sugar
1/2 tbsp salt

Put milk and butter on stove together and scald. Beat eggs and sugar together and add scalded mixture of milk and butter. Cut bread in small squares and put in buttered baking dish. Pour mixture over bread and bake in oven at medium heat for 45 minutes. Place baking dish in pan of water while in oven. See recipe for sauce below.

Sauce:

1 block butter
3/4 cup sugar
3 tbsps warmed cream
    or milk

3 or 4 tbsps bourbon whiskey
    or sherry

Cream together butter and sugar and add cream or milk. Flavor with whiskey or milk.

HELEN'S APRICOT DESSERT BARS - B & W

Combine 2 1/2 cups (2 20 oz cans) cooked apricots and 3/4 cup sugar and 1/4 cup apricot juice. Cook for 5 minutes until thickened. Sift together 2 cups flour, 1 teaspoon salt, and 1/2 teasoon soda. Cream 3/4 cup butter or margarine and 1 cup sugar. Blend in flour mixture. Add 1/2 cup shredded coconut and 1/2 cup chopped nuts. Press 3 cups of crumb mixture in a 9 x 13 pan. Bake at 400° for 10 to 15 minutes. Spread apricot mixture over hot crumb layer and sprinkle on remaining crumb mix. Bake 20 to 25 minutes more in 400° oven.

BAKED CUSTARD - W

Caramelize 1 cup sugar and add 1/2 cup boiling water. Simmer until no sugar granules remain. Pour 1/2 in ring mold. With pastry brush, coat sides of mold. Store remainder. Place 1 pint of half & half in top of double boiler and scald. Beat 1/2 cup sugar, 3 whole eggs, 2 egg yolks, and 1 tablespoon vanilla in bowl. Add milk and mix well. Pour in mold and bake at 350° for 1 hour. Put mold in pan of water while baking. Empty on flat plate.

YUMMY CHEESE CAKE SQUARES - W

1 (24 oz) package cream cheese, softened
1 cup sugar
5 eggs

1/2 cup lemon juice
1 tbsp vanilla
Graham cracker lined baking pan

Make graham cracker crust according to directions on package. Line bottom and sides of baking pan, 9 x 13 inches. Use large pan for party squares so they will be thinner. Bake at 375° for 6 to 8 minutes. Use a mixer to beat cream cheese, sugar and eggs until smooth. Stir in lemon juice and vanilla. Pour into graham cracker crust. Bake at 350° for 30 minutes (25 for larger pan). Remove from oven. Spread top with sour cream mixture consisting of 1 cup sour cream, 2 tablespoons sugar, and 1 teaspoon vanilla. Bake 5 minutes longer. Cool and cut in small squares. Freeze for several months if packaged in air tight, moisture/vapor proof containers. Makes about 90 (1 inch) squares.

FRUIT BARS - W

1 cup butter or margarine
2 cups sugar
3 eggs
1 tsp baking soda
2 tsps water
1 (8 oz) package chopped dates
3 cups sifted flour

1 tsp cinnamon
1 tsp nutmeg
1/4 tsp cloves
1/8 tsp salt
1 cup chopped nuts, walnuts,
  or pecans
2 tbsps sugar

Cream butter and sugar; beat until light. Add eggs one at a time, beating well. Combine baking soda and water; blend into creamed mixture. Add dates. Sift flour, spices, and salt. Gradually add to creamed mixture. Blend in nuts. Chill several hours. Shape into rolls 10 inches x 3/4 inch on floured board. Put 2 rolls on each cookie sheet and flatten with fingers to 1/4 inch. Sprinkle with sugar. Bake 15 to 18 minutes to a 350° oven. While hot, make diagonal slices 1 to 1 1/2 inches apart to form bars. Cool on rack.

SPICE BARS - W

1 spice cake mix
1/4 cup cooking oil
3 eggs

Raisins and nuts
Water

Bake 20 minutes. Glaze with mixture of 1/4 cup butter, 1 cup powdered sugar, 1 teaspoon vanilla, and water. Bake at 350˙.

MOM'S LADYFINGERS - B

1/2 cup sifted cake flour
1/2 cup sifted confectioner's sugar
1/2 tsp vanilla extract

1/4 tsp lemon extract
1/8 tsp salt
3 eggs, separated

Beat egg whites until stiff, but not dry. Beat in sugar gradually. Beat egg yolks until thick; fold into egg whites, then fold in extracts, flour, and salt. Shape into 4 1/2 inch fingers on baking sheet covered with heavy paper. Sprinkle with additional confectioner's sugar and bake in moderate oven at 350° for 10 to 12 minutes. Press together in pairs. Makes 12 cakes.

MOM'S GUMDROP BARS - B

2 cups cake flour
1/2 tsp cinnamon
3 eggs
2 cups brown sugar

1/4 cup evaporated milk
1 cup soft gumdrop candy,
   cut into small pieces
1/2 cup chopped nuts

Sift flour, salt, and cinnamon together. Beat eggs until light, then beat in sifted sugar. Add milk gradually. Add flour mixture in thirds, beating each time until smooth after each addition. Add gumdrops and nuts. Spread on greased pan and bake in oven at 350° for 35 minutes. Cut into bars 4 inches x 1 inch thick. Spread top with favorite frosting and decorate with sliced gumdrops. Makes almost 40 bars.

HOLIDAY SOFT BARS - B

2 eggs, well beaten
1 cup sugar
3/4 cup cake flour
1 tsp baking powder

1/4 tsp salt
1 cup raisins
1 cup finely chopped pecans

Beat eggs and add sugar. Sift all dry ingredients together and add raisins and chopped pecans. Add flour mixture to sugar and egg mixture. Beat until smooth. Line 6 x 11 baking dish with wax paper. Pour in dough 1/2 inch high. Bake at 350° for 40 to 45 minutes. Makes 24 1 x 3 inch bars.

BROWNIES - B & W

Melt (14 oz) package Bakers German Sweet Chocolate and 3 tablespoons butter over very low heat. Stir, then cool. Cream 1 3 ounce package cream cheese with 2 tablespoons butter. Gradually add 1/4 cup sugar. Cream till fluffy. Blend in 1 egg, 1 tablespoon flour, and 1/2 teaspoon vanilla. Set aside. Beat 2 eggs till light colored. Pour batter over top zigzagging knife through batter to marble. Bake at 350° for 35 to 40 minutes.

COCONUT KISSES - B

1 1/3 cups can sweetened
   condensed milk
1 tsp vanilla extract
1/4 tsp lemon extract

1/2 cup chopped pecans
1/8 tsp salt
3 cups shredded coconut

Combine ingredients and drop from teaspoon onto greased cookie sheet. Bake at 375° for 10 minutes. Remove from oven and take off cookie sheet while hot. Keep separated on wax paper until cool. Place in glass cookie jar to keep fresh.

RAISED MUFFINS - B

1 cake yeast
1/4 cup warm water
1 cup scalded milk
3/4 tsp salt

4 tbsps sugar
2 tbsps shortening
3 1/2 cups sifted flour
1 egg, beaten

Soften yeast in lukewarm water. Add scalded milk to salt, sugar, and shortening. When lukewarm, add yeast and 1 1/2 cups flour. Beat thoroughly. When very light, add beaten egg and remaining flour. Mix well and let rise until doubled in bulk. Shape into small balls and place in greased muffin pans. Brush tops with egg whites, slightly beaten, and sprinkle with chopped nuts. Let rise and bake in hot oven at 425°. Makes 2 dozen.

CARAMEL LOUISIANA PECAN ROLLS - B

1/2 recipe standard roll
3 tbsps butter
1/2 cup brown sugar

3/4 cup chopped pecans
3/4 cup cooked fig preserves

When dough is light, roll out and spread with softened butter. Sprinkle with brown sugar and nuts. Roll up. Slice and place cut side down on greased baking sheet. Let rise. Bake at 400° for about 25 minutes. Makes 12.

MARTHA'S TEXAS DELITE - W

Crust:

1 cup self rising flour
2 tbsps brown sugar

1/2 cup pecans
1 stick oleo

Mix and press in 9 x 13 rectangular pan. Mix and layer in pan:

8 ozs cream cheese
8 ozs cool whip

1 cup powdered sugar

Mix 2 small boxes instant chocolate pudding with 3 cups milk and pour in pan. Spread 2 (8oz) tubs cool whip over all. Sprinkle with chopped nuts and cherries. Chill for 1 hour.

MILLION DOLLAR COOKIES - B

1 cup shortening
1/2 cup white sugar
1/2 cup brown sugar
1/4 tsp soda
1/4 tsp salt

1/2 cup chopped nuts
2 cups flour
1 egg
1 tsp vanilla

Cream together sugar and shortening. Add 1 well beaten egg and dry ingredients, and nuts and vanilla. Form into small walnut size balls. Roll in granulated sugar. Dip glass in sugar and press cookies. Bake at 350° for 10 to 12 minutes.

MAMA'S TEA TIME TASSIES - W

Pastry:

1 (3 oz) package cream cheese
1/2 cup oleo or butter (1 stick)

1 cup sifted flour

Soften cheese and butter to room temperature. Mix in flour. Roll into balls the size of marbles. Chill for 1 hour. Press into small baking forms.

Filling:

Beat together 1 tablespoon soft butter, 3/4 cup brown sugar, 1 egg, 1 teaspoon vanilla, and a dash of salt. Cover dough with broken pecans. Put 1 teaspoon filling over pecans and top with pecan halves. Bakes at 325° for 25 minutes.

PECAN CRESCENTS - W

2 cups unsifted all purpose flour
1 cup oleo, softened
1 cup ground pecans
1/2 cup unsifted confectioner's
** sugar**

1/8 tsp salt
3/4 tsp vanilla extract
1/4 tsp almond extract

Vanilla Syrup:

Vanilla bean, cut up
2 cups sifted confectioner's sugar

Combine flour, butter, nuts, 1/2 cup sugar, salt, and extracts. Mix with hands till thoroughly combined. Refrigerate, covered, for 1 hour. Make vanilla syrup. In food processor, combine vanilla bean and 1/4 cup sugar and blend. Combine with rest of sugar. Preheat oven to 375°. Shape cookies in balls and then roll. Place 2 inches apart on ungreased sheet. Curve each to make crescents.

TEA CAKES FOR 100 - W

3 cups butter or oleo
1 qt sugar
8 eggs
2 1/4 qts flour

3 1/3 tbsps baking powder
2 tsps salt
2 tbsps vanilla

Cream butter and sugar. Add eggs and beat till well blended. Add flour, baking powder, salt, and vanilla to cream mixture. Mix well. Drop cookies on greased cookie sheet. Bake at 375° for 10 to 12 minutes.

TEA CAKES - W

1 cup margarine or butter, melted
2 cups sugar
3 eggs
4 tbsps milk

1 tsp vanilla
3 tsps baking powder
2 3/4 cups flour

Mix first five ingredients together; then stir in flour and baking powder. Drop by teaspoonfuls. Pat down to form cake. They may be cooked on ungreased cookie sheet. Cook at 350°.

OLD FASHIONED TEACAKES - B

1 cup sugar
1/3 cup shortening or lard
1 egg
1/2 tsp nutmeg
1/2 tsp vanilla

2 1/3 cups all purpose flour,
    sifted before measuring
1/4 tsp salt
1/3 tsp soda
1/3 cup buttermilk

Grease baking sheet lightly. Start oven ten minutes before baking. Set to moderately hot (425°F). Measure sugar and shortening into mixing bowl and grease well. Add egg and beat until smooth and fluffy. Stir in nutmeg, vanilla, and salt. Stir soda into buttermilk and add flour and buttermilk, alternating in 2 or 3 portions, beginning and ending with flour. Stir gently until just smooth between additions. Remove 1/3 of dough at a time to a floured pastry cloth and roll out about 1/8 inch thick. Sprinkle lightly with sugar and cut with 1/2 inch cutter. Lift out with pancake turner onto baking sheet. Bake for 8 to 10 minutes. Makes 36 teacakes.

Glace A La Vanille

CHAPTER XII

"Glace a la Vanille"

(desserts, candies)

Also in eighteenth century New Orleans, one found the ice cream peddler—a black man who balanced a gallon freezer on his head and sold custard ice cream on the streets. He had a big spoon, a glass and a small spoon. After he served sidewalk customers and they had finished, he wiped the glass and spoons with a rag he draped over his left arm, then went on his way.

The more discriminating customers, adults and children, would bring their own container and spoon and he would serve them with a scoop from a big spoon.

This chapter deals with desserts from old time custard ice cream to more fancy ones.

PICTURE EXPLANATION

The day the ice cream man came by was always a special day, for it was a rare treat. Here, Ethel pictures our little girls, with money in hand, ready to try the ice cream.

FRENCH CUSTARD ICE CREAM - W

4 cups heavy cream   1 1/2 cups sugar
6 egg yolks   Flavoring to taste

While bringing cream to a boil, whisk sugar and egg yolks in bowl till thick. Carefully whisk in boiling cream. Return to heat and stir over low heat till mixture is slightly thickened and custard coats spoon. If mixture curdles slightly, pass through fine sieve. Add flavoring. Cover and chill up to 24 hours. Churn and freeze as directed in ice cream freezer. Makes 1 quart.

OLD TIME FREEZER CUSTARD ICE CREAM - W

Scald one quart milk and one cup cream together. Add one cup of sugar, 3 eggs, and one tablespoon flour beaten together. Cook mixture 20 minutes. When cool, flavor and freeze.

For vanilla: add 1 teaspoon vanilla to mixture.

For fruit: add 1 cup of any well mashed fruit (figs, peaches, strawberries)

For chocolate: melt 2 squares chocolate with 1/2 teaspoon cinnamon, 1 tablespoon sugar, and 2 tablespoons milk. Add to basic custard while custard is hot and beat with egg beater.

SPANISH FLAN - W

1 can condensed milk   1 tsp vanilla
1 cup sugar   1 cup evaporated milk
6 eggs (4 whole and 2 yolks)

Preheat oven to 375°. Caramelize sugar for bottom of mold. Make a syrup of 1 cup sugar and 3/4 cup water. Boil for 5 minutes. Add condensed milk, eggs, vanilla, and evaporated milk. Pour mixture in a pan or mold and put in another pan with water in the bottom. Bake at 375° for 45 minutes.

KAT'S GELATIN COOL WHIP DESSERT - W

2 packages unflavored gelatin
1/2 cup cold water
1 cup boiling water

1 pt sherbert (any flavor)
1 (9 oz) carton cool whip

Put gelatin in a large mixing bowl. Sprinkle 1/2 cup cold water over it and let it sit for 1 minute. Then pour 1 cup boiling water over it and stir till well dissolved. Add 1 pint of sherbert and mix well with wire whisk. Add cool whip and mix well again. Add food coloring of choice and spoon mixture into dessert glasses. Place in refrigerator and leave till serving time. Serves 6. To double, use a 12 ounce carton of cool whip.

STRAWBERRY DESSERT - W

1 box white cake mix
1 lg box strawberry jello

1 box frozen strawberries
1 lg cool whip

Use about a 13 x 9 inch cake pan. Mix cake and cook according to directions on box. While cake is cooking and just before it is done, pour 2 cups boiling water on strawberry jello. When cake is done, take a fork and stick it as full of holes as you can. With a tablespoon, pour the hot jello over the hot cake. It will absorb the liquid. Cool cake and refrigerate. When ready to serve spread with cool whip and top with strawberries. Refrigerate.

CHARLOTTE RUSSE - W

1 1/2 dozen ladyfingers, halved
2 1/2 tsps gelatin, soaked in 1/4
  cup cold water, then dissolved
  in 1/2 cup boiling water
2/3 cup sugar

1 pt whipping cream
1 oz sherry or whiskey
  (optional)
4 eggs separated

Heat egg yolks with sugar till very light, adding flavoring, gelatin, and cream. Fold in egg whites, beaten stiff. Line large bowl with ladyfingers and pour mixture over this or make individual servings. Chill several hours before serving.

NEW ORLEANS BABA - W

2 eggs
1/2 cup sugar
1 cup flour, sifted

1 1/2 cups water
1 cup sugar
2 ozs rum

Beat eggs and sugar until light and frothy. Mix well with flour. Pour into buttered molds or paper cups. Bake at 350° for 15 to 20 minutes. Make syrup of sugar and water and bring to a boil. Add rum to syrup and pour over cakes until they are thoroughly soaked. Decorate with whipped cream. Yields 6 to 8 babas.

CHOCOLATE FONDUE - W

8 squares (8 ozs) semi-sweet
  chocolate
1 (15 oz) can sweetened
  condensed milk

1/2 cup milk
Orange liqueur, creme de menthe
  or plain mint flavoring

In a saucepan, melt chocolate. Stir in condensed milk and plain milk till well blended. Heat thoroughly. Add liquor or mint flavoring and pour in fondue pot. Place over heat. If it thickens, add more milk. Use as a dip for angel food squares, banana or pineapple chunks, or strawberries.

LYNN'S MERINGUE SHELLS - W

4 egg whites or 1/2 cup egg whites   **Pinch of salt**
1 cup sugar   **1 tsp lemon juice**

Beat egg whites till stiff. Add salt, sift in sugar, and add gradually. Beat well after each addition. When about half of sugar is added, add lemon juice, a little at a time, alternating with sugar. Beat till stiff and glossy. Drop by big spoon on brown paper. Bake in slow oven (275°) for 1 1/2 to 2 hours till slightly browned. Remove from brown paper and store in an airtight container. Cut top off each when ready to use, fill with ice cream and top with fruit. Makes 12 to 14 medium. Note: 4 egg whites should make 1/2 cup.

NANNIE'S CREAM PUFFS - W

1 cup water   **1/2 cup butter**

Bring to a boil and stir in 1 cup flour. Keep stirring until it forms a paste. Take off fire, let cool, and stir in 3 unbeaten eggs. Beat 5 minutes. Drop with tablespoon on greased pan. Cook at 375° for 15 minutes. Turn heat off and cook another 20 minutes. DO NOT OPEN DOOR.

Filling:

Let 4 cups milk heat till skim forms on top. Mix in 2 cups sugar, 1/2 teaspoon salt, 12 tablespoons flour, and 4 eggs. Mix well. Add 1 teaspoon vanilla and hot milk and cook till thick.

LEMON SAUCE - B

1/2 cup sugar
1 tbsp corn starch
2 tbsp lemon juice

Nutmeg
2 tsp butter
1 cup boiling water

In a double boiler, combine and mix the corn starch and sugar. Add the boiling water and a pinch of salt. Boil until thick and clear. Continue cooking over hot water for 20 minutes. Beat in the butter, lemon juice and nutmeg. Then mix in the grated rind of the lemon.

MAPLE SAUCE - B

1/2 cup water
1/2 cup walnut meat

1 lb (2 cups) maple sugar
or 2 cups brown sugar

In a double boiler put in the sugar, add the water slowly stirring constantly, until it reaches the thread stage (the water should be 230-235 F). Add the finely chopped walnut meat. This sauce can be used hot or cold over custard or ice cream.

RAISIN SAUCE - B

1/2 cup seeded raisins
1 cup boiling water
3/4 cup sugar
1/2 tsp lemon juice

1/4 cup chopped citron
1 tsp corn starch
1 tbsp butter

Slowly simmer the citron and raisins in water over a low heat until raisins are tender (about one hour). Sift together the sugar and the corn starch, then add the raisin mixture. Mix well and continue cooking for ten minutes more. Add the butter and lemon juice. Cook a few minutes longer and the sauce is ready for serving.

AUNT B'S MARSHMALLOW MINT SAUCE - B

1/2 cup sugar
1/4 cup water
1 egg white, beaten stiff

1 drop oil of peppermint
Green coloring
8 marshmallows

Cook sugar and water until it makes a thin syrup (220-230 F). Cut up the marshmallows in small parts and add to the syrup. Slowly pour the mixture over the egg white, gradually beat firmly. Add the peppermint and tint with the green food coloring to a delicate green. This sauce is good over chocolate ice cream or custard.

SOUTHERN ORANGE SAUCE - B

1 chopped mint leaf
5 tbsp butter
1/2 cup sugar
1/2 cup water

3 egg whites
2 oranges (juice from the oranges)
1 1/2 tbsp lemon juice

In a large bowl, cream the butter and sugar. In a double boiler add water and let it come to a rolling boil. Then in another bowl beat egg whites until stiff. Then add orange juice, lemon juice, mint, and continue beating until light and foamy.

STRAWBERRIES LOUISIANE - B

1 pt strawberries
1/2 cup sweetened condensed milk
1/4 tsp salt

1 tbsp lemon juice
3/4 cup pineapple juice
1 cup shredded coconut

Hull and wash strawberries. Cut into bite size pieces and place in a shallow bowl. Combine condensed milk, salt, lemon juice, pineapple juice and lightly mix until smooth. Mix this mixture with strawberries or place on top. Chill 2 hours or longer. Before serving, sprinkle coconut over the top. Makes about 6 servings.

SPICE PUDDING - B

1 egg, beaten
1/2 cup sugar
2 cups milk, scalded
1 1/2 cups bread crumbs
1 tsp cinnamon
1/2 tsp cloves

1/2 tsp allspice
1/4 tsp nutmeg
1/8 tsp salt
1 cup raisins (soak in hot water)
1 tbsp melted butter

Combine ingredients in order given, mix thoroughly. Pour into greased baking dish. Set in pan of hot water in oven at 350 degrees and cook for 35 to 40 minutes or until firm. Serve hot with a chocolate sauce or with raisin sauce. Makes 6 servings.

COCONUT CUSTARD - B

2 ripe coconuts
1 1/2 qts milk
2 tbsp flour
1/2 tsp salt
1 1/2 cups sugar

6 egg yolks
6 egg whites
1 1/2 cups heavy cream,
    whipped

Crack coconuts and reserve the liquid inside. Pare brown part of meat, grate or grind kernels in food chopper. Put these gratings in double boiler over hot water with milk. Cook 5 minutes. Cool until it can be handled; strain the coconut milk into a bowl through a fresh dish towel, wringing to extract each creamy drop. Discard grated kernels. Return milk to double boiler along with reserved coconut liquid. Mix together the flour, salt, and sugar. Sift the mixture into cooking milk and mix well. Cool about 2 minutes longer, stirring diligently. Beat egg yolks lightly. Stir into the coconut milk. Flavor to taste and cook 2 minutes more.

If it is to be frozen in refrigerator, first let mix cool. Put into trays, freeze for 2 hours, then mix in the egg whites, beaten stiff, and the whipped cream. Return to the refrigerator freezer the trays or dessert containers. Freeze till firm. Makes 8 to 10 servings.

REALLY GOOD!

CARROT PUDDING - B

You know those figs or other canned fruit you put up this summer. Well you can use them now. Just cut down on the molasses about half and do not forget to soak your raisins for best results. Other dried fruits can be used also. Soak as well.

1 1/2 cup bread crumbs
1/4 tsp salt
1 1/2 tsp baking powder
1 tbsp shortening, butter
   or margarine
1/2 cup grated carrots
1 cup molasses

1/2 cup raisins
1/2 cup figs
1/2 cup chopped nuts of
   your choice
2 tbsp lemon juice
1 tsp grated lemon rind

Combine salt and baking powder, mixing well. Add crumbs and add remaining ingredients, mixing thoroughly. Fill greased mold 2/3 full and steam 3 to 4 hours. Serve with raisin or lemon sauce. Serves about 6.

PEACH PUDDING - B

1/4 cup sugar
1/2 tsp salt
1/2 tsp vanilla
2 cups milk

3 eggs beaten
4 to 6 slices dry bread
6 peaches, sliced or 1 lg can
   peaches, drained

Beat eggs until smooth. Add sugar and beat again. Add milk, then mix together. Dip whole slices of bread into mixture. Place bread into greased baking dish. Make a layer of bread, then a layer of peaches until you fill the dish. Pour any remaining liquid over the top. Set dish in larger pan of hot water and bake in oven at 350° from 30 to 40 minutes or until firm. Serve hot with any pudding sauce. You can omit bread and use dry cake slices or ladyfingers.

BREAD PUDDING - B

2 cups day old bread, toasted on
    both sides and broken up into
    small pieces
4 cups scalded milk
2 eggs
1/2 cup sugar

1/4 tsp salt
1/4 tsp nutmeg
1 tsp vanilla
1/2 cup raisins, apples
    or peaches

Soak bread in milk until soft. Beat eggs and add sugar. Beat again adding salt, nutmeg, vanilla and fruit. Mix thoroughly with bread mixture. Pour into greased baking dish and set in pan of hot water. Bake in oven at 350° for 55 to 60 minutes or until knife inserted 1/2 inch into center comes out clean. Serve warm or cold with any sauce. Serves 8.

HARD SAUCE - B

1/3 cup butter
1 cup powdered, granulated
    brown or maple sugar

1 tsp lemon, vanilla or almond
    extract

Stir the sugar and extract together in a large boil. Cream the butter until very soft. Cover with a cloth and set in a cool place until ready to use. Any spice may be used in place of the extract such as nutmeg, powdered cinnamon or grated lemon rind. Use one or the other. Cream or milk may be added with more sugar to make more sauce. This sauce can be served with a hot pudding of any kind.

PRALINES - B

1 cup sugar
1 cup brown sugar
1/2 tsp baking soda
1/8 tsp salt

1 cup buttermilk
2 tbsps butter
1 1/2 cups chopped pecans
1 tsp vanilla

In heavy 4 quart saucepan combine sugars, baking soda, butter, milk, and salt. Stir over low heat until sugar is dissolved. Boil over moderate heat until candy thermometer registers 230° or syrup becomes thread stage. Remove from heat. Add butter, nuts, and vanilla. Beat candy until it starts to become thick and sugary. Then place saucepan over low heat to prevent candy from becoming too hard before it is dropped into patties. Dip by tablespoonfuls onto waxed paper, forming patties about 3 inches in diameter. Cool. Remove from paper and wrap individually in waxed paper. Makes about 15 patties.

POPCORN BALLS WITH SYRUP - B

1 tbsp butter
1 cup sugar
1 cup syrup

1/2 tsp salt
4 qts popped corn

Melt butter. Add sugar, syrup, and salt. Boil on medium heat until thread like. At 260°, pour over corn. Stir corn thoroughly while pouring syrup over it. Butter hands lightly. Shape into medium size balls. Makes 12 to 14.

PEANUT BRITTLE - B

1 1/2 cups shelled peanuts
1/4 tsp salt
1 cup sugar

1/2 cup corn syrup
1 1/2 tbsps butter
1/2 tsp lemon extract

Sprinkle nuts with salt and warm in oven. Put sugar, corn syrup, and warm in pan. Stir until it boils. Wash down sides with wet pastry brush and cook to 295° or until mixture is very brittle when tried in cold water. Add butter, lemon extract, and nuts. Pour into a shallow greased pan. As soon as it can be handled, turn the mass over and pull and stretch it out as thin as possible. Break into irregular pieces. Place in cans or in a box.

RICE PUDDING - B

1/2 cup cooked rice
1/2 qt milk
1/2 tsp cinnamon or nutmeg

1/2 cup sugar, white or brown
1/2 tsp salt

Mix all ingredients into a bowl. Pour into greased baking dish. Bake at 275° for 1 hour. Stir frequently the first half hour. Serves 6. Add 1/2 cup raisins or 2 eggs during the last half hour. Be sure to beat eggs slightly before adding. Soak raisins in hot water 1 hour. Drain and then add to rice mixture.

SWEET POTATO PUDDING - B

1 cup milk
1/2 cup sugar
1/2 tsp salt
3 tbsps butter
1 tsp nutmeg

2 cups mashed sweet potatoes
2 eggs, separated
1/2 cup raisins
1/2 cup chopped pecans

Peel and grate sweet potatoes. Beat eggs and add milk, butter, and salt. Stir in grated potatoes and add spices and pecans. Pour into a buttered dish. Bake at 350° for about 2 hours or until pudding is almost caramelized.

CAN'T FAIL DIVINITY - W

2 cups sugar
1/2 cup water
Pinch of salt
1 pt marshmallow creme

1/2 cup chopped nuts or
     candied fruit
Cherries, drained
1 tsp vanilla extract

Mix sugar, water and salt in saucepan and cook till small amount of mixture forms a hard ball when dropped in a cup of cold water. Place marshmallow creme in a mixing bowl and beat in hot syrup slowly. Continue beating until thick. Fold in nuts or fruits and vanilla and drop from spoon on wax paper. It really works and melts in your mouth!

PEANUT BUTTER BON BONS - B

2 cups smooth peanut butter
1/2 cup butter or oleo
4 1/2 cups (16 ozs) sifted
  powdered sugar

2 cups Rice Krispy cereal
1 (16 oz) package semisweet
  chocolate chips

In saucepan, melt peanut butter and butter. In large bowl, combine powdered sugar and cereal. Pour peanut butter mixture over cereal and sugar mixture. Blend together with hands. Form into balls of desired size. Chill till firm on cookie sheet. Melt chocolate pieces in double boiler. Put several tablespoons of paraffin in double boiler and wait for it to melt before putting in chips. Will not harden without paraffin. Dip balls in chocolate and roll. Lift out, using teaspoon. Put on wax paper to dry. Place in air tight tin.

CARAMEL CANDY - W

While 4 cups sugar and 1 cup milk are boiling, caramelize 1 cup sugar in skillet. Pour melted sugar in first mixture and cook till it forms a ball in water. Add 3/4 block of butter or oleo and beat till creamy. Chopped pecans can be added at this point. Drop on wax paper.

KAT'S TWENTY MINUTE MOUSSE - W

2 envelopes Knox unflavored
  gelatin
1/2 cup cold water
1 cup boiling water

2 cups (1 qt) sherbet, any flavor
1 container (9 oz) frozen
  whipped topping, thawed

In large bowl, sprinkle unflavored gelatin over cold water. Let stand for 1 minute. Add boiling water and stir till gelatin is completely dissolved. With wire whip or rotary beater, blend in sherbet till melted; blend in whipped topping. Put in food coloring the color of the sherbet, if desired. Stir till well blended. Spoon into dessert dishes and chill 15 minutes. Makes about 8 servings. Can make ahead and keep in glasses in refrigerator. Great after a large meal.

GREEN MINTY TOPPING - W

1 cup prepared whipped topping   Green food coloring
1/4 tsp mint extract

Mix all ingredients well and store in refrigerator. Makes enough topping for ten individual desserts or one large dessert.

NEVER FAIL 5 MINUTE FUDGE - W

2 tbsps butter
1/3 cup evaporated milk
1 1/3 cups sugar
1/2 tsp salt
2 cups miniature marshmallows

1 1/2 cups (16 oz package)
    semisweet chocolate pieces
1 tsp vanilla
1/2 cup chopped nuts

Combine butter, evaporated milk, sugar and salt in a saucepan over medium heat. Bring to a boil. Cook 4 to 5 minutes, stirring constantly. Start timing when mixture starts to bubble around the edges of the pan. Remove from heat and stir in marshmallows for 5 minutes. Place in buttered 8 or 9 inch square pan. Allow to cool and cut into squares.

NEAPOLITAN DELIGHT - W

2 cups peaches, cubed and drained
2 cups sugar
1 qt orange juice

3/4 cup apricot brandy
1/4 cup lemon juice

Stir and freeze. Serve with one tablespoon apricot brandy on top. Serves 8.

BROWN BETTY - B

1/3 cup butter, melted
2 cups bread crumbs
2 cups sliced apples
1/4 tsp cinnamon
1/4 tsp nutmeg

1/2 cup sugar
1/2 tsp vanilla
1/2 cup water
1 lemon, rind and juice

Mix butter and crumbs. Place alternate layers of crumbs and apples in buttered baking dish, using crumbs for first and last layers. Sprinkle each layer of apples with combined water, lemon juice, rind, sugar, and spices. Cover and bake in moderate oven at 350° for 30 minutes, then remove cover and bake an additional 45 minutes. You may use any fruit for this recipe. Serves about 6.

HOT LEMONADE SPICED FRUIT - B

2 (6 oz) cans concentrate lemonade
Water (2 lemonade cans full)
1/2 cup raisins, soaked in
   hot boiling water
4 pear halves

4 peach halves
2 tbsps cinnamon
2 tbsps cloves
2 bananas, cut in 2 chunks

Mix concentrate for lemonade with water and spice. Arrange well drained fruit in deep baking dish and pour the lemonade mixture over fruit. Bake in moderate oven at 350° for about 20 minutes. Serves 4 to 6. Serve with favorite sauce from one of our sauces in the sauce section.

COCONUT AND BANANA - B

1/2 cup shredded coconut
2 tbsps grated lemon rind or
   lemon juice
1/2 tbsp lime juice

2 tbsps butter or margarine,
   melted
4 firm ripe bananas

In a well greased baking dish, cut bananas crosswise or smaller. Baste with butter or margarine, then baste with juices and grated lemon rind. Sprinkle coconut over the bananas. Bake for 15 to 20 minutes in a 375° oven or until coconut is browned and bananas are tender. Pierce with a fork. To add color, add your pineapple, cherries, and serve hot with your favorite sauce.

Lagniappe

"LAGNIAPPE"

(leftovers, foreign foods, soul food)

In Cajun French, "lagniappe" means "a little something extra." Our chapter deals with just that!

Soul foods are basic foods from the black culture; leftovers are recipes to stretch the food dollar; and no Louisiana cookbook can be complete without foreign foods. In addition to Louisiana's first settlers of French, Spanish, Black, and Indians, there are colonies of Belgians, Czechoslovakians, Germans, Mexicans, Cubans, Filipinos and Orientals, to mention only a few. You'll find authentic recipes from the above cultures, all of which help make Louisiana cuisine colorful and delectable. Since we are both superstitious and don't like the number 13, this chapter, which is the last, will not be numbered. Just as the name implies, it is a little something extra!

PICTURE EXPLANATION

In our final chapter, Ethel pictures our girls tossing a blanket in the air filled with the ingredients that go into making our cooking "Colorful Louisiana Cuisine".

Leftovers have always been big in creole cooking and the thrifty cook takes advantage of all of these.

Leftover stale bread became toasted bread crumbs, stored in a jar for au gratin dishes. It was also used for making bread puddings and bread muffins. The true creole bread pudding was always made with stale French bread.

Leftover mashed potatoes were used for croquettes or quenelles. Cold boiled potatoes were used for french fries, country fries, potato salad, and casserole potatoes.

Leftover meats were used for making croquettes or boulettes.

Leftover turkey, chicken or rabbit was used in making gumbos.

Leftover rice was used for calas, puddings, and jambalaya.

Leftover vegetables were used for soup and casseroles.

Hambone was used for seasoning vegetables and dried beans.

LEFTOVER MEAT PIE

Dash of salt
2 to 2 1/2 cups cooked ground
  meat or ground steak, cooked
1/2 small carrot, grated
1 small potato, grated or finely
  chopped

1 tomato, mashed up
Pie crust dough for top and
  bottom crust

Mix meat, carrot, potato and tomato and salt. Line bottom of pie pan with bottom crust, spread in above ingredients with water to moisten. Cover with top crust and bake at 400 to 425° for 30 to 35 minutes or till done.

CREAMED TURKEY - B

1/4 cup fat (margarine or butter)
1/4 cup flour
3 cups broth and milk
2 cups cut up canned boned turkey

Salt and pepper to taste
1 cup cooked or canned peas,
  drained if you like

Melt fat in pan, stir in flour. Drain broth from the canned turkey and add enough milk to make 3 cups. (If peas are used, drain liquid from vegetables and add enough milk and broth to make 3 cups.) Slowly add milk and broth to flour mixture. Stir and cook over medium heat until mixture comes to a boil. Lower heat and cook until thick, about 3 minutes. Add turkey, salt, pepper and peas, if used. Heat. Serve over hot cooked bulgur, rice or toast. Makes 6 servings, about 3/4 cup each.

PORK AND RICE CASSEROLE - W

2 cups chopped cooked pork
1 can Rotel tomatoes
1 can tomato paste

Chopped onions & green peppers
1 can mushroom stems & pieces
1 cup cooked rice

Sauté vegetables and add tomatoes, paste, mushrooms and pork. Let mixture cook down and season with salt, pepper, cajun seasoning, oregano, bay leaf. Add rice to mixture and put all in casserole. Top with Italian Bread Crumbs and parmesan cheese. Bake at 350° for 20 to 25 minutes.

CREAMED CHICKEN & MACARONI - W

Melt oleo, add flour and make a white sauce. Add a cup of sour cream, pimentos, a small can of green peas and a small can of onions. Add a cup of chicken bouillon (made from cubes) and a can of cream of chicken soup. Cook till warm through. Add 2 cups cooked chicken and 2 cups cooked macaroni. Season to taste. Pour in casserole dish and top with mozzarella cheese and Italian bread crumbs. Cook in 350° oven 20 to 25 minutes.

TURKEY CASSEROLE - B

3 tablespoons chopped onion
1/3 cup chopped green peppers
3 tablespoons fat
1 tablespoon salt
6 tablespoons flour
1 stalk celery

1 1/2 cups milk
1 can cream of chicken soup
1 cup chopped turkey
1/3 cup grated cheese
1 recipe biscuits

Brown onion and green pepper in melted fat; add salt and flour. Blend until moistened; add milk and soup. Cook until bubbly hot and thick, stirring occasionally. Add turkey. Pour into greased baking dish. Roll biscuits to form rectangle 1/4 inch thick. Sprinkle grated cheese over dough and roll like jelly roll. Cut 1/2 inch thick, place on casserole. Bake in preheated oven for 15 minutes. Reduce heat to 425°F and bake until swirls are browned. Serves 6.

QUICK JAMBALAYA - B

1/2 cup butter
1/2 cup chopped onion
1/2 cup chopped bell pepper
1 clove garlic, chopped

2 cups diced ham
1 lb cooked, peeled shrimp
1 can tomatoes
2 cups precooked rice

Sauté vegetables in butter until soft. Add ham and shrimp and cook over low heat. Add tomatoes and seasoning. Cover and simmer for a few minutes. Stir well and add rice. Continue to simmer a short while longer. Sausage or cooked chicken can also be added.

COUS COUS

2 1/2 cups cornmeal
1/2 teaspoon salt
1 teaspoon baking powder
1/2 cup milk
1/2 cup water
1 tablespoon dripping from fried meat

Mix cornmeal, salt, baking powder together, add milk and water together, then pour over dry ingredients. Add drippings. Warm small amount of fat in a pan and pour in batter. Lower heat and stir constantly for about 15 to 20 minutes. Serve as a cereal with milk, can add sugar if desired.

For 5 years while I was managing the shopping center, we had an International Festival honoring the foreigners living in our area. A cookbook was published and from that came the following recipes that were prepared on our festival day.

ITALIAN MEAT SAUCE
Amerita Ladies Auxiliary

1 1/2 lbs ground beef
1 lg onion, chopped
2 cloves garlic, minced
1 cup seasoned bread crumbs
1 (1 lb) can tomatoes, cut up

2 (6 oz) cans tomato paste
1 tsp sweet basil
3 tbsps sugar
Salt and pepper to taste

Mix meat and bread crumbs together. Cook meat, onion, and garlic until meat is browned and onion and garlic are tender. Add remaining ingredients and 5 cups water. Bring to a boil, reduce heat and simmer, covered, for 2 hours. Remove cover, cook about 1 hour or until sauce is thick. Stir occasionally. Serve over hot spaghetti. Sprinkle with Romano cheese. Serves 6.

SAUSAGE AND CABBAGE DINNER
Belgian-American Club

1 head Savoy cabbage
1 tsp salt

2 lbs yard pork sausage

Preheat oven to 350°. Wash and chop cabbage. Cover with water, add 1 teaspoon salt and partially cook. Drain well. Place cabbage in baking dish and top with sausage. Puncture sausage skin in several places. Cover and bake for 1 to 1 1/2 hours or until sausage is done. Remove cover last 15 minutes or so, for sausage to brown.

VLEESKROKETTEN
(Meat Croquettes)
Belgian-American Club

4 tbsps butter
4 tbsps flour
2 cups milk or bouillon
1 lb chicken, pork or beef,
  cooked and cut finely

2 onions, chopped fine
1 lemon
1 tbsp parsley, cut fine
3 eggs
Crumbs

Brown the onions in butter. Dissolve the flour with the 2 cups liquid and add to onion to make a thick sauce. Stir in lemon juice and parsley. Remove from heat and let cool. Stir in the egg yolks and finely chopped meat. Spread mixture on a plate and refrigerate about 4 to 6 hours. Roll into balls. Beat egg whites lightly. Add 1/4 teaspoon salad oil and 2 teaspoons cold water; stir well. Roll balls in the egg white mixture, then in crumbs. Fry in deep fryer until golden brown.

POTATO CHEESE CROQUETTES
Belgian-American Club

2 lbs potatoes, peeled
2 1/2 tbsps grated parmesan
  cheese
2 eggs

Salt and pepper to taste
1/4 tsp nutmeg
1 tsp cooking oil
Crumbs

Cook potatoes with a little salt until done. Drain and let cool. Mash the cooled potatoes fine, or squeeze through colander. Add 1 egg, parmesan cheese, and seasonings. Mix thoroughly, spread out on a flat plate, and refrigerate for several hours. Beat the second egg lightly and mix in cooking oil. Form the potato mixture into balls or form into rolls the size of fingers. Roll the balls or fingers in the crumbs then lightly into the beaten egg and then again into the crumbs. Cook in deep fryer until golden brown. These crumbed croquettes can be frozen for several weeks and then deep fried.

CHESTNUT STUFFING
British Wives Club

2 lbs chestnuts
1 pt stock or milk
6 ozs bread crumbs
2 heaped tbsps chopped parsley
2 eggs, beaten

2 ozs shortening
A little grated lemon peel
Salt and pepper to taste
1 heaped tbsp sugar

Slit ends of chestnuts and boil in water, then shell and skin. Simmer in stock or milk till tender (about 30 minutes). Remove from pan and drain. Add crumbs, parsley, melted shortening, lemon peel, seasoning, and sugar. Bind with beaten eggs. Use to stuff neck of turkey, chicken, etc.

TOAD IN THE HOLE
British Wives Club

1 lb small pork sausage links
2 eggs
1 1/2 cups milk

1 cup flour
1/2 tsp salt

Pierce sausages with fork, place on a 13 x 9 inch baking pan, bake in a very hot oven (450°) for 15 minutes until brown, shaking the pan occasionally to brown the links evenly. Meanwhile, beat eggs with milk, flour, salt to make a light batter. Remove sausage from baking pan. Drain off all but 4 tablespoons fat. Pour the batter into the hot pan, quickly arrange sausages in the batter, return at once to the oven to bake about 25 minutes until crust is well puffed and brown. Serves 6.

SCONES
British Wives Club

3 1/2 cups all purpose flour
5 tbsps double acting baking powder
3/4 cup margarine
1 tsp salt

1/2 cup sugar
4 eggs
1/2 cup milk
1/2 cup golden raisins

Preheat oven to 425°. Grease large cookie sheet. In medium bowl, with fork, mix flour, baking powder, salt, and sugar. With pastry blender cut in margarine until mixture resembles coarse crumbs. Stir milk into remaining beaten eggs; stir this mixture into flour mix. Stir until well mixed. Add raisins. Turn dough onto floured surface. Lightly roll dough until 3/4 inch thick. Cut dough into 4 inch squares, then into 2 triangles. Place 2 inches apart on cookie sheet, brush with reserved egg and sprinkle on a little sugar. Bake 10 to 15 minutes until golden. Serve warm with butter, or split and fill with jam and whipped cream, if desired.

ENGLISH TRIFLE
British Wives Club

Sponge cake or ladyfingers
Sherry (if desired)
1 small package Jello (any flavor)
Whipped cream

1 small package vanilla pudding mix (not instant)
Jam (any kind)
1 can salad fruit

Split sponge cake and spread with any kind of jam. Place these in bottom and round sides of glass bowl. Make up jello, pour over cake, put in fruit and place in refrigerator till set. Make vanilla pudding, let cool, then pour over jello mixture. Put back in refrigerator until cold, then decorate top with whipped cream. NOTE: A little sherry may be sprinkled over the cake if desired, before jello is poured on.

BELGIAN MOLASSES COOKIES
British Wives Club

Cream together:
> **1 cup butter**
> **1 cup shortening**
> **1 cup sugar**

Add:
> **1 cup molasses**
> **1 tsp baking soda dissolved in a little hot water**
> **Approximately 4 1/2 cups flour**

Sift with half of the flour:
> **1 tsp nutmeg**
> **1/2 tsp cloves**
> **3/4 cup finely ground almonds**
> **1/2 tsp ginger**
> **1 tsp cinnamon**

Add flour to make a dough which can be worked into rolls for slicing. Let stand overnight in refrigerator and slice very thin to bake. Bake in a 350° oven for 10 minutes.

LANCASHIRE PARKIN
British Wives Club

1 lb oatmeal	**1/2 lb brown sugar**
2 tsps baking powder	**5 ozs black treacle (molasses)**
1 tsp ground ginger	**4 ozs syrup (karo)**
1/2 tsp salt	**1 egg**
1/4 lb butter	**Milk to mix**

Mix together oatmeal, baking powder, ginger and salt. Mix in butter. Beat egg well, mix in sugar, treacle and syrup and add to oatmeal. Add sufficient milk to make a soft mixture of slow pouring consistency. Grease small roasting tin or 2 (1 lb) bread tins well and half fill with mixture. Bake in top half of moderate oven (350°) for 40 to 50 minutes and cut in squares before it gets cold.

FELIXSTOWE CAKE
British Wives Club

1 cup water
2 cups dried fruit
1 cup brown or white sugar
3 ozs margarine
2 cups self rising flour

1 tsp mixed spice
1 tsp soda
Pinch of salt
1 egg

Put first four items in pan and bring to boil. Boil for 10 minutes. Cool, then work in rest of ingredients. Lastly, add beaten egg. Bake in moderate oven (320°) for 1 hour.

GINGER SNAPS
British Wives Club

4 ozs self rising flour
4 ozs golden syrup
Juice of 1/2 lemon

4 ozs sugar
4 ozs butter
1/4 oz ground ginger

Put the butter and sugar and lemon juice and syrup into a saucepan and melt them slowly. Sift the flour and ginger together and add to the ingredients in the pan, warm gently but do not cook. Remove from the heat and put teaspoonfuls of mixture on a well greased baking sheet three inches apart (about five will go on an ordinary baking sheet). Put into a moderately hot oven and cook till they are nicely browned. Leave for a moment before removing them from the tin, then quickly take them off, turn them over. and loosely roll them around the handle of wooden spoon. This must be done quickly as they soon begin to crisp. Refill the tin with more mixture and proceed as directed. Oven should be on 370° and place pan on middle rack.

YORKSHIRE PUDDINGS
British Wives Club

1 cup all purpose flour sifted
  before measuring
1/2 tsp salt
1/8 tsp pepper

2 lg eggs, at room temperature
1 c. milk, at room temperature
4 tbsps hot fat from roasting pan

Bake these individual puddings while the roast rests before carving. Make batter at least 30 minutes before baking, several hours ahead if more convenient. Mix flour, salt,and pepper in a medium sized mixing bowl and then make a hollow all the way to the bottom of the bowl. Break eggs into the hollow and pour in the milk. Beat eggs and milk with a fork; when mixed, gradually beat in the flour a little at a time until a smooth batter is made. Pour into a pitcher for easy pouring later; cover and let stand at room temperature. About 10 minutes before roast finishes cooking, heat a pan for 12 large muffins in the oven. When roast is done, remove from oven and set on a plate in a warm place. Remove muffin pan from oven and turn up oven to 450°. Spoon about 1 teaspoon of hot fat from the roasting pan into each heated muffin cup. Pour batter into cups, filling each one half to two thirds full. Bake about 10 minutes until puddings are puffed and begin to brown. Turn down oven to 375° and bake for 10 minutes longer, until well browned. Remove pan from oven and loosen puddings with a spatula or knife. Serve immediately.

SCOTCH EGGS
British Wives Club

1 lb sausage meat
8 hard boiled eggs
1/2 cup flour seasoned with
  1/2 tsp salt and 1/4 tsp pepper

2 eggs, slightly beaten
1 cup fine bread crumbs
1/2 tsp sage
2 tbsps finely chopped parsley

Combine sausage meat, 1/2 teaspoon sage, 2 tablespoons finely chopped parsley. Pat mixture into 8 rounds. Surround each hard boiled egg with a sausage pattie. Roll the eggs in the seasoned flour then in the beaten eggs and finally in the bread crumbs. Fry in deep hot fat for 10 minutes until the sausage is cooked. Serve hot or cold.

QUEEN OF PUDDINGS
British Wives Club

2 tbsps butter
2 1/4 cups milk
1/4 cup sugar
3 egg yolks

1/2 cup bread crumbs,
  freshly made
1/2 cup red raspberry preserves
Grated rind of 2 lemons

Butter a 8 inch pie plate. Place remaining butter, milk, lemon rind, and sugar in saucepan. Heat to simmering point. Remove from heat and cool to room temperature. Strain the milk and discard lemon rind. Stir in egg yolks and bread crumbs. Place in pie dish and bake 350° oven for 30 minutes. Spread pudding with preserves to prepare meringue. Beat 2 egg whites, 1/8 teaspoon salt, 1/8 teaspoon cream of tartar, until soft peaks form. Beat in 1/2 teaspoon vanilla and 1/2 cup sugar gradually. Spoon over pudding. Return pudding to oven and bake for 15 minutes until meringue is lightly browned.

SAVOURIES OF COLD MEAT
British Wives Club

1/2 lb cold cooked meat
  (beef, etc.)
1 fried or boiled onion
1 tsp Worcestershire sauce

1 lb cooked mashed potatoes
1 egg
Salt and pepper to taste
Bread crumbs

Bread crumbs, mince meat and mix with potatoes, chopped onions, pepper and salt, sauce and egg yolk. Make into patties, brush with beaten egg whites, toss in bread crumbs, and fry in hot fat to a golden brown.

SHRIMP CANTONESE
Chinese

3 cups hot cooked rice
12 ozs peeled, deveined raw
  shrimp, halved lengthwise
2 tbsps butter, margarine, or
  vegetable oil
2 cups diagonally sliced celery
2 cups sliced onions

1 qt (8 ozs) fresh spinach leaves
1 (16 oz) can fancy mixed
  Chinese vegetables
1/4 tsp pepper
1/4 cup soy sauce
1 1/4 cups chicken broth
2 tbsps cornstarch

While rice is cooking, sauté shrimp in butter for 1 minute or until shrimp turn pink, using a large skillet. Add celery and onions. Cook, stirring, for 2 minutes. Add spinach and Chinese vegetables which have been rinsed and drained. Cover and cook 1 minute. Blend pepper, soy sauce, chicken broth, and cornstarch. Stir into shrimp/vegetable mixture. Cook, stirring, until sauce is clear and thickened (about 2 minutes). Serve over beds of fluffy rice. Makes 6 servings.

KOLACHE
Czechoslovakian - American Club

1/4 cup warm water
1 package yeast
1 cup lukewarm buttermilk
1/2 cup shortening
4 to 4 1/2 cups flour

1/2 cup sugar
1 tsp salt
1/2 tsp soda
2 eggs

Dissolve yeast in warm water. Add buttermilk, shortening, sugar, eggs, and half the flour sifted with the soda and salt. Beat 5 minutes at medium speed of electric mixer. Gradually add enough flour to make a soft dough. Turn onto lightly floured board and knead until smooth and elastic, about 8 minutes. Place in greased bowl, turning to grease top. Cover and let rise until double in bulk. Punch down. Let rise again until almost doubled. Roll dough to 1/2 inch thickness and cut 1 1/2 inch rounds. Place on greased baking sheet and brush wth melted shortening. Let rise until almost doubled. Make deep depression in center; fill with any desired filling. Let rise again until doubled. Bake at 350° for 15 to 18 minutes.

Cream Cheese Filling: Combine 8 ozs Philadelphia cream cheese, softened, 1 egg yolk, 1 teaspoon vanilla, and sugar to taste.

Fruit Filling: Prunes, apricots or any fresh fruit cooked until thick and sweetened to taste.

Poppy Seed Filling: Use filling as it comes from can.

BABOVKA
(Pecan Roll, Coffee Cake)
Czechoslovakian - American Club

1 cup milk	2 packages active dry yeast
1/2 cup butter	1 cup lukewarm water
1/2 cup sugar	2 eggs
2 tsps salt	6 cups sifted flour

Scald milk. Stir in butter, sugar and salt. Cool to lukewarm. Dissolve yeast in lukewarm water. Add yeast, eggs and 2 cups flour to milk mixture. Beat until smooth. Gradually add enough remaining flour to make a soft dough. Turn out on floured surface; let rest 10 minutes. Knead until smooth; about 5 minutes. Place in greased bowl. Cover and let rise in warm place until doubled, about 1 1/2 hours. Punch down. Let rise again until doubled, about 45 minutes. Divide dough in half. Roll out each into 18 x 12 rectangle. Spread with filling. Roll up each into jelly roll. Curl each roll loosely into coil on greased baking sheet. Let rise until doubled, about 45 minutes. Bake in 350° oven for 40 minutes.

Nut Filling: Beat together 2 eggs, 1/2 cup honey, and 1/4 cup melted butter. Stir in 3 cups chopped nuts, 2 tablespoons cinnamon and 1 teaspoon vanilla.

ESTONIAN WARM POTATO SALAD

1 qt hot potatoes, diced	1/4 cup vinegar
1/4 cup onion, chopped	Salt, pepper, sour cream, and
1/3 cup hot beef stock	parsley
1/4 cup oil	

Combine potatoes, onion, stock, and seasoning. Blend oil with vinegar and pour over salad. Refrigerate and marinate overnight. Before serving, add enough sour cream to coat potatoes. Mix lightly and garnish with parsley.

ESTONIAN MASHED RUTABAGA

2 1/4 lbs rutabaga
Water, salt
2 tbsps butter
2 tbsps flour

3/4 cup milk or half & half
1/2 tsp salt
1/2 tsp ground nutmeg

Cut rutabaga in small cubes and boil in small amount of lightly salted water till tender. Either mash with potato masher or use a mixer. Melt butter in saucepan; add flour and stir till light brown. Add milk. Stir sauce in mashed rutabagas. Bring to a boil. Add salt and nutmeg. Put in baking dish and run in 350° oven for 20 minutes.

PUTO
(Rice Cakes)
Filipino - American Club

2 eggs, unbeaten
1 cup sugar
1 1/2 cups or 2 small cans
   evaporated milk

2 cups rice flour (Bisquick can
   be substituted)
1 tsp baking powder
1 tsp vanilla

Mix eggs with sugar and beat for 2 to 3 minutes. Add milk. Beat thoroughly until well mixed. Add flour and baking powder. Beat until lumps are dissolved (about 2 to 3 minutes). Add vanilla. Put in muffin pans lined with paper cup cakes. Steam for 25 to 30 minutes. Serve with butter, cheese, or grated fresh coconut. Serves 6 to 8.

PANSIT
(Philippine Noodles)
Filipino - American Club

1 1/2 package noodles, soaked in hot water for 5 to 10 minutes
1 lg onion, chopped fine
4 cloves garlic, chopped fine
3 tbsps soy sauce
4 tbsps vegetable oil
1/4 tsp Accent
1/2 bay leaf
2 cups cabbage, cut in strips
1 c meat, chicken, sliced in strips
2 carrots
1 box soybean curd, fried and chunked
1 stalk celery, chopped

Sauté garlic, onions, chicken meat, bay leaf for a few minutes; stir in soy sauce, add bean curd, stir thoroughly and cover for 2 minutes. Add celery, carrots, cabbage and cook covered for 5 minutes, or until vegetables are half cooked. Add noodles, mixing well until noodles are done. Sprinkle Accent and mix; garnish with sliced boiled eggs and green onions.

PHILIPPINE FRIED RICE
Filipino - American Club

3 cups cooked rice (long grain type)
1 cup diced ham, cooked
5 strips bacon, fried and crumbled (save 2 tbsps bacon fat)
1 bell pepper
2 med size carrots, diced
2 tbsps soy sauce
1 tsp fish sauce
Salt and pepper to taste
2 eggs, scrambled
2 cloves garlic, crushed
3 green onions, finely chopped

Using oil derived from frying bacon, fry garlic until brown. Add ham, bacon, pepper, carrots, and stir fry for 5 minutes. Add rice and continue to cook over low heat for 10 minutes. Add soy sauce, fish sauce. Season with salt, pepper to desired taste. Add eggs and cook for 2 minutes. Serve hot. Serves 6 to 8.

LUMPIA
Filipino - American Club

1 can Soyameat, chopped in
  small pieces
1 can bean sprouts
3 cloves garlic,chopped
1/2 lb string beans, sliced
1 can bamboo shoots, sliced
1/2 tsp accent
3 tbsps soy sauce
Salt to taste

1 can water chestnuts, sliced
1 med onion, chopped fine
1 package frozen green peas
3 tbsps oil
1 Irish potato, chopped fine
12 to 24 pieces spring roll
  wrappers:
1 cup water
1 cup flour blended

Brush, using a barbeque brush, in slightly greased pan, moderately heated on top of stove. Sauté garlic, onions, Soyameat, soy sauce. Add remaining ingredients and cook for 5 to 10 minutes (half cooked); add salt and accent to taste. Drain off all juice as dish cooks. Place 2 tablespoons mix on each wrapper and roll, then fold both ends. Deep fry. Serve hot with or without sauce.

FRIED LUMPIA
Filipino - American Club

1/2 lb ground lean beef
1 small can water chestnuts,
  minced
3 green onions, minced

2 lg onions, minced
2 tbsps soy sauce
Accent and salt to taste
1 package wonton wrapper

Mix all ingredients and wrap in wonton wrapper. Deep fry in hot oil.

ABOBO
(Chicken)
Filipino - American Club

1 chicken, regular size
1/2 cup vinegar
1 clove garlic
Salt and pepper to taste

1/2 bay leaf
Lard
1/2 cup water
1 small onion, chopped

Clean the chicken, cut into pieces. Add the salt, minced garlic and pepper to the chicken. Put in a pan and add the bay leaf, vinegar and water. Cover and let simmer until the chicken is tender and the liquid has practically evaporated. Add fat and fry meat and chopped onions until brown. Serve hot or cold.

EMPANADA
Filipino - American Club

Pastry:

Mix together 2 slightly beaten egg yolks, 3/4 cup water, 1/3 cup sugar, and 1 teaspoon salt. Add to 4 cups flour. Mix to a stiff dough. Knead until a fine texture is obtained. Toss on floured board and roll very thinly, almost like paper. Powder with sifted cornstarch to keep from sticking. Stretch dough gradually while rolling. Take end of dough and brush surface with melted butter. From this end, roll the dough like a jelly roll, brushing the surface with more butter until the whole roll is about 1/2 inch thick. Cut into 1 inch thick portions. Flatten each, cut side up, and roll portion into rounds. Place a tablespoon or more of meat filling in each.
Brush each piece with cold water, half way round, and close to edge. Fold and press edges together or trim with fluted pastry cutter. Heat plenty of fat in deep pan. When it browns a piece of bread in 60 seconds, drop each empanada and fry until golden brown. Drain before serving.

Filling:

Sauté 2 segments of minced garlic, 1 large onion, chopped, 1 chopped tomato (or tomato sauce), 1 cup ground veal, 1 cup ground pork, 1 cup ground chicken, salt, pepper, Accent, and 1 teaspoon sugar in 1 tablespoon fat. Cook until meat is tender. Cool before using. Add a slice of hard boiled egg and slice of sweet pickle before serving.

LEBERKLOESSE
(Liver Dumplings)

This is a typical South German dish and your family will enjoy the unique method of preparing liver.

1 lb chicken livers	1 1/2 tsps salt
2 slices white bread	1/2 tsp pepper
2 egg yolks	2 tbsps flour
1/4 cup soft butter	2 egg whites
2 tsps chopped onions	5 cups soup stock
2 tbsps chopped parsley	

Skin and remove the fiber from the liver and mince or chop it until it is very fine. Soak the bread in water for a few minutes and wring dry. Beat the egg yolks into the soft butter and add the liver and the soaked bread. Put in onion, parsley, salt, pepper, and flour and mix well. Beat the 2 egg whites until stiff and fold them into the other ingredients. Shape the mass into 1 1/2 inch balls. Bring the soup stock to a boil and gently place the balls in it. Cook them for 5 or 6 minutes. Serve them with the soup. Or drain them and serve soup extra, following it up with the dumplings served with sauteed onions. Serves 6.

KOURABIETHES #2
Greek

1 lb sweet butter (draw out salt)	2 tsps vanilla
1/4 cup confectioner's sugar	1 oz mastika (optional)
1 egg yolk	5 to 6 cups cake flour

Melt one pound of sweet butter and carefully pour into mixing bowl, being sure to leave salt and water out. Refrigerate until soft consistency, then put in electric beater and whip until light and fluffy. Add the powdered sugar, egg yolk, vanilla and mastika, beating thoroughly after each addition. Add flour a little at a time until a soft dough is formed that can be handled easily. Take about a teaspoonful at a time and roll into a small ball. Place on cookie sheet (which has been previously prepared by covering with 4 layers of newspapers topped with one layer of white shelf paper, not greased). Make a small indentation with finger on center of each, center with nut or clove if desired, and bake at 350° for 15 minutes. When done, sprinkle liberally with powdered sugar while still hot.

GREEK SALAD

1 lg head lettuce
3 cups potato salad
Roka leaves or watercress
2 tomatoes, cut in 6 wedges each
1 cucumber, cut lengthwise into
   8 fingers
1 avocado, cut into wedges
4 portions Feta cheese
1 green bell pepper, cut into
   thin rings

4 slices cooked beets
4 boiled, peeled shrimp
4 anchovy fillets
12 black olives
4 spring onions
1/2 cup white vinegar
1/4 cup each olive and salad oil,
   blended
Oregano

Line a large bowl with outside lettuce leaves. Place 3 cups of potato salad in center. Shred remaining lettuce and make a bed around potato salad. Arrange roka leaves or watercress on top of this. Place the tomato wedges around the outer edge of the bowl. Put the cucumber fingers between the tomatoes. Now put the avocado wedges around the potato salad. Arrange Feta pieces over salad. Now add pepper rings over top. Add the spring onions at right angles to each other around the center. Place a slice of beet between each of these. Top each beet with one of the shrimp, then an anchovy on each shrimp. Add black olives over the bowl. Sprinkle with vinegar and then with the blended oil. Sprinkle the oregano over all and serve at once. Serves 4 hungry people. Serve with Italian or French bread.

SOPAPILLA RECIPE
Hispanic Culture Club

1 cup flour
1 tsp shortening
1 tsp baking powder

1/2 tsp salt
1/4 cup buttermilk
1/4 cup water

Mix like biscuit dough and roll out about 1/8 inch thick, cut in 3 inch triangles and squares, drop in deep fat, baste with spatula until brown.

HOMINY CASSEROLE
Hispanic Culture Club

2 (#2 size) canned hominy
1 cup scalded milk
1 cup bread crumbs
1 cup grated cheese
2 eggs, slightly beaten
1 tbsp butter

2 tbsps hot chili sauce
1 tbsp chili powder
2 tbsps grated onion
1 tbsp chopped parsley
Salt and pepper to taste
1 tbsp chopped green pepper

Mix all ingredients in order given and place in buttered casserole dish, reserving some crumbs for top. Bake in 350° oven for 40 minutes.

SPANISH OMELET
Hispanic Culture Club

8 eggs
3 tbsps butter
Salt and pepper to taste
8 lg tomatoes, cubed

4 onions, chopped
Pinch of garlic
3 small jalapenos
5 tbsps fat

Cook tomatoes slowly for 10 minutes. Fry onion and garlic in hot fat. Combine tomatoes and the onion and garlic and simmer for 3 hours, adding hot water as necessary. Set aside. Beat eggs lightly, just enough to blend yolks and whites. Add salt, pepper, and milk for a creamier omelet. Melt butter in hot omelet pan and let it run over the bottom and sides of pan. Pour in mixture and cook slowly. As it cooks, prick with fork so the egg on top will run under sides. When evenly cooked, increase heat so the omelet will brown underneath. Pour sauce over omelet or fill ends of platter with sauce before serving.

MEXICAN STEAK
Hispanic Culture Club

1 lb round steak
1 tbsp vinegar
1 button garlic, minced
2 tbsps flour
1 tsp salt
1 tsp pepper
2 tbsps shortening
2 small onions, chopped

1 (14 oz) can Enchilada sauce
1 (14 oz) can tomatoes
2 tsps chili sauce
1/2 tsp sugar
1/2 cup water
2 lg potatoes, sliced
2 (4 oz) cans whole green chilies

Rub meat with vinegar, pour in garlic, flour, salt, and pepper. Cut in 1 inch strips. Brown well. Reduce heat and cook meat 20 minutes longer. Add remaining ingredients and continue cooking for 1 hour. Serves 6.

COCIDO DE ARROZ CON POLLO
(Chicken & Rice Stew)
Hispanic Culture Club

1 stewing chicken, cut into pieces
3 cups boiling water
1/2 tsp salt
6 whole cloves
4 to 6 peppercorns
1/4 tsp powdered ginger
1/4 tsp mace
2 tbsps raisins

1/2 tsp cinnamon or 2 sticks
1/4 tsp pepper
7/8 cup butter
3 lg onions, sliced on bias
3/4 cup uncooked rice
2 cups chicken stock
1/2 tsp saffron
1/2 cup chicken broth

Simmer chicken in boiling salted water until tender. Drain; save stock. Remove bones; brown chicken meat lightly in oven. Grind spices together on mortar. Melt butter; sauté onion slices. Put in heavy frying pan with cover. Add rice, chicken stock, raisins, and ground spice mixture to onions. Cover tightly; cook over low heat. Simmer together; discard saffron. When rice is soft outside and slightly tough in center, add chicken broth with saffron and chicken. When rice is tender, serve at once.

SPINACH WITH PEPPERS
Hispanic Culture Club

3 tbsps canned green chilies,   6 tbsps fat
  chopped   3 cups cooked spinach
1 tbsp minced pimento   1 tsp salt
3 tbsps minced onions   2 tbsps lemon juice

Cook green chilies, pimento and onion in fat. Add spinach and salt, heat thoroughly, add lemon juice and serve. Serves 6 to 8.

BAKED TOMATOES AND CORN
Hispanic Culture Club

2 cups stewed tomatoes   1 tbsp butter
2 cups cut, cooked corn   1/2 tsp salt
1 green bell pepper, chopped   Dash of pepper
1 small onion, chopped   1 cup dry bread crumbs
2 tsps hot chili sauce   2 tbsps grated cheese

Simmer tomatoes about 5 minutes. Add corn, green pepper, onion, hot chili sauce, butter, salt, and pepper, and cook slowly 15 minutes. Place alternate layers of vegetable mixture and bread crumbs in greased baking dish ending with layer of crumbs. Sprinkle cheese over top and bake in hot oven (400°) about 20 minutes or until brown. Serves 6 to 8.

MEXICAN STUFFED SQUASH
Hispanic Culture Club

5 small squash
1/4 lb ground beef
2 tsps hot chili sauce
1 small onion, minced
1 small tomato, minced

2 buttons garlic
1 tsp salt
1 tsp thyme
1 tbsp butter

Select green squash 5 to 6 inches in length. Cook until tender. Scoop out the inside, do not break the skin. Fry the beef brown, add chili sauce, onion, tomato, thyme, salt, and garlic. Add a bit of water to the beef and the vegetables and cook dry. Stuff the squash with the mixture. Place in baking pan in moderate oven (325°) with the butter, and bake until the skins of the squash are brown. Serves 5 to 6.

CHICKEN ENCHILADA CASSEROLE
Hispanic Culture Club

12 tortillas
1 cooked chicken, chopped
  and boned
1/2 cup ripe olives, drained
1/2 (4 oz) can green chilies
4 green onions, chopped
Salt and pepper to taste

1 1/2 c. grated cheddar cheese
2 cups chicken stock
1 (10 1/2 oz) can cream of
  mushroom soup
1 (10 1/2 oz) can cream of
  chicken soup

Cut tortillas into quarters. In greased casserole dish, arrange a layer of tortillas, and a layer of chicken, olives, chilies, onions, and cheese. Repeat layer. Mix chicken stock, mushrooms and chicken soup and pour over mixture. Top with more grated cheese. Bake for 45 minutes at 350°.

PAPAS CON QUESO
(Potatoes With Cheese)
Hispanic Culture Club

6 small potatoes
1 tbsp butter, heaping
3 tbsps cream
1 egg

Cheese
Salt to taste
Chopped parsley

Cook potatoes until done. Mash well with butter, cream, salt, and egg. Beat well. Shape potatoes into balls. With handle of teaspoon, make a hollow place in the ball and fill with a cube of cheese. Grease each potato ball with a bit of lard and place in a hot oven (450°) and brown. Serve balls sprinkled with chopped parsley, and garnished with slices of tomatoes.

TAMALE PIE
Hispanic Culture Club

1/2 cup corn meal
1 1/2 cups water
1/2 tsp salt
1 1/2 cups milk
1 tbsp shortening

1 onion
1 cup ground raw meat
1 1/4 cups tomatoes
Red pepper and chili powder

Cook corn meal, water, and salt until mixture begins to thicken. Add milk, cook about 10 minutes longer; stir constantly to prevent sticking. Fry chopped onion in shortening, add meat and cook until meat begins to brown. Add tomatoes, salt, red pepper, and chili powder. Line a deep baking dish that has been buttered with 3/4 of the corn meal mush, pour in meat mixture and cover with remaining mush. Cook in moderate oven about 45 minutes. Serves 6.

GHRY BEE
(Lebanese Butter Cookies)
Syra - Meric Club

2 cups melted butter
1 1/2 cups granulated or
   superfine sugar

3 1/2 cups flour
Walnut halves

Mix cooled butter and sugar and cream well. Add flour. (Test small amount by rolling a ball in palms of hands. If too soft, add more flour until of right consistency). Shape dough into egg shape or round balls and place on an ungreased baking sheet. Make indentation in center of cookie and place a walnut half in indentation. Bake in moderate oven at 350° until bottom of cake is slightly golden, about 15 to 20 minutes; cakes remain white on top. Remove from oven and cool, then sprinkle top of cakes with confectioner's sugar. Let stand overnight to cool before removing from pan.

RAW KIBBIE
Syra - Meric Club

2 lbs lean round steak ground
   fine (heavy beef)
2 cups cracked wheat, fine

Season to taste with salt, red
   pepper, allspice, cinnamon, mint

Wash wheat in cold water and drain. Season with salt, mint, cinnamon, red pepper, allspice. Let stand for 1 hour. Mix well using ice water to moisten wheat. Add meat and mix thoroughly using the water to make soft.

BUL KO KI
(Korean Dish)

2 lbs sirloin tip, sliced in thin
    2 inch strips
2 med carrots, shredded
1 small onion, thinly sliced
2 green onion, cut into 2 inch
    long slices
1/3 cup soy sauce
1/8 tsp pepper

1/8 tsp MSG
1/8 tsp garlic powder or 1 clove
    garlic, minced
1/8 tsp ginger powder
2 tsps sugar
2 tsps roasted sesame seed
1 tsp sesame oil

Mix all ingredients together. Pan fry and serve with rice. Pan fried juice makes good gravy.

330

MIHSHEE MALFOOF
(Stuffed Cabbage Rolls)
Syra - Meric Club

1 lb ground lamb or beef
   (include both lean and fat)
1 cup rice, washed and drained
1 lg or 2 med head of cabbage
1/2 cup melted butter

Salt, pepper and cinnamon
   to taste
6 cloves garlic, unpeeled
1/2 cup lemon juice

In a bowl, combine meat, rice, butter and spices and mix well. Set aside. Carve out thick core from center of cabbage and drop cabbage into boiling salted water, cored end down. Boil about 5 minutes until leaves are softened for easier separation of leaves. While boiling, loosen each leaf with a long fork; remove separated leaves and rest of cabbage from water and place in a pan or bowl until cool. Remove heavy center stems or ribs from leaves and set aside. If leaves are large, cut in half or palm size. Lay outside leaves (usually too large to roll) in bottom of 4 quart saucepan and enough cabbage ribs to fill the bottom of pan. Fill each leaf with about 1 to 1 1/2 teaspoons of stuffing and roll firmly in shape of cigar, gently squeezing rolled cabbage to be sure it is firmly closed. Lay cabbage rolls neatly side by side in rows, alternating and making several layers. Scatter cloves or garlic among layers. Put leftover cabbage leaves and ribs on top layer of rolls, then place an inverted plate and press down. Add water and salt to reach slightly above inverted plate. Cover and cook on medium heat for 40 minutes. Add lemon juice and cook 10 minutes more. (Lift plate or saucer off of cabbage rolls before adding lemon juice in order for the juice to penetrate all layers).
Variation: Tomato sauce may be added to stuffing mixture, adding moisture to filling. After all rolls have been arranged in layers and plate or saucer pressed over top, add can of tomatoes, mix with 1 cup water and salt to reach slightly above plate. Cook, uncovered, over medium heat for approximately 40 to 50 minutes. Do not add lemon juice.

MIHSHEH WAROK INIB B' LAH'M
(Stuffed Grape leaves)
Syra - Meric Club

5 dozen grape leaves
1 cup rice, washed
1 lb meat, chopped

1 tsp salt (more or less to taste)
1 tsp allspice (more or less
  to taste)

Place grape leaves on tray or waxed paper and set aside. Mix rice, meat and spices together and blend well. Take 1 grape leaf at a time, place 1 tablespoon of filling across leaf and fold sides away from you. Arrange stuffed leaves in pan and alternate the direction with each row; sprinkle salt on tops. Cover with a plate; cover with water to cover top of plate. Cook, covered, on medium heat for about 40 minutes, or until rice is done. Add lemon juice if desired, squeeze juice of 1 lemon on top of the grape leaves before you start to cook.

BAKLWA
(Lebanese pastry)

1 (1 lb) box Fillo Strudel Dough　　　3/4 cup melted butter

Filling:

1 1/2 lbs pecans (may be mixed
   half and half with walnuts)
   ground

1 cup sugar (optional)

Syrup:

1 cup water　　　　　　　　　　2 cups sugar
1 tsp lemon juice　　　　　　　　1 tbsp rose water

Boil sugar and water until syrupy. Add lemon juice and rose water. Set aside. Grease 12 x 15 inch pan (must be deeper than cookie tray) with butter. Carefully separate fillo sheets and lay 1 sheet at a time in buttered pan. Brush each layer with melted butter, using pastry brush or small paint brush (paint brush with soft bristles spreads butter evenly, and more area is covered than with pastry brush. Reserve this brush as you would pastry brush for later use). Continue with single sheets in this manner until 1/2 the dough is used (approximately 20 sheets). If dough breaks in handling, patch it and brush with butter. Mix filling or use only ground nuts. Distribute the filling evenly over the dough about 1/4 inch thick. Spread other half of dough, buttering each layer carefully. Using sharp knife, cut into squares or diamond shaped pieces (about 2 inches each square). Bake 1 hour in preheated 300° oven, or until golden brown and crisp. (Temperature varies according to type oven; regulate accordingly). Remove from oven and pour syrup over tray while hot. Set aside to cool. Be sure it is completely cooled before removing individual pieces to serve. Be sure to use all of syrup mixture; properly glazed, will keep indefinitely and retain its flavor. Seal tightly to store. Baklawa may be frozen, also. Prepared Fillo Strudel leaves are available packaged in 1 pound cartons. If you are not familiar with where it may be purchased, consult with a Lebanese friend for this information. In the filling, some prefer to leave off mixture of sugar with nuts, since heavy syrup is used after cooking, making it unnecessary to use more sugar in preparing filling. Use your own taste in making this decision.

KHANOM PONG TOD
(Thai Style Fried Bread)

1 lb fresh shrimp	3 eggs
12 slices white sandwich bread	1/2 cup finely chopped onions
1 tsp salt, pepper	1/4 cup chopped carrots
1 lb ground pork	2 tbsps cornstarch

Leave bread out on a platter for 2 hours to dry. Trim crusts off each slice. Cut each piece into 4 squares. Mix pork, shrimp, onions, and carrots. Add salt, pepper, and eggs. Mix well and spread mixture on the bread. Heat 3 to 4 cups of oil in a wok or pot. Drop breaded shrimp side down into oil and fry for 30 seconds; turn and fry on the other side for another 30 seconds. Both sides should be golden brown. Serve hot.

PELAU
Trinidadian - Tobago

1 chicken or beef equivalent	1 onion
2 cups precooked French cut string beans	5 cloves garlic
	Parsley
2 cups rice	Hot pepper, salt, and black pepper to taste
1 cup sliced or shredded carrots	
	1 tbsp sugar
1 bell pepper	1 tsp oil

Cut meat or chicken into small pieces. Wash and highly season with chopped bell pepper, onion, garlic, parsley, hot pepper, salt, and black pepper to taste. Cover seasoned meat and place overnight in refrigerator. Following Day Cooking Instructions: Using the teaspoon of oil moisten skillet, heat and sprinkle sugar in skillet. When sugar begins to get a dark color and bubble, put seasoned meat in, stirring constantly until meat becomes a golden brown color. Add 1 cup of water occasionally, cover and allow meat to become about three quarters of the way cooked. Day 2: In meat which has been three quarters of the way cooked, place enough water to accommodate rice. Turn heat down to a medium temperature. Put in the string beans, then rice and thinly sliced or shredded carrots and thoroughly mix all ingredients once. Cover pot and allow to cook until rice is fully cooked, but not over cooked. Must be on a medium or low heat. Stir pelau only to a minimum degree to prevent sticking. Makes 6 to 8 servings.

There are many Indian tribes in Louisiana and right in our Central Louisiana area, we boast of the Clifton/Choctaw tribe 28 miles from Alexandria in Clifton and the Tunica Indians in Marksville. The following 2 recipes came from the Clifton/Choctaw tribe leader's wife, Anna Neal.

INDIAN FRIED BREAD

4 cups plain flour   3 tbsps baking powder
2 tsps salt   2 cups tap water

Mix all dry ingredients in a medium bowl. Make well in middle of flour mixture. Pour water, small amount till the flour mixture is sticky. Use all flour mixture, mixing with hands till all flour is used up. Pat dough with cooking oil. Let stand for 20 to 30 minutes before frying. Heat oil in skillet about 400°, pinch a small dough, flatten or stretch dough about 4 to 6 inches and drop in hot oil. Let brown on one side, turn and do same. Ready to eat with preserves, syrup, honey, or with main meal. Makes about 12 to 15 fried breads, depending on size used. If dough gets sticky, use little flour on before frying.

INDIAN COOKIES

1 cup flour   1/3 cup corn meal
1/3 cup shortening   1 egg
1/3 tbsp sugar   1/3 tsp baking powder
1/3 tsp nutmeg   1/3 tsp lemon extract
Dash of salt   3 tbsps raisins

Cream shortening, sugar, and egg. Add flour and corn meal and continue creaming. Add other ingredients. Drop on buttered cookie sheet. Bake at 350° until brown.

SOUL FOODS

SAUSAGE STEW - B

2 lbs link style pork sausage,
   cut in bite sizes
1/2 cup chopped onion
8 to 10 ripe tomatoes
1/2 cup uncooked rice

4 potatoes, pared and sliced
1/2 cup green pepper
1 cup diced okra
Salt and pepper to taste
2 tbsps butter

In 2 tablespoons butter, sauté 1/2 of the onion. Cover bottom of large roasting pot with remaining onions. Add 1/2 of the tomatoes on top of the onions. Spread rice over tomatoes. Then add chopped potatoes. Season each layer. Add sausage and cover with remaining tomatoes. Add diced okra and season. Cover and cook for 1 1/2 hours on low heat or until vegetables are tender. Serves 5 to 6.

OLD FASHION CABBAGE SOUP - B

1 lb ground pork or lean beef
1 lb salt pork or 6 slices bacon
1 lg head cabbage, cut into
   small pieces

2 cans stewing tomatoes
6 cups water
Salt and pepper to taste
1 bay leaf

Brown meat and drain off fat. Add cabbage, stewing tomatoes, salt, and pepper to meat. Mix well, then pour 6 cups water over mixture. Add bay leaf. Cover and cook for 1 hour. Serves 6 to 8.

HAM HOCKS 'N GREENS - B & W

3 1/2 pounds ham hocks
1 pound mustard greens washed
   and drained
8 ounces turnip greens, washed
   and drained

8 ounces collard greens, washed
   and drained
1 8 1/2 ounce package corn
   bread mix

In large kettle or Dutch oven, brown ham hocks. Add 1 quart water and bring to boiling. Add greens and return to boiling. Reduce heat; cover and simmer 1 1/2 hours. Meanwhile, prepare and bake combread mix according to package directions; cut in squares. To serve, ladle out greens and juices ("Pot liquor") into serving bowl; garnish with hard-cooked egg slices, if desired. Serve ham hocks in another bowl. Spoon juices over corn bread squares. Makes 4 servings.

CHICKEN BONE SOUP - B

1 (5 lb) stewing hen or frying
  chicken
1 stalk celery
1 carrot, diced
1/2 cup onion, chopped

2 tbsps parsley
1 1/2 tsps salt
1/4 tsp pepper
1 bay leaf

Season chicken and place in dutch oven. Cover with water and add onion, celery, bay leaf, carrots, and parsley. Bring to a rolling boil. Lower heat and cook covered for 1 1/2 hours or until chicken is falling off bone. Remove bones and cook 1/2 hour longer on low heat. Serve over cooked rice. Makes 4 to 6 servings.

RED BEAN SOUP

1 1/2 cups red beans
6 1/2 cups water
4 carrots, cut in cubes
1 green pepper, chopped
1/4 cup parsley, chopped
1/4 cup celery, with tender
  leaves chopped

3 garlic cloves, chopped
1 1/2 tablespoons salt
1/2 tablespoon black pepper
2 tomatoes, finely cut
1 tablespoon tomato paste
1/2 cup olive oil, peanut oil
  or salad oil

Wash beans and cook in water about 1 1/2 hour. Add the vegetables and seasonings and cook half an hour more. Add tomatoes and tomato paste and cook 15 minutes longer or until beans are soft. A little before the cooking time is over, add the olive oil and cook 15 minutes more. Olive oil is easier to digest if not cooked long. Serve hot or cold. Serves 6.

CABBAGE TOMATO SOUP

1 medium head of cabbage
  shredded
1 large can tomato juice or
  V8 juice
Beef bouillon made from
  stock or cubes
1 medium onion, sliced

Minced garlic
1 tsp salt
1 tsp sugar
1 tsp lemon juice
1/2 tsp tabasco
2 cups water

Combine all ingredients and heat to boiling. Reduce heat, cover and simmer till cabbage is tender. Serve with toasted croutons and parmesan cheese sprinkled on top.

LAGNIAPPE

We leave you with an old Southern superstition that one must eat black eyed peas and cabbage on New Year's Day to have good luck and money through the year. Whether this originated with the whites or blacks, I could not trace.

I, for one, would never go against the custom and for those of you who have never tried it - who knows how lucky or wealthy you could have been? For those of you who practice the custom, who knows how poor or unlucky you would have been, if you hadn't.

For Black eye peas, follow the recipe in the vegetable chapter for cooking any dried bean or pea.

Cleaning Up For Company

CANDIES

CHEESE AND EGGS

COOKIES

VEGETABLES

Bon Soir

Bon Appetit!